IMAGES
of America

NASSAU

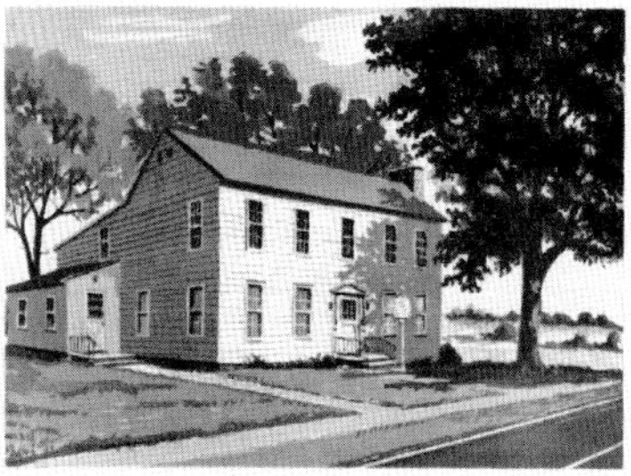

NASSAU TOWN HALL
Built prior to 1816 Remodled in 1968

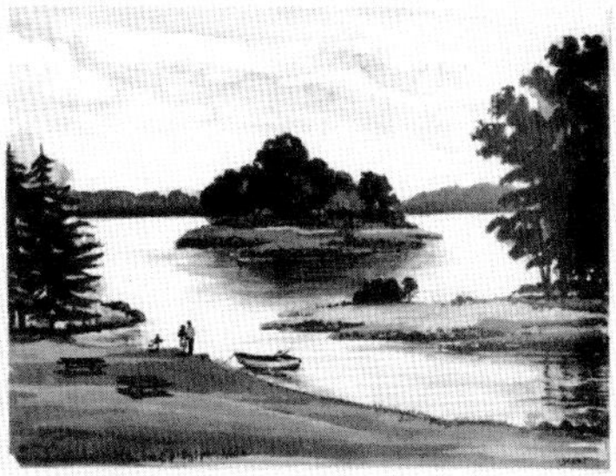

BURDEN LAKE
One of the many centers of water sports, this lake is the northern boundary of the town.

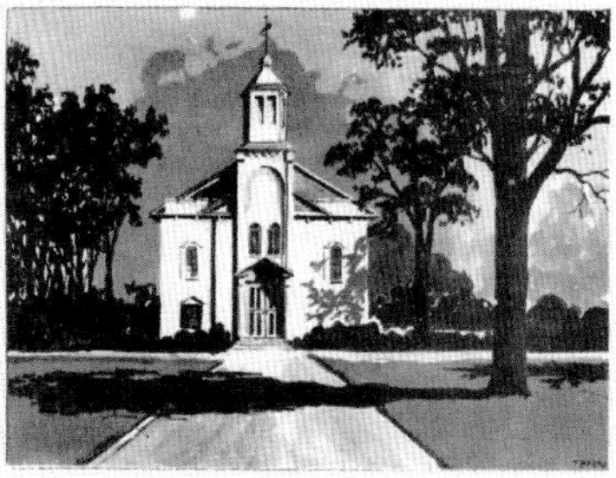

GRACE UNITED METHODIST CHURCH
Built 1833 Remodeled and Expanded 1923
Provides an adjacent church hall for full social and Sunday School activities.

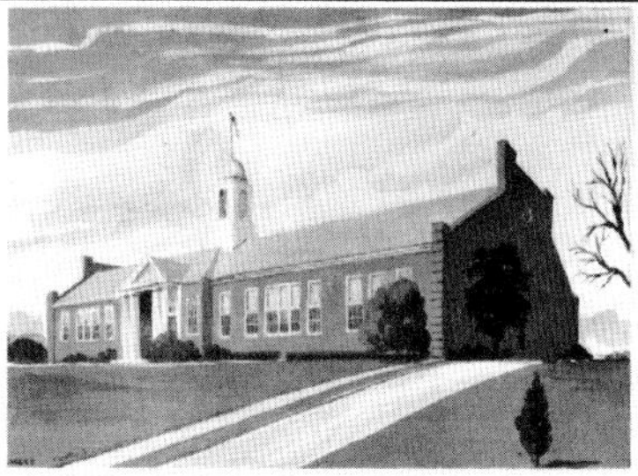

DONALD P. SUTHERLAND ELEMENTARY SCHOOL
Built 1939
Named in honor of its former principal and long time area resident.

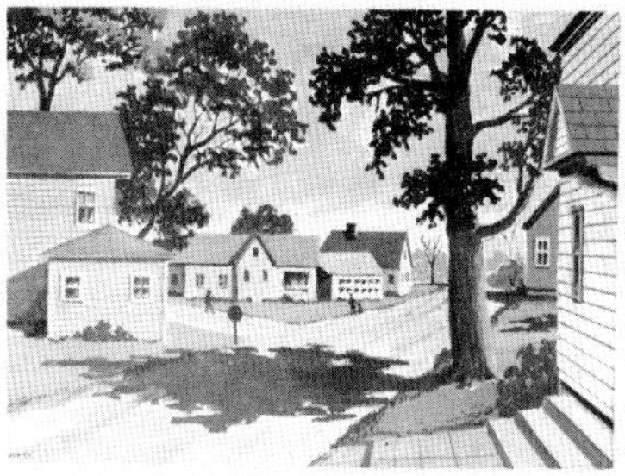

MILLERS CORNERS
Typical of the many picturesque by-ways seen as you travel the area.

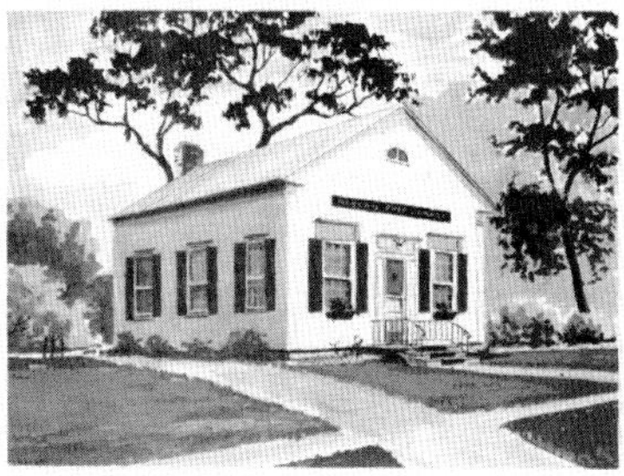

NASSAU FREE LIBRARY
Organized 1881 Incorporated 1893
Purchased this 1835 house from the Dutch Reformed Church and has occupied the premises since 1892. Recently purchased adjacent property from St. Mary's Catholic Church for expansion program.

Organized attempts by Nassau's business owners and merchants to join together to promote the community date back at least to the 1920s. In earlier days, these types of individuals often served as elected officials in the community. The Nassau Businessmen's Association existed from the 1950s through the 1970s, and was the most influential of these groups. Its aim was to promote growth and business opportunities in anticipation of the large-scale suburban expansion that was so confidently predicted. The images and captions in this 1972 association brochure, entitled *This is the Town of Nassau N.Y.*, evoke a mood of optimism and confidence. (Courtesy of the author's collection.)

ON THE COVER: Nassau's existence was based on the location of available waterpower, and the subsequent growth of industry depended on it. In the spring of 1895, George D. Borst and his brother-in-law Ray W. Lock purchased Nassau Mills. In the fall of that year, the mill was at capacity, grinding rye purchased from local farmers for 1¢ per pound. Mills have stood on that property, at the end of Elm Street and Lake Avenue (formerly Wall and Mills Streets, respectively), since the 1700s. Last used commercially for the imprinting of ballpoint pen barrels by a business called Speedy Sales, the ancient building currently sits vacant. (Courtesy of the author's collection.)

IMAGES
of America

NASSAU

Kurt Vincent

ARCADIA
PUBLISHING

ISBN 978-0-7385-9938-0

Published by Arcadia Publishing
Charleston, South Carolina

Printed in the United States of America

Library of Congress Control Number: 2012955731

For all general information, please contact Arcadia Publishing:
Telephone 843-853-2070
Fax 843-853-0044
E-mail sales@arcadiapublishing.com
For customer service and orders:
Toll-Free 1-888-313-2665

Visit us on the Internet at www.arcadiapublishing.com

Contents

ACKNOWLEDGMENTS

When first asked by the publisher if I would consider this project, my first reaction was, "Do they know Nassau, New York, is not the same as Nassau County, New York?" When I was assured they did, I started thinking, "Why not?" The subject matter has always been of interest to me, and Nassau has many fascinating stories and bits of history that are not immediately apparent. So, with that, I started. This final product could not have been possible without the help of many others.

Without the resources of the Nassau Free Library, there would be no book. Its local history collection is rich with photographs, clippings, and personal memories that would surely have disappeared if not for the library's stewardship. Librarian Pat Sahr was gracious and supportive from the start, and all the other volunteers expressed a keen interest and a helpful attitude about the project. And a special acknowledgement goes to someone long dead: Leroy Allendorph, whose photo album, donated to the library, serves as a window to the past. With images of almost every structure in Nassau village, his album shows exactly what life looked like more than 130 years ago.

Thanks go to the members of the Nassau community, past and present, who shared their family photographs. All are credited, but, in particular, Judy Marquette was a wonderful source—her relatives were talented photographers, and, luckily, much of their work survived the years, including rare glass-plate negatives.

Then there were my "detectives," those who helped identify why and when a photograph was taken and who the mystery people in photographs are. While they were not always successful, my thanks go to Marion Blair, Jane Konisky, Diane McGrath, Margaret Van Deusen, Marcia Valenty, Steven and Nancy Cooper, Russell "Hoppy" Decker, Norman Young, Don Carpentier, Paul Sanford, Keith Prior, Rita Lebrum, and Wayne Morrow.

Finally, as this is being written, Archie Sherman has recently left us. Having spent more than half of his 97 years in Nassau, he was a rich source of information, wit, and optimism.

Unless otherwise noted, all images are courtesy of the author's collection.

INTRODUCTION

Phillipstown, New Stores, Union Village, Clark's Corners, Greenman Terrace, Braeside, and Edgewood Acres are all names out of the past. Some have remained familiar, but most have been lost in time. Each represents a time in history, when hopes, dreams, human struggle, and endeavor marked the part of the world we now call Nassau.

While Nassau is only nine miles from where Henry Hudson's ship the *Half Moon* arrived in September 1609 at what is now Castleton, development was slow to come. In 1756, Thomas Pownall drew one of the first maps showing the Valatie Kill and Kinderhook Lake. North of the lake, he noted, "the land here but indifferent, hilly and stony, producing white & black oak, and ash and hickory in valleys." The movement of English settlers from the east and south brought the first settlers to the area.

Missionary David Brainerd arrived from Stockbridge, Massachusetts, in 1743 to attend to the Mahican Indians living in a settlement near a bend of the Kinderhook Creek, at a place called Kaunaumeek. Just a year later, he persuaded the group to return with him to Stockbridge as the French and Indian War intensified. He was disliked by the Dutch because he sought to aid the very people driven off their lands by unscrupulous land transfers. Later, a family named Brainard (spelled with an *a*) settled in the area for which it is now named.

In May 1760, Mahican chief Keshomack conveyed land north and south of present-day Nassau Lake to Hugh Wilson and Joseph Primmer. Quaker Jonathan Hoag, who arrived in 1775 from Dutchess County, found Nassau "in a state of nature," with only a tavern and one or two houses. By the spring of 1786, Hoag and his partner Moses Vail had built a store on Church Street, and Vail had built his house on Elm Street. The name New Stores was adopted for the fledgling crossroads.

The name Phillipstown, in honor of Phillip Van Rensselaer, was generally applied to the areas east of the Valatiekill. By 1798, visitors reported that "about thirty houses" had been built in the village, and the growth brought another name change, this time to Union Village. In 1806, the town of Nassau was formed from parts of Petersburgh, Stephentown, and Schodack, comprising a land area of 45.2 square miles. The population at the time numbered 2,501, making it the largest settled area in southern Rensselaer County.

Growth continued with the development of agriculture and industry in the hamlets and settlements of Hoag's Corners, Brainard's Bridge, East Nassau, Denault's Corners, Dunham Hollow, the Alps, North Nassau, and Miller's Corners. In 1808, the name of Union Village changed again, becoming Nassau, and, soon after, the entire town took on the same name. The people of Nassau exercised determination, worked hard, and developed a sense of place.

Nassau has seen three major phases in its development: the initial founding and early growth; the move away from the land to industry; and the period after World War II, when the population grew and Nassau became a suburban bedroom community rather than a place where people worked close to home.

Much of the growth of Nassau was determined by highways. One of the earliest highways passed from the south along today's McClellan Road towards Schodack Landing. Another entered from the direction of Malden Bridge, and, farther off, Stockbridge. A chain of turnpikes extended from the state line in Lebanon, in Columbia County, through East Nassau and Nassau village to Albany and westward on to Buffalo. In the earliest days, travelers from the east avoided crossing the wild Kinderhook Creek by circling around Curtis Mountain and fording the stream at a wider spot near East Nassau. All of these routes still exist today.

Nassau has also had its share of problems. One that remained constant was water; there was either too much or too little. With factories and workshops located close to streams, spring flooding and summer deluges often washed away bridges and mills. Nassau village proposed and dismissed numerous plans to provide sufficient drinking water to homes, including tapping into Nassau Lake, Lyon's Lake, and, in one plan, a swampy pond east of the village. When it was disclosed that summer guests from a tourist home popular with New York City vacationers often bathed in the pond, that idea was also dropped.

Over the years, townspeople have fought back against the tyranny of feudal landlords, welcomed immigrants into their communities, and sent servicemen and women to every conflict from the Revolutionary War to the hostilities in the Middle East in recent years. Mills, factories, and workshops created all types of products, from flour and pork sausage to the woolen fabric that covered Ford Model T seats. Workers forged raw iron into farm plows, and girls and mothers stayed home sewing piecework for Troy wholesalers.

When trolleys rolled through Nassau when the annual fair was in session, the *Albany Evening Journal* wrote, "Nassau's streets were black with people." A canopy of leaves from publicly maintained trees shaded village streets during the heat of summer. And when the news reached Nassau in 1919 that the hostilities in Europe were over and an armistice had been signed, former mayor A.O. Kosegarten fired a ceremonial cannon from atop John VanValkenburgh's hill in celebration. These stories, and hundreds of others, are the collected heritage that has been left to us. But there is also a more tangible heritage. Much of what is physically left of the old Nassau—houses, business structures, and places of worship—is still here.

Hopefully, as readers looks at the old images in this book, they will see the beauty and history in what once was. While one new village in Nassau was created less than 20 years ago, the other, older village toys with the idea of dissolution. Crossroads are nothing new for Nassau; indeed, they are what started it all so many years ago. Our choice today is whether we look confidently to the future while respecting the past and using it as our guide, or whether we stumble shortsightedly ahead, cutting away at what makes us unique, strong, and proud.

One

Old Nassau

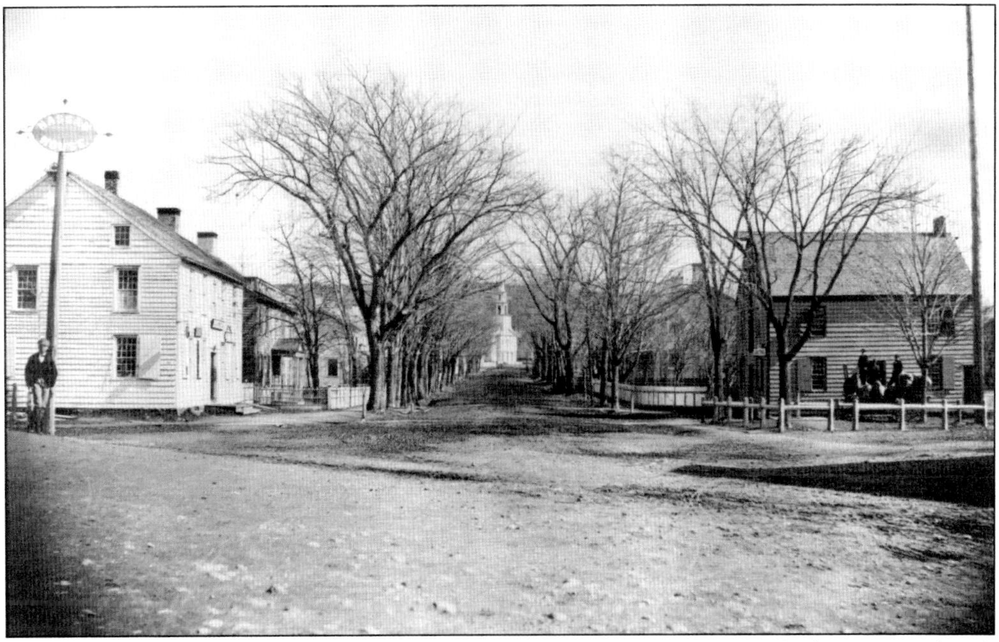

This is one of the earliest surviving photographs of Nassau. The 1868 view looks east up Church Street, which later became US Route 20. This route helped form the crossroads that made Nassau village an early center in the town. In 1786, Church Street served as the boundary between the lands of early settlers and partners Jonathan Hoag and Moses Vail, to the north, and those of Thomas Tobias, to the south. (Courtesy of Nassau Free Library.)

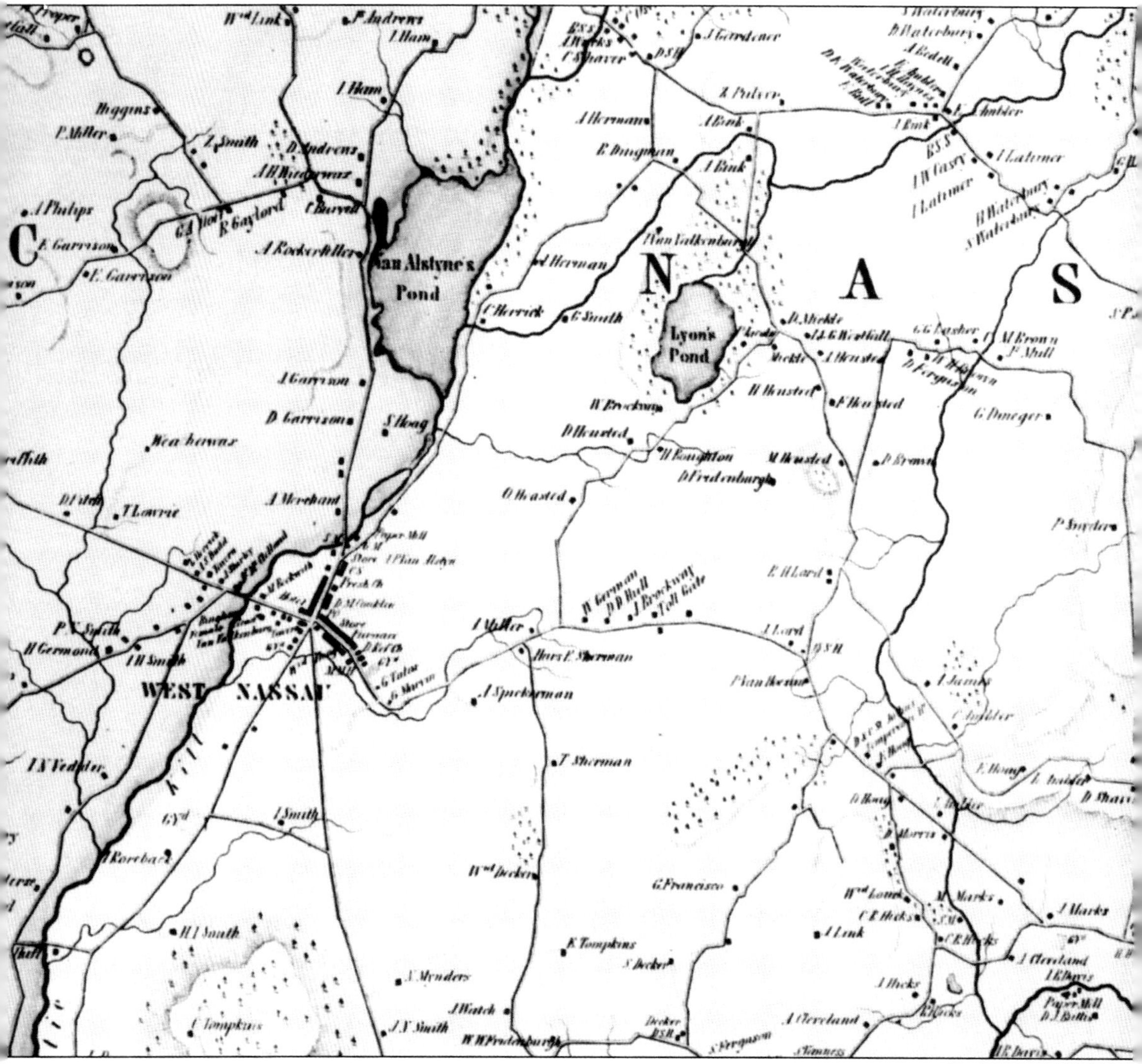

This 1854 Whitlock's map of Rensselaer County shows the basic network of roads and the early development of Nassau village. VanAlstyne's Pond and Lyon's Pond are now known as Nassau Lake and Lyons Lake, respectively. Interestingly, Nassau village is indicated as West Nassau, to differentiate it from East Nassau. The origin of many of today's road names can be traced to the family names of early property owners. Examples include Lords Hill Road, Bliss Schoolhouse Road, and Duesenbury Hill Road. (Courtesy of Village of Nassau.)

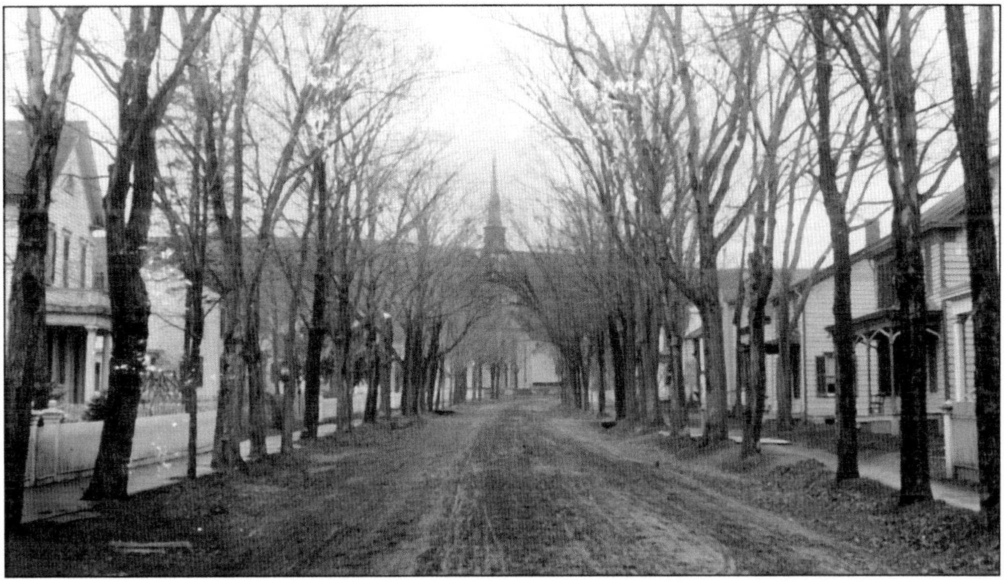

Looking east up Church Street from the village center, the view in this 1890s photograph shows many buildings that still stand today, as well as impressive trees and not-so-impressive road conditions. At the bend in the street stood the second of three Reformed church sanctuary buildings built in Nassau. (Courtesy of Nassau Free Library.)

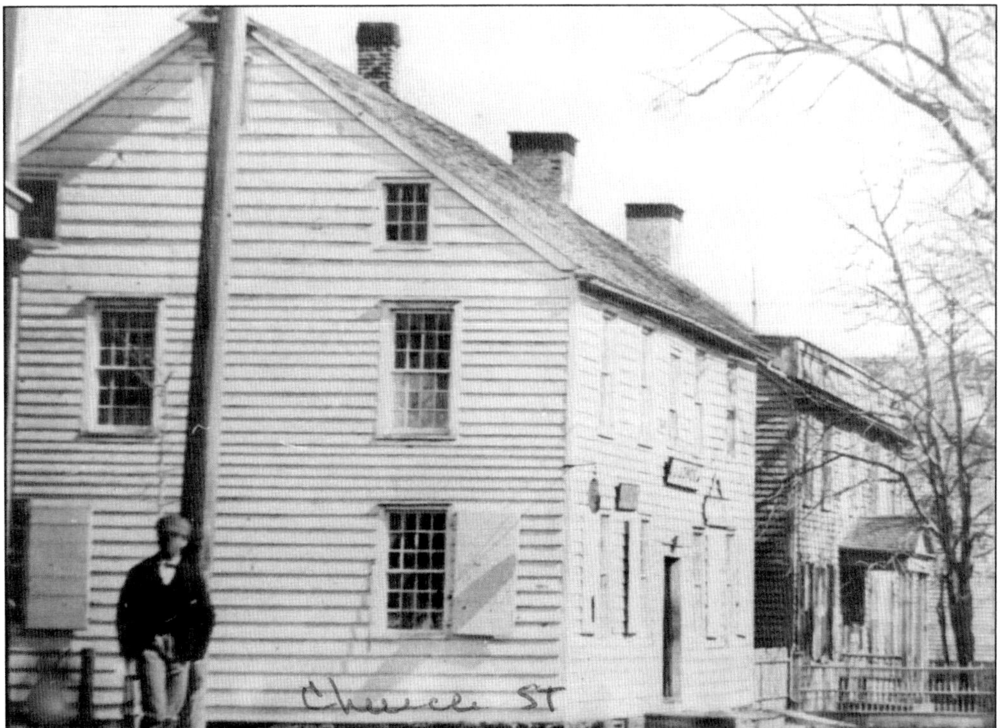

Records indicate that the corner of Church and Elm Streets has been the location of a variety of commercial enterprises since at least 1786. This photograph shows the L. Jones store in 1868. The second floor housed a wagon factory. (Courtesy of Nassau Free Library.)

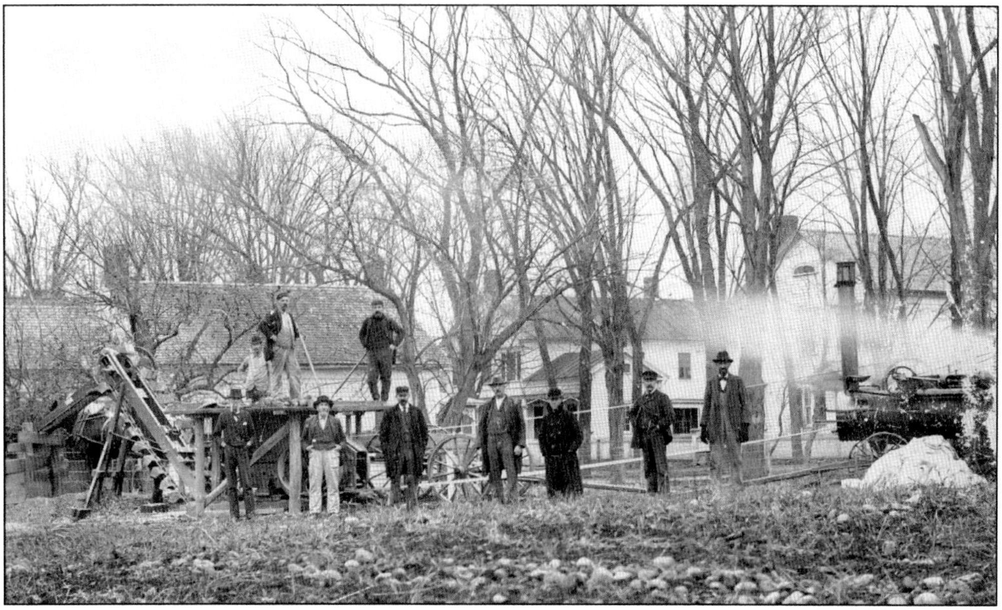

An early steam-powered sawmill is seen in this 1890s photograph of a work party on the west side of Elm Street. To the rear, past the row of trees, is the Methodist parsonage. Around this time, land that had previously been used for farming was divided to make way for new development. (Courtesy of Nassau Free Library.)

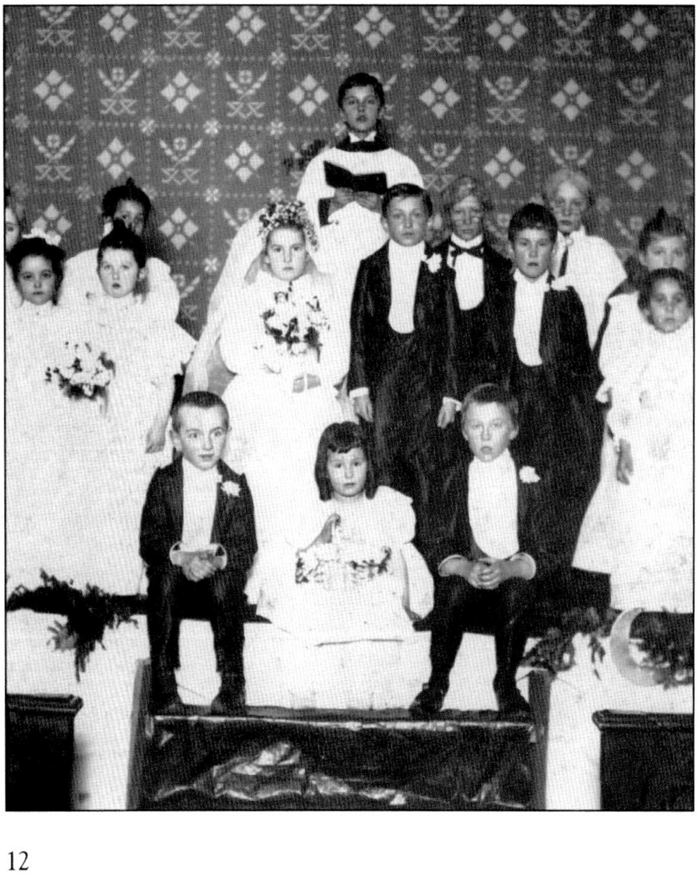

This photograph, taken on December 20, 1898, in the Reformed church shows a Tom Thumb wedding, a popular social event of the period inspired by P.T. Barnum's circus publicity stunts. This group includes Ruth Winters as the bride, Howard Shufelt as the bridegroom, and Clarence Kirby as the minister. (Courtesy of Nassau Free Library.)

Prior to the age of instant entertainment, people gathered together in clubs and societies for education, socializing, and an opportunity for social networking. The Sunshine Society, Nassau Wheelmen, the Order of the Easter Star, and the Nassau Youth League were just some of these groups. Here, ladies in an afternoon music circle meet for their annual summer picnic. (Courtesy of Nassau Free Library.)

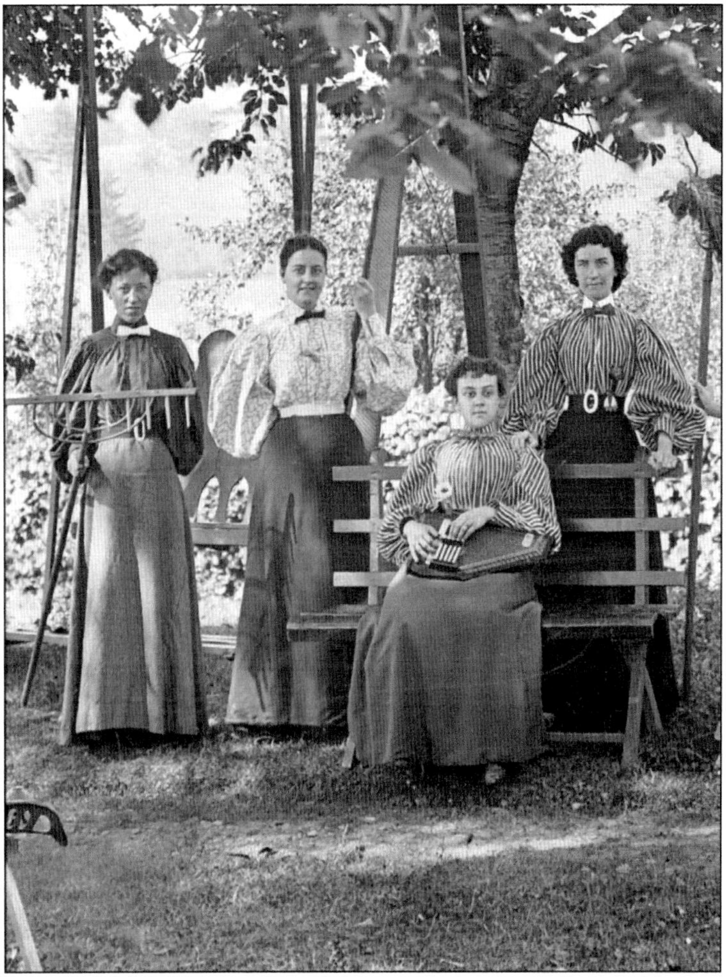

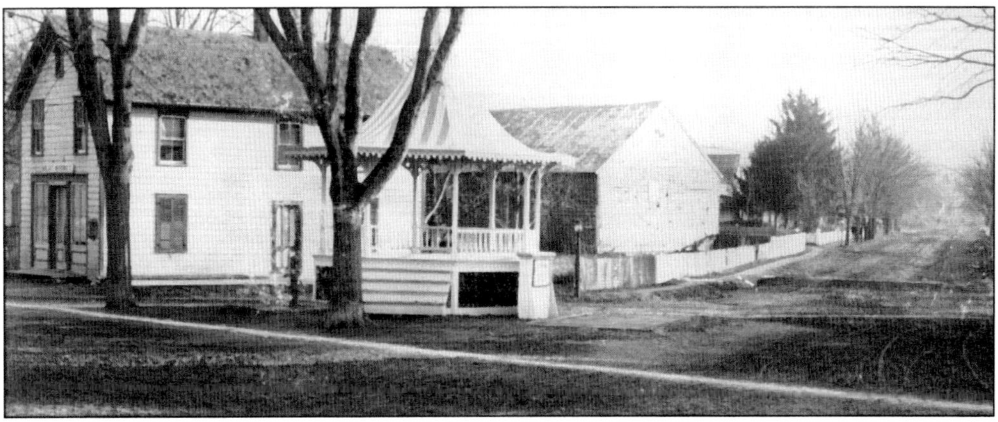

Nassau village was incorporated in 1819. This photograph, taken about 70 years later, shows the center square with the bandstand. To the right of the bandstand are the public scales used to weigh wagonloads of goods going to and from local mills. In 1881, when the Nassau Free Library was organized, it used an upstairs room in Clapper's Meat Market (left). Malden Street is on the right.

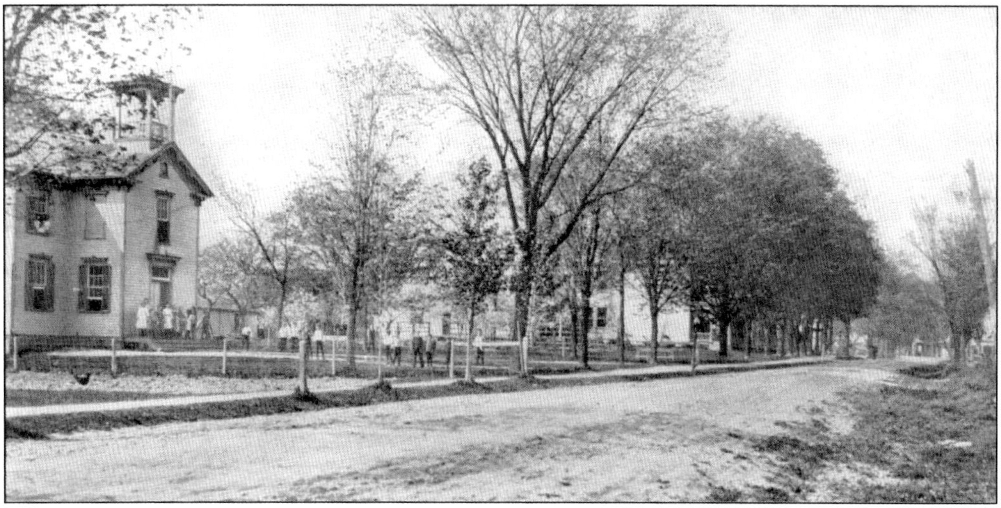

Around the time this c. 1900 photograph was taken, there were 14 independent school districts within the town, each with one school building. Districts were based on what was considered a normal walking distance for students: about four miles. The Nassau Union School, seen here on Chatham Street, was the largest. At this time, only the west side of Chatham Street was developed. Since 1948, the structure has been part of the Nassau Hose Company firehouse.

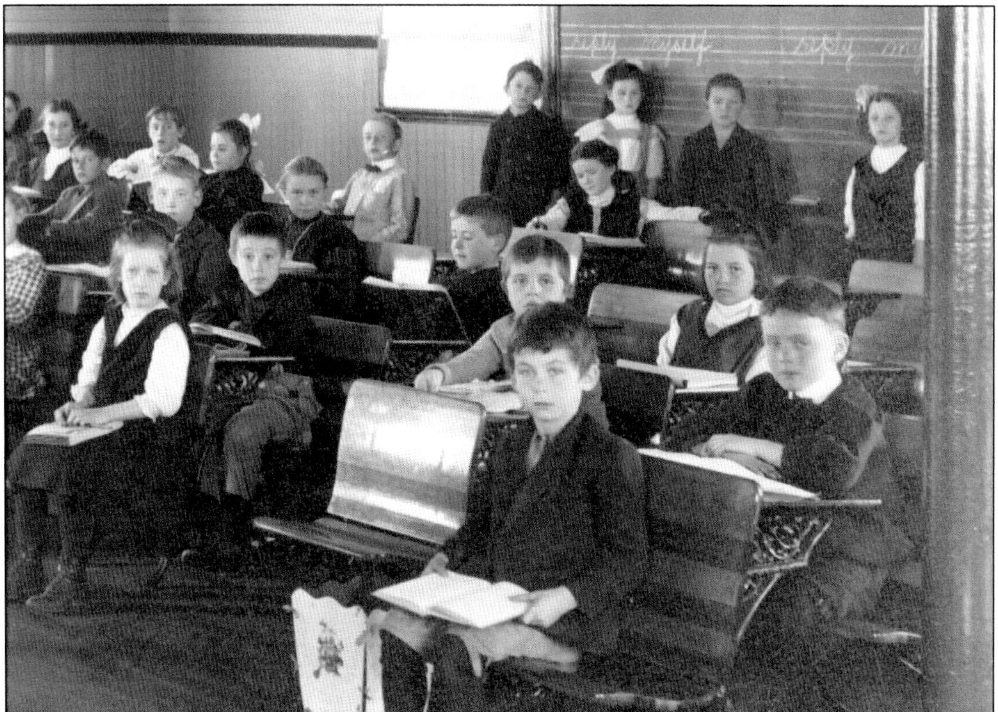

At the Nassau School, seen here, grades one through four were on the first floor, and grades five through eight were on the second. Leonard Chandler and William McKever are two members of this class. A windup Victrola provided military music for outside recreation. The Nassau School often had 50 to 60 students. By comparison, the Bunker Hill School had only 17. (Courtesy of Nassau Free Library.)

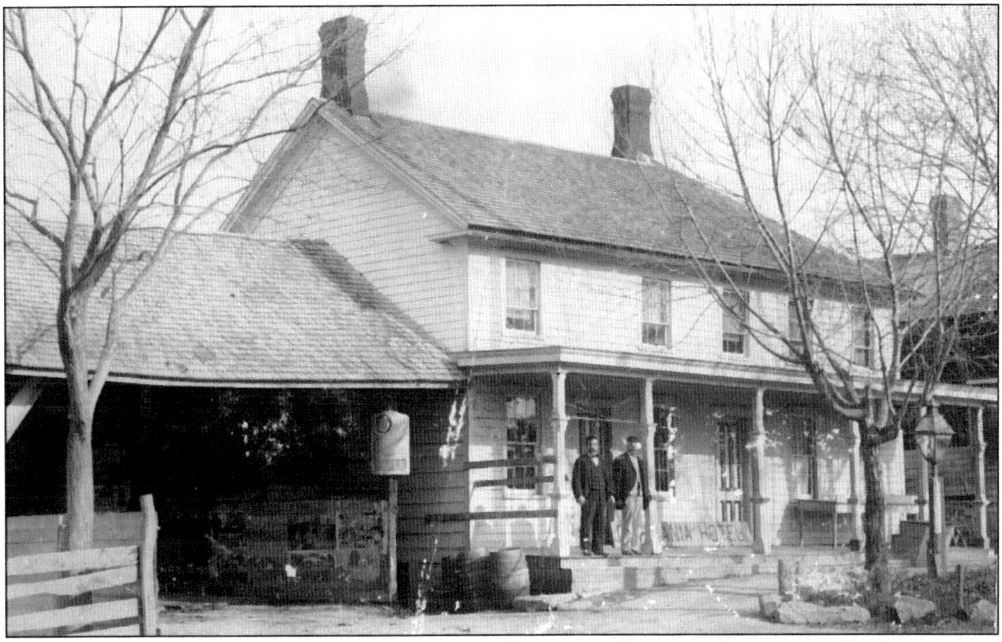

The Germania Hotel, also known as Krutznacker's Hotel, is seen here open for business on Albany Avenue. A sign to the left advertises Dobler Beer, from Albany. To the right is a kerosene streetlight, which was lit nightly by the village lamplighter. Lights burned until 10:00 p.m., and until 11:00 p.m. on Saturdays. (Courtesy of Nassau Free Library.)

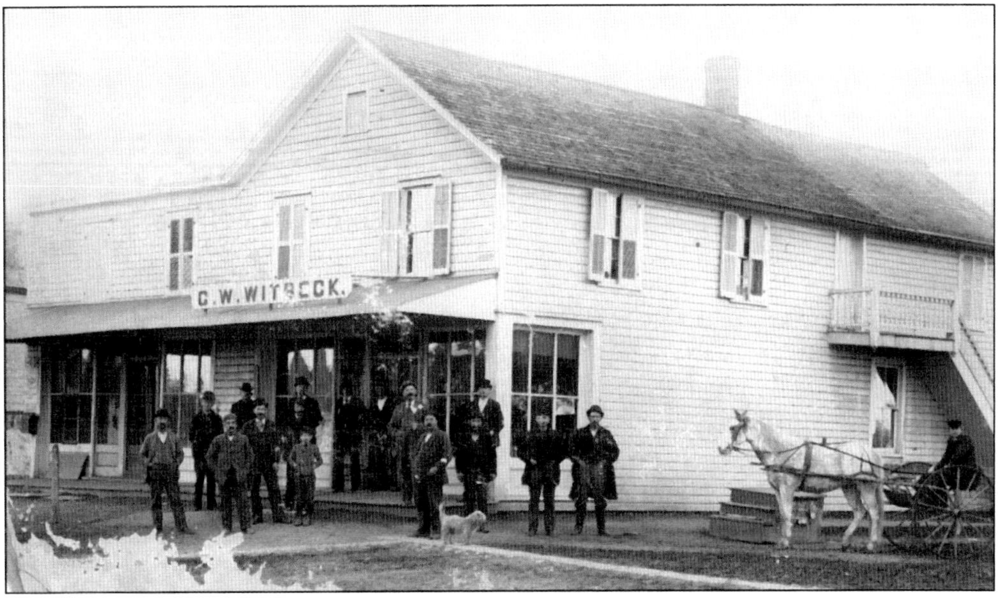

Business in Nassau village drew customers from the surrounding farms. General merchandise stores existed for decades opposite each other at the village square. This group poses in front of the G.W. Witbeck store on Chatham Street. Later, Charles West's store occupied the same location. (Courtesy of Nassau Free Library.)

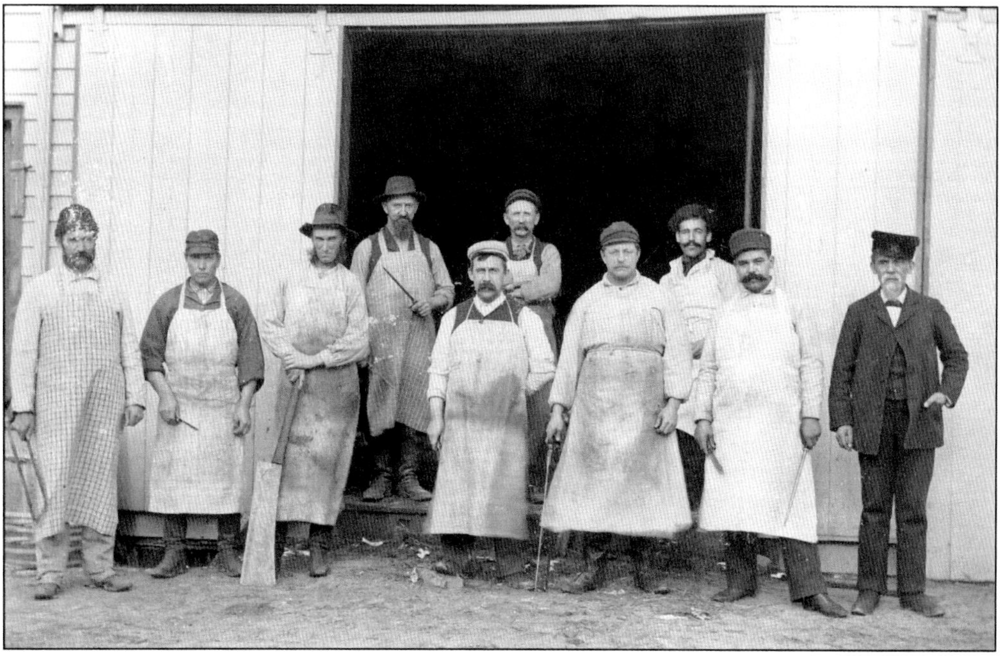

Starting in the 1870s, the David F. Winters family operated a pork-packing business on Elm Street. Here, family members and employees display tools of the trade in front of the business. They are, from left to right, David, Horace, and Oscar Winters, William Shufelt, William Kirby, George Miller, J.S. Weber, unidentified, Orlando Allendorph, and A. Cooke. There was also a sausage factory on Malden Street; the structure is now an apartment building. (Courtesy of Nassau Free Library.)

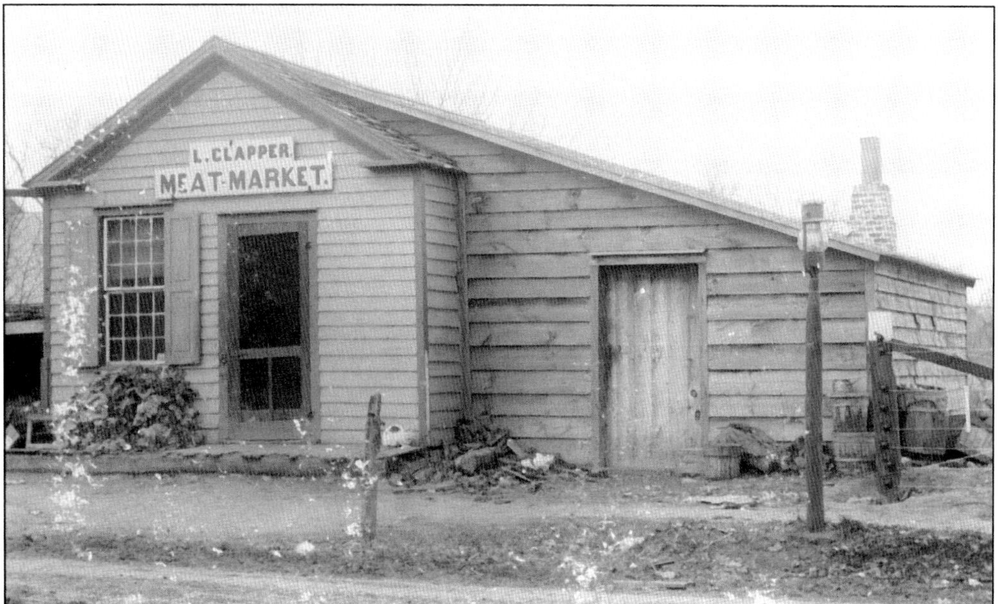

The Clappers were merchants who ran a number of businesses in Nassau for several generations. For many years, a market was on the south side of Church Street, adjacent to the village square. This market was on Elm Street, behind the Nassau House Hotel. (Courtesy of Nassau Free Library.)

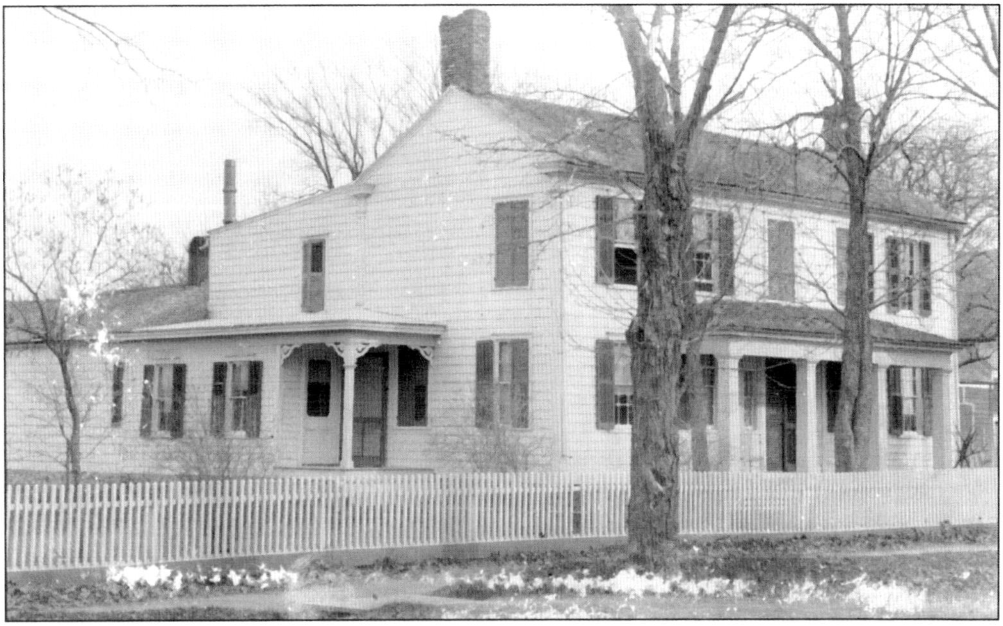

An active 80-acre farm until the early 1900s, with hayfields extending to the rear of Elm Street, 19 Church Street was one of three large, adjacent Federal-style homes. St. Mary's rectory, across the street, and an earlier home on the current site of St. Mary's Church made up the trio. This building is now the town hall. (Courtesy of Nassau Free Library.)

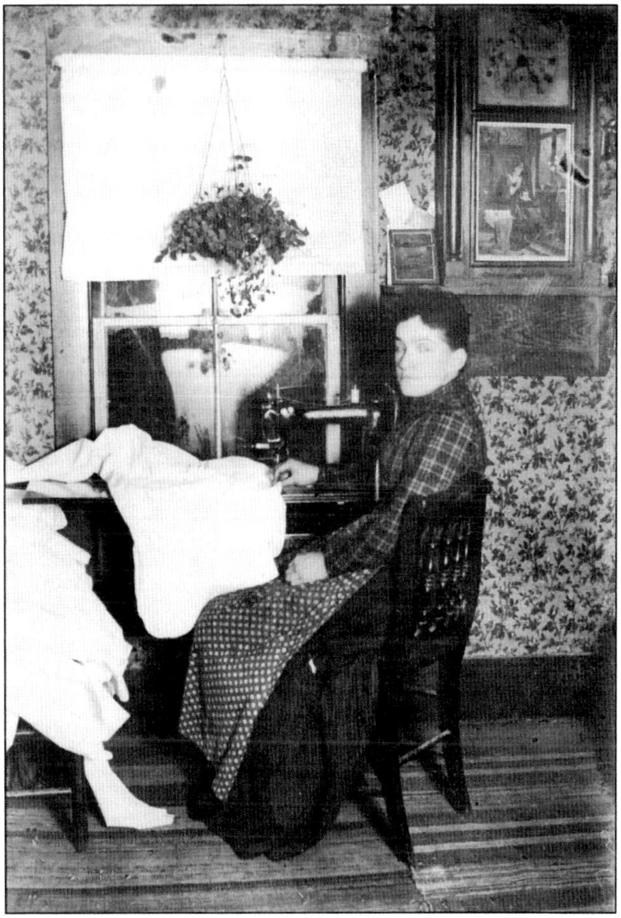

Early commercial industry was not limited to shops and factories. Women working at home provided many families with additional income. Piecework for Cluett & Peabody shirtmakers, in Troy, was common throughout Rensselaer County. Lillian Garrison Velie is seen taking a break from making shirts in 1892. (Courtesy of Judith Marquette.)

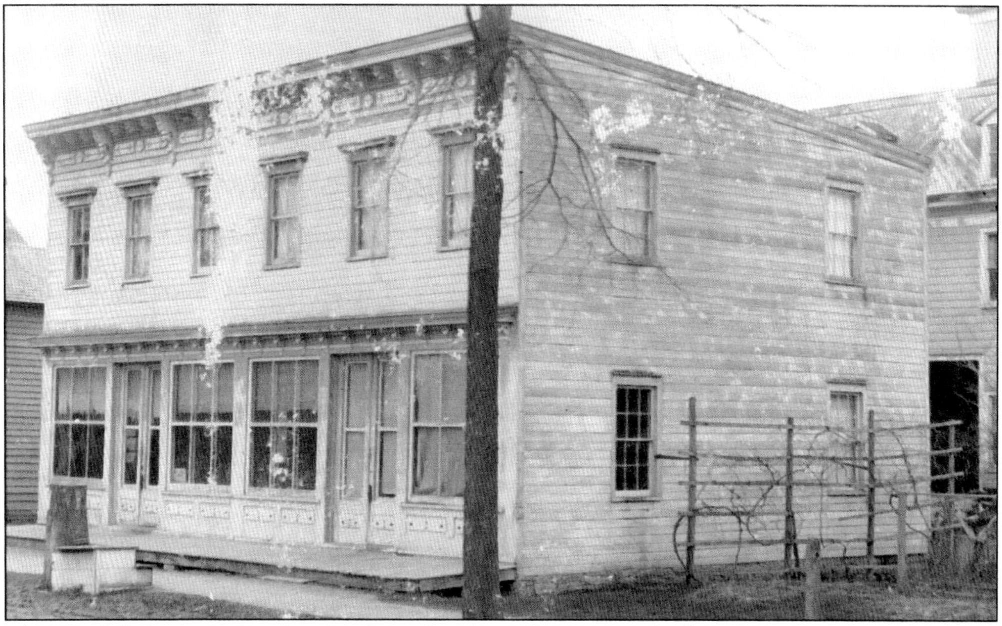

The VanSalisburys were a family of woodworkers who operated a furniture store in this building on Elm Street for many years. As was common in those days, they also made wooden coffins. Around 1900, the family divided the ground floor into two storefronts and opened Nassau's first undertaker's parlor. (Courtesy of Nassau Free Library.)

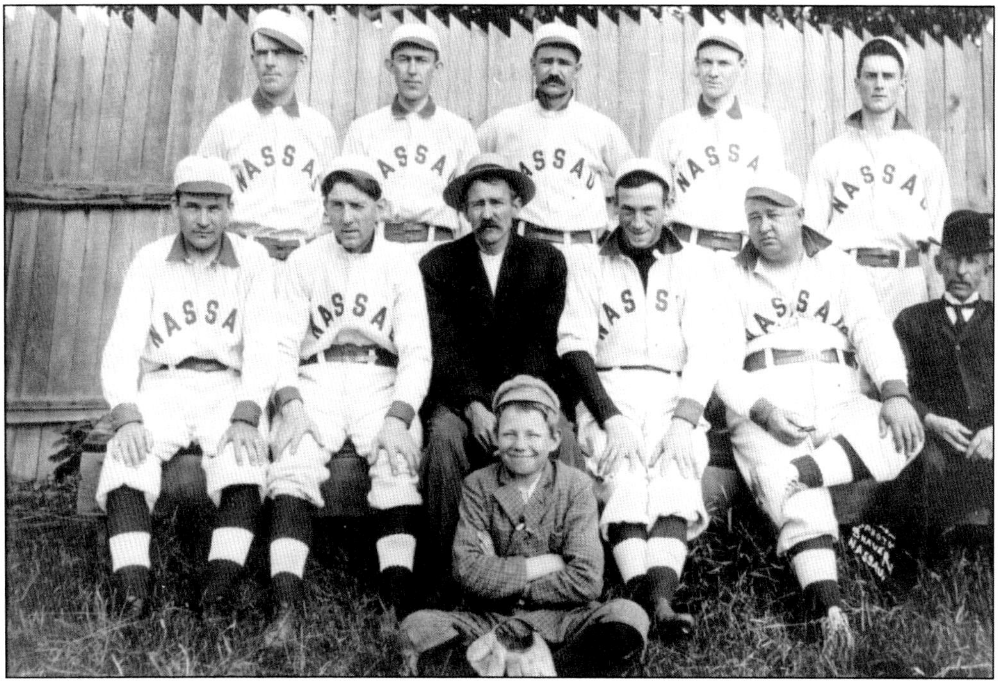

Baseball has long played a part of social life in Nassau. This town team includes, from left to right, (first row) Clayton Roth, unidentified, Charles Kosegarten, unidentified, Harry Bateman, and George Seeley; (second row) John Vandenberg, Harry Bull, Otto Kosegarten, Ralph Cooper, and Guy New. Team mascot Fritz Kosegarten is in front. (Courtesy of the Schodack Town Historian.)

Two

GETTING TO NASSAU

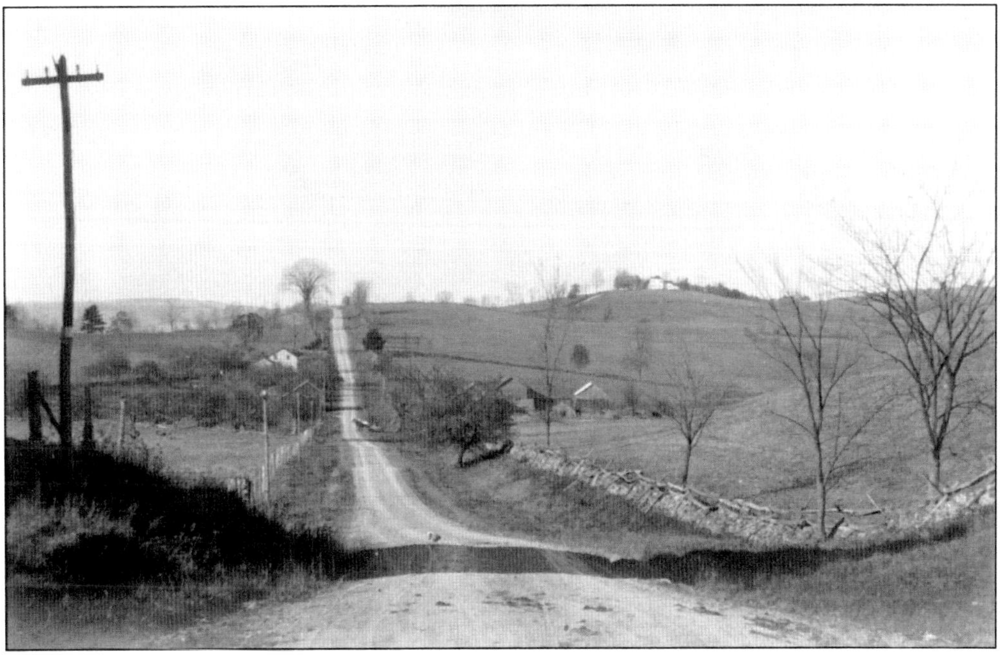

This 1880s photograph is thought to have been taken in the area of Lord's Hill, east of Nassau village. It was named after the Lord family, early settlers who farmed the property. The open fields produced hay and wheat and provided grazing land for herds of farm animals. Firewood was also a sought-after commodity, which led to the close trimming of open fields.

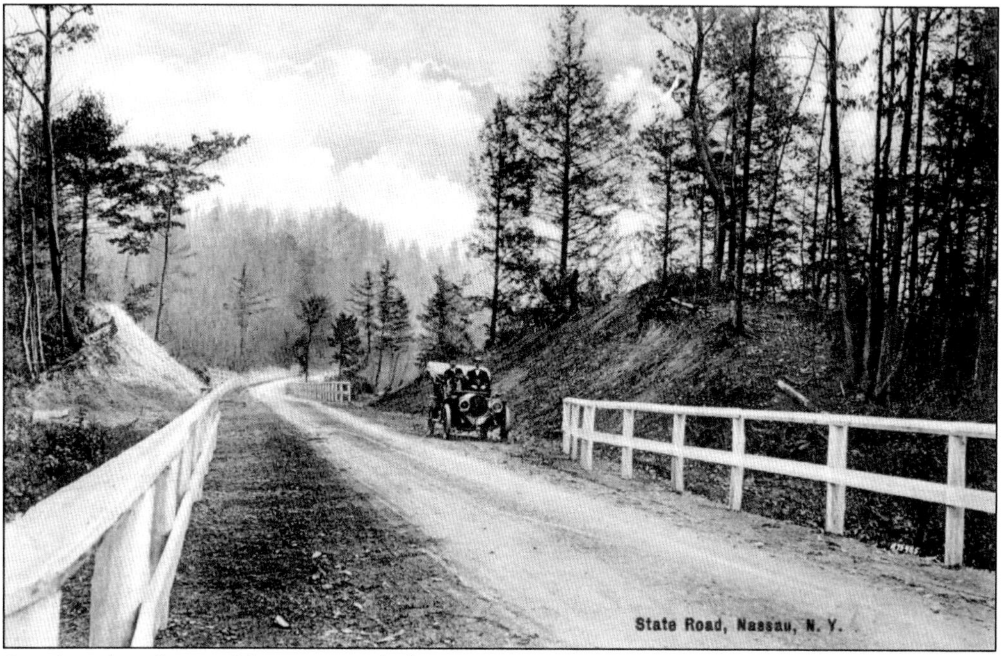

Simply referred to as "the state road" for many years, US Route 20 continues to be the main route through the village and town of Nassau. As early as 1808, permission was requested from the state legislature to incorporate a turnpike extending from Nassau to New Lebanon. East of Nassau village, Kinderhook Creek presented the greatest barrier for a direct route east. In 1813, Joseph Brainard built a bridge over the creek and charged a toll to cross.

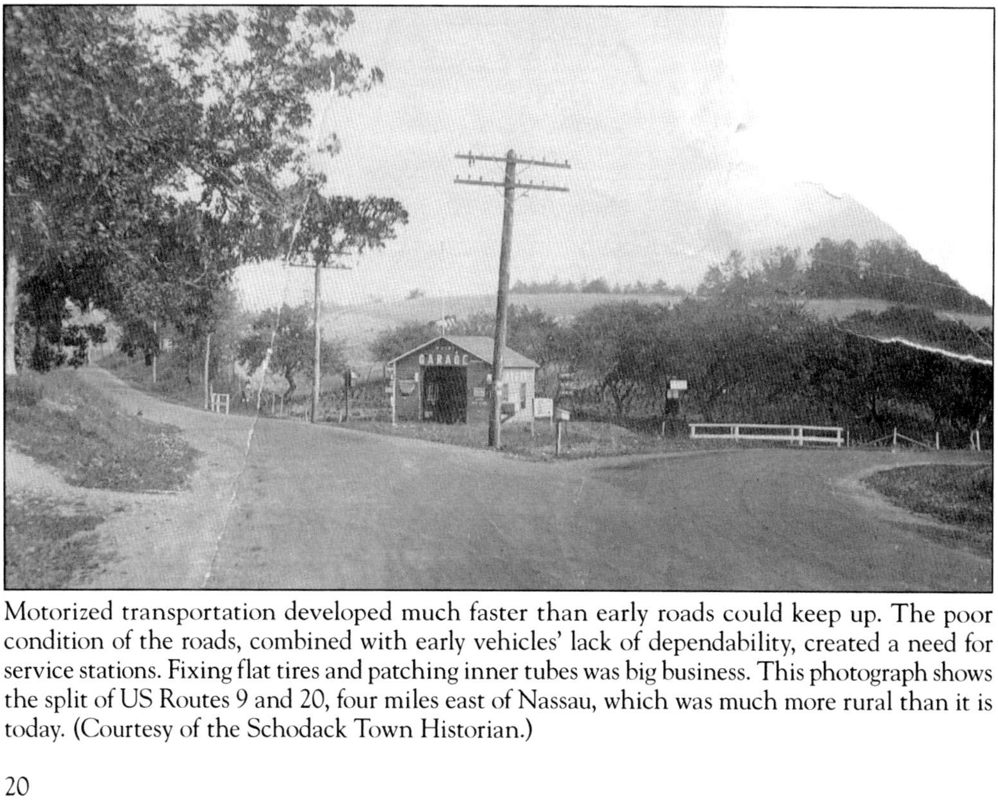

Motorized transportation developed much faster than early roads could keep up. The poor condition of the roads, combined with early vehicles' lack of dependability, created a need for service stations. Fixing flat tires and patching inner tubes was big business. This photograph shows the split of US Routes 9 and 20, four miles east of Nassau, which was much more rural than it is today. (Courtesy of the Schodack Town Historian.)

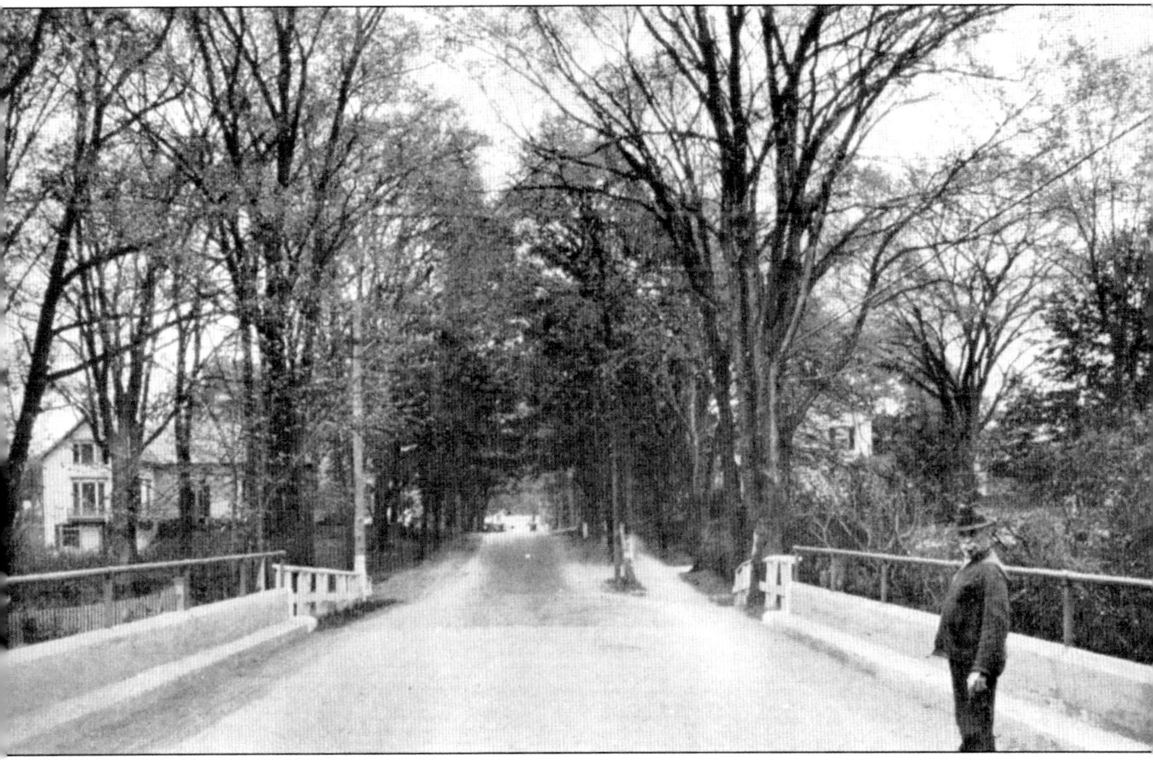

Ever since Nassau was created from parts of surrounding towns, including parts of Schodack in 1806, the Valatiekill stream has formed the border Nassau and Schodack. Flowing south to meet Kinderhook Creek in Valatie, the stream was the route the earliest Europeans used to explore the area. Nassau youth who grew up in the days of the first automobiles admiringly watched car owners using the stream to wash their cars. George Koons, of McClellan Road, is seen here walking across the bridge into Nassau village. His daughter Florence worked at the Piano Action Factory, and he would often join her for lunch. Even the little Valatiekill could flood, and periodic flooding threatened the stability of the bridge until the 1930s.

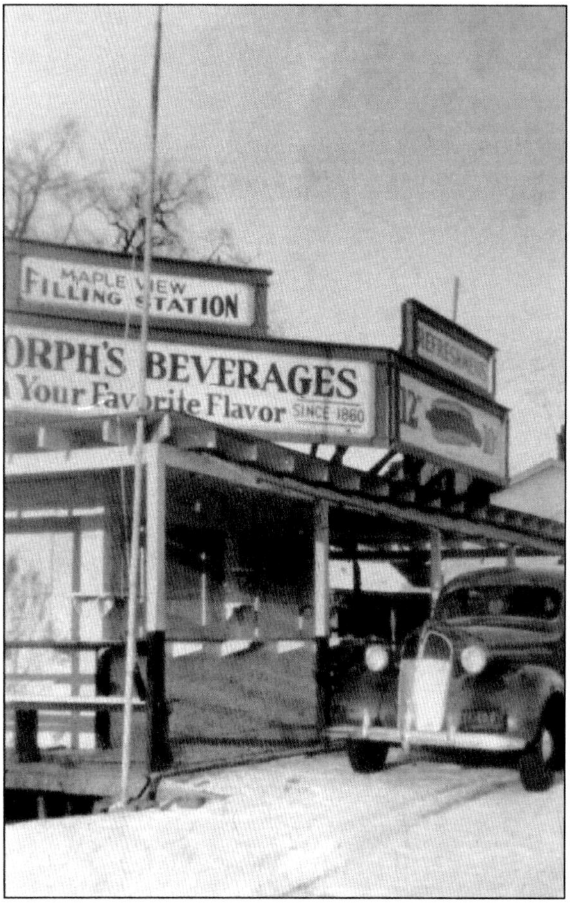

A service infrastructure built up as vehicle use increased. Maple View Filling Station is seen here in the 1930s. Better known as a hot dog stand, the business was located on US Route 20, east of Nassau village in the vicinity of Lyon's Lake Road. Reisdorph's Beverages were a locally bottled brand of sodas.

Seward Clapper and Leland Francisco opened the first Nassau Garage in a small barn opposite the trolley station on Albany Avenue, west of the Germania Hotel. It was replaced by a larger structure in the same location after fire destroyed this building. (Courtesy of Nassau Free Library.)

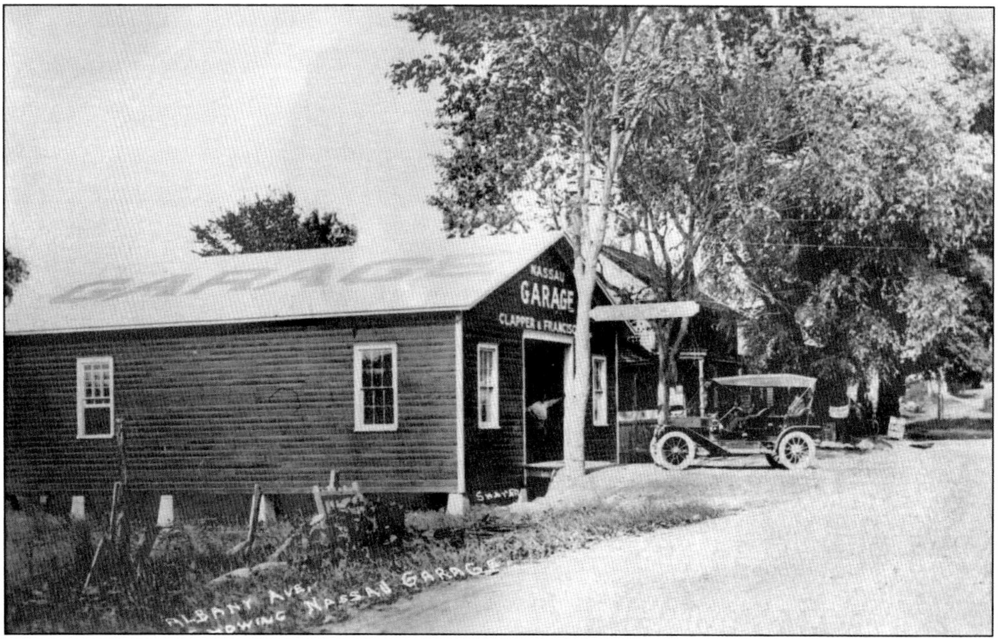

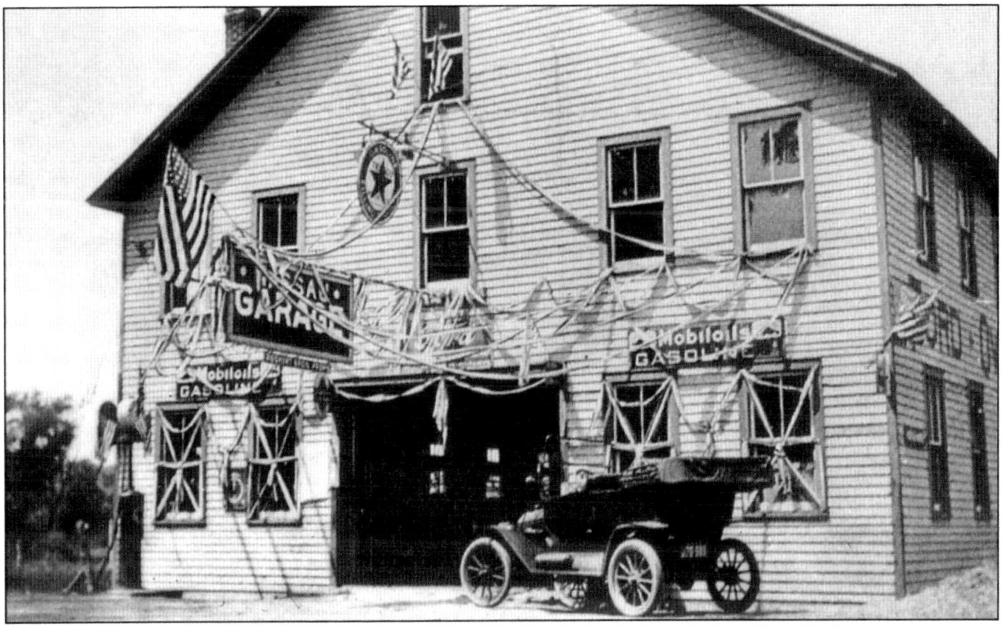

The rebuilt Nassau Garage was the largest automobile repair shop in Nassau. It also served as a machine shop. When a mechanical part broke, the rule was "repair rather than replace." An early Locomobile touring car was converted to serve as a tow truck. When this building burned in the late 1920s, village elders questioned the need for gas stations in the village.

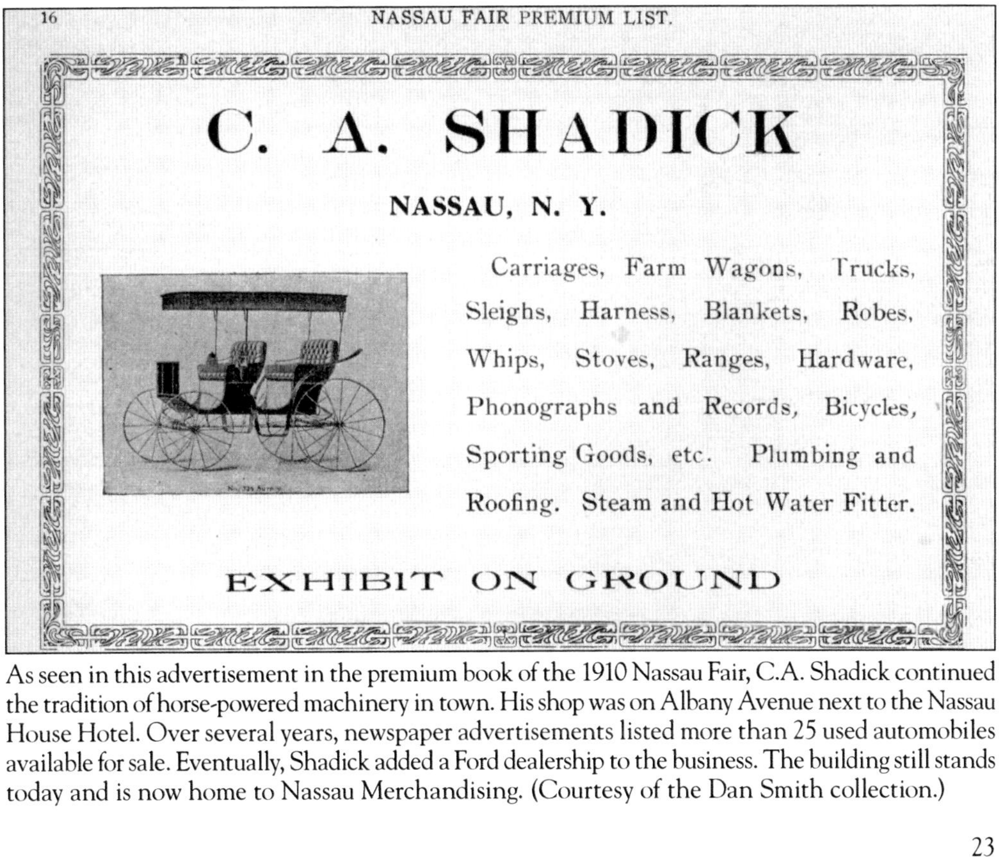

As seen in this advertisement in the premium book of the 1910 Nassau Fair, C.A. Shadick continued the tradition of horse-powered machinery in town. His shop was on Albany Avenue next to the Nassau House Hotel. Over several years, newspaper advertisements listed more than 25 used automobiles available for sale. Eventually, Shadick added a Ford dealership to the business. The building still stands today and is now home to Nassau Merchandising. (Courtesy of the Dan Smith collection.)

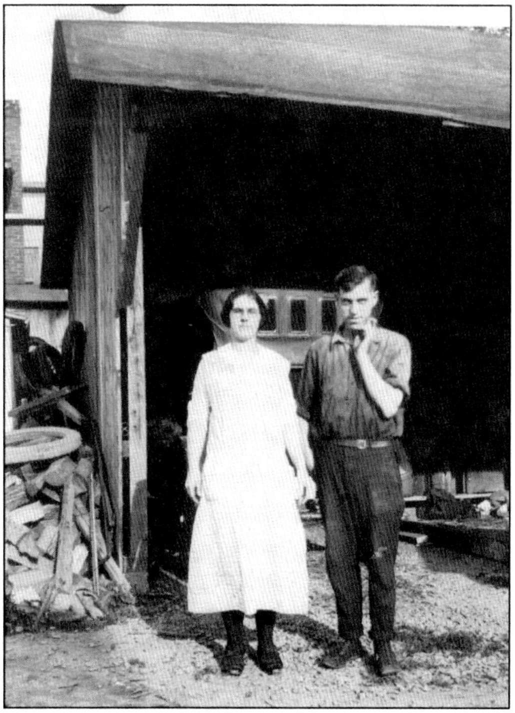

Sturm's Garage operated for many years on upper Church Street, just at the village limits. The Sturms were a farm family from Schodack before coming to Nassau. Frank and Elizabeth Sturm are seen at left in front of the garage. Early records show Frank's occupation as teamster and then a blacksmith. He was drafted into World War I and opened the garage after the war. Three generations of the family operated the business, selling gas and automotive supplies and offering repairs. In the early 1940s, they also sold Durant automobiles. Sturm's was the first area garage with towing services robust enough to deal with the growing number of trucking accidents on US Route 20 through the 1950s. The advertisement below, from the 1927 Nassau Fair premium book, misspells the family name as "Strum." (Left, courtesy of the William Sturm family; below, courtesy of Nassau Free Library.)

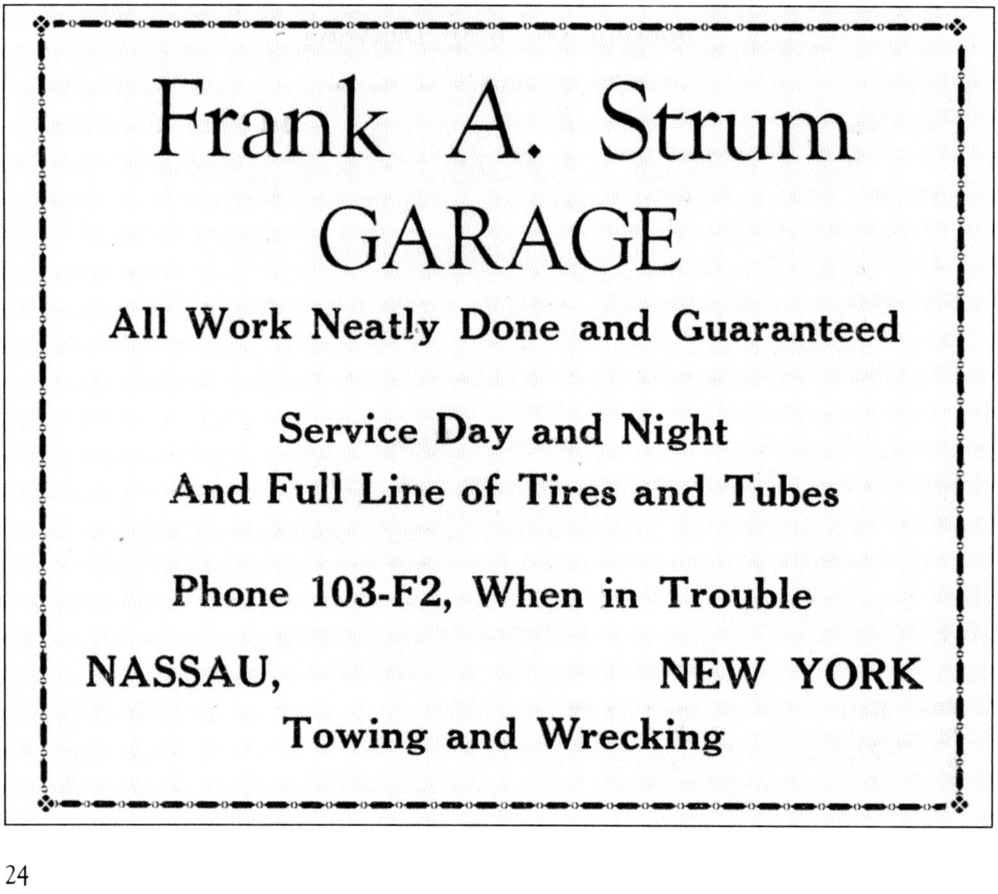

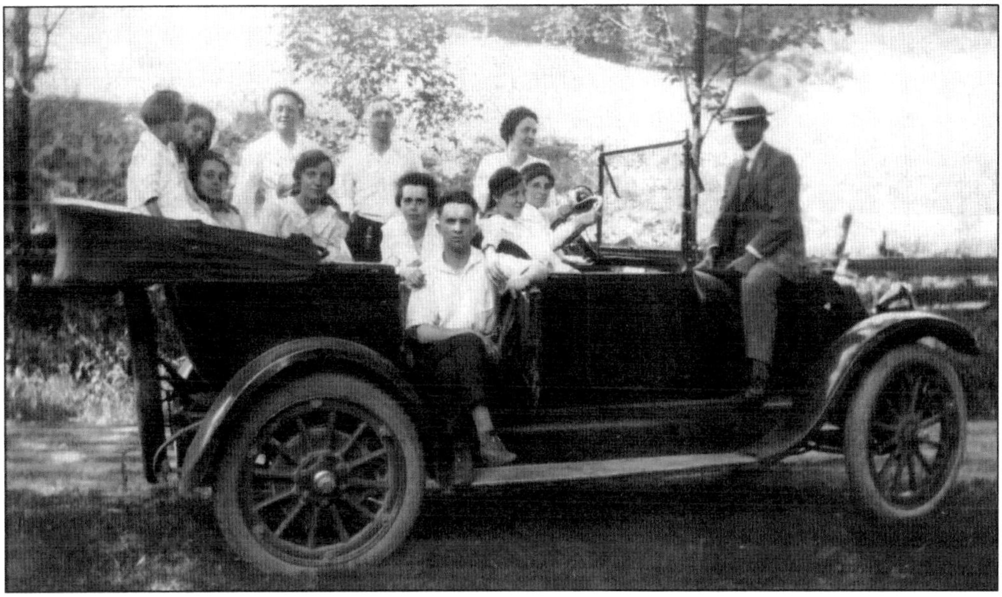

The Bull family and their friends enjoy an outing to Tassawassa Lake in 1919 in a Studebaker touring car. Horace Bull, a stockbroker and investor in Albany, was one of Nassau's wealthiest residents. The family lived on Elm Street. (Courtesy of the Schodack Town Historian.)

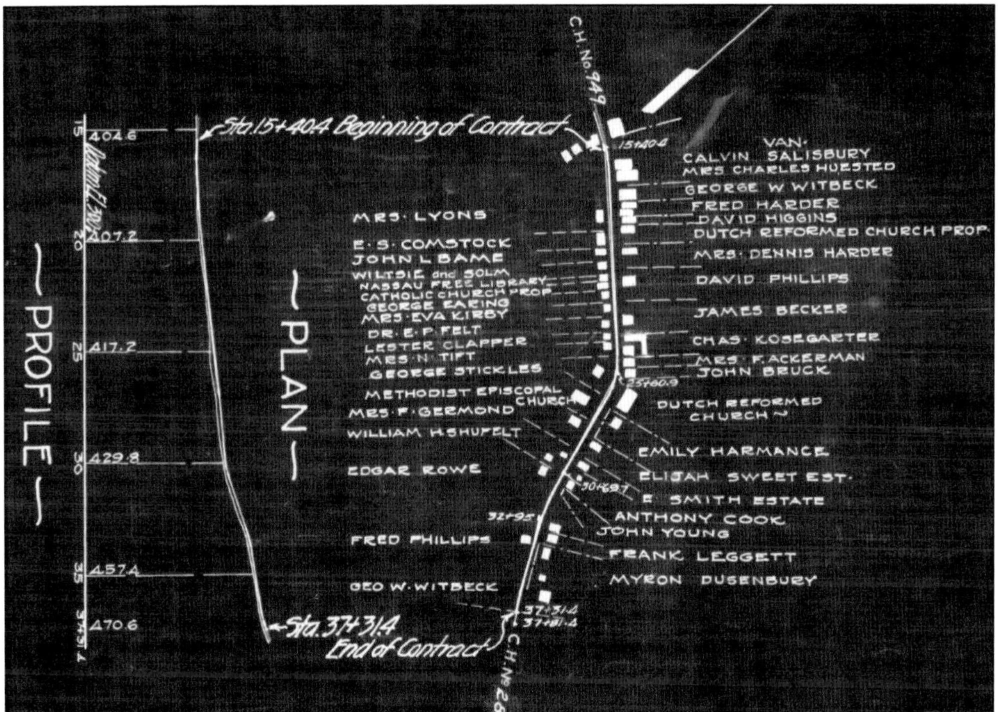

In 1911, New York State approved funds to pave the state highway for the first time. Prior to that, the surface of oil-packed gravel was dusty in the summer, muddy in spring and fall, and limited to horse-drawn sleighs in winter. This detail from the construction blueprints offers a glimpse of the project, from the center of Nassau village east up Church Street.

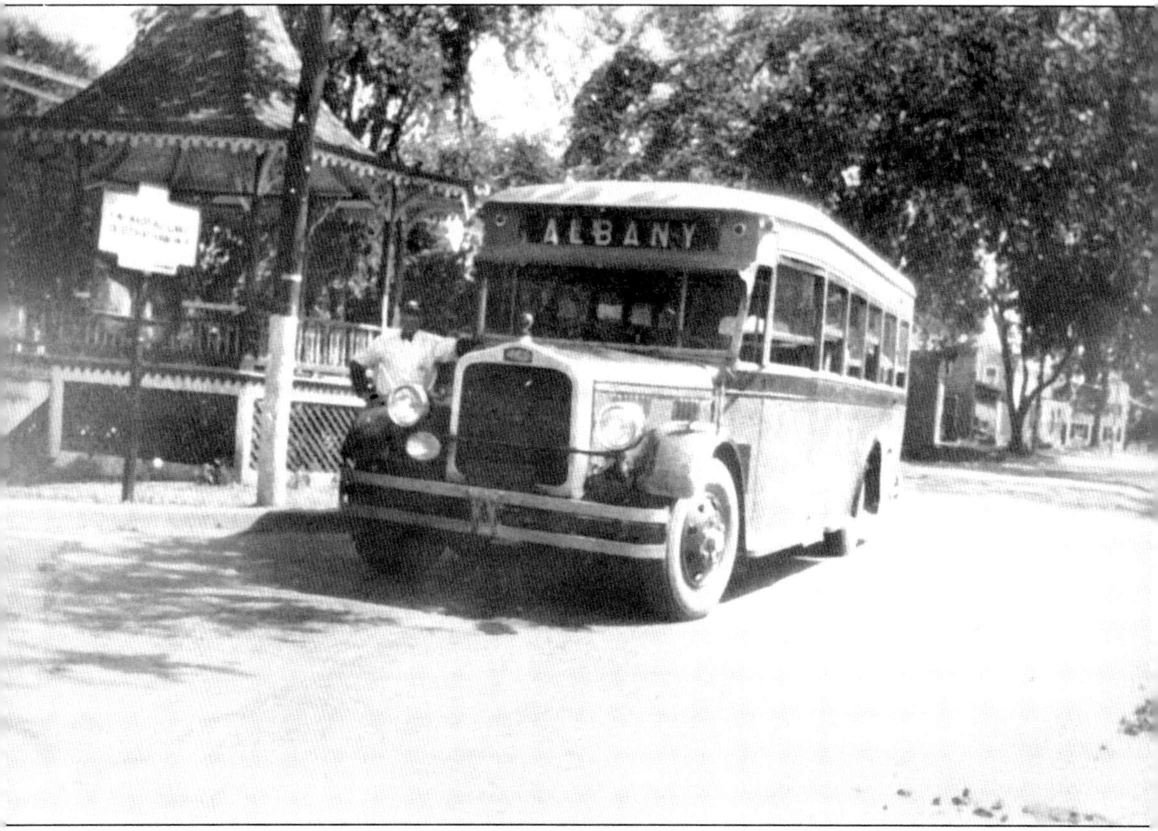

In December 1929, rail traffic ended on the Albany Southern Railroad trolley route. To fill the gap, United Transportation of Albany was mandated to continue servicing the route, and it started running busses. The Albany bus is seen here in 1932 waiting at the village square for passengers. While access to towns south of Nassau was lost, much of the former route northwest to Albany was maintained. It is because of this that, to this day, the limited bus service from Nassau to Albany still travels via Nassau Lake and East Schodack. (Courtesy of Judith Marquette.)

Three

The Village Square

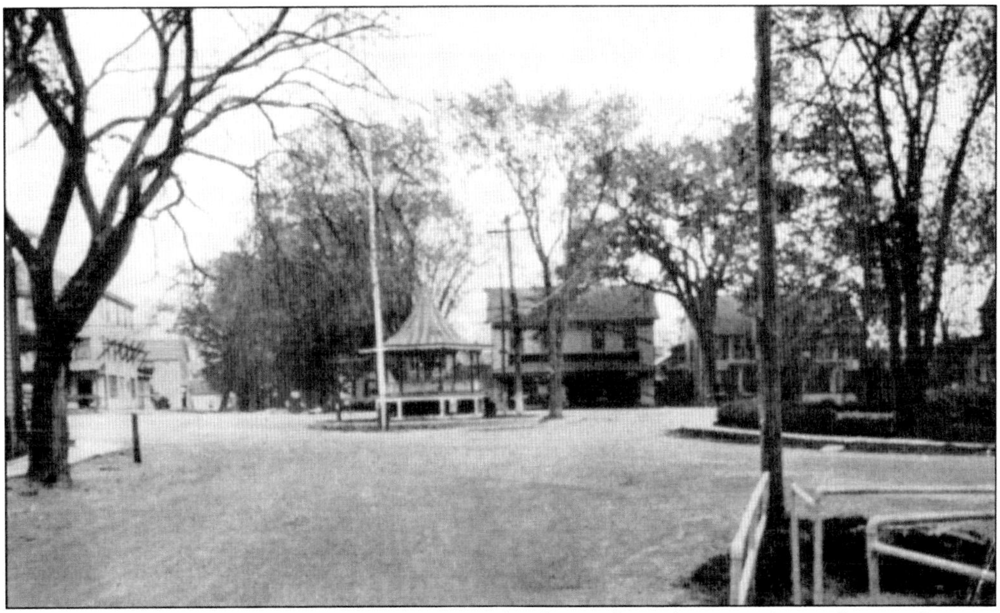

Clusters of homes and businesses dotted Nassau's landscape from the time of its earliest settlement. Stores, mills, and taverns often attracted additional development in the vicinity. But Nassau village was always the largest community in the town, and was the only incorporated village for the first 192 years of town history. It was also the inspiration for the renaming of the town itself. The area of the village of Nassau is only about one square mile, but for most of its years, it has been home to a large portion of the town's population. The growth of Nassau started with a store, a tavern, and a freshwater spring at what became the village square. The view in this photograph looks north on Chatham Street towards Elm Street. Church Street is to the right and Albany Avenue is to the left.

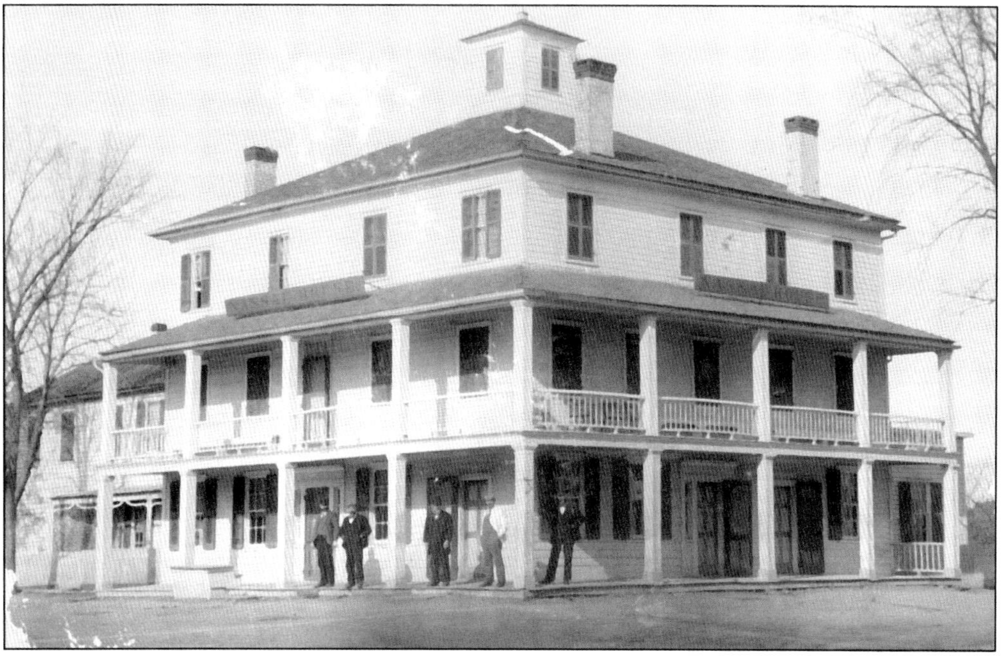

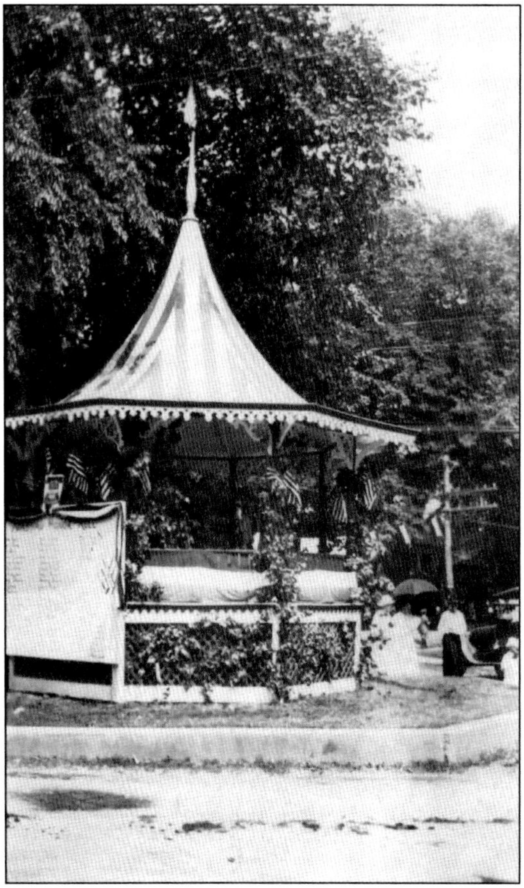

Although it went through a number of names, the hotel above stood on the corner of Albany Avenue and Elm Street for years. Around 1800, Jacob Witbeck built the Nassau House Hotel there. A focal point for community life, it was the scene of political meetings and dinners and included a tavern, a courtroom, and a stagecoach stop. The hotel was noted for its 60-foot ballroom, and because former president Martin Van Buren attended Sunday dinner there in the 1840s. A hotel survived at that location until 1955, when it was demolished to make way for a gas station. (Courtesy of Nassau Free Library.)

This ornate bandstand became the centerpiece of Nassau's village square in the Civil War era. With a dramatic pointed roof and gingerbread trim under the eaves, the structure was predated by a freshwater spring, and then, for many years, a public hand pump.

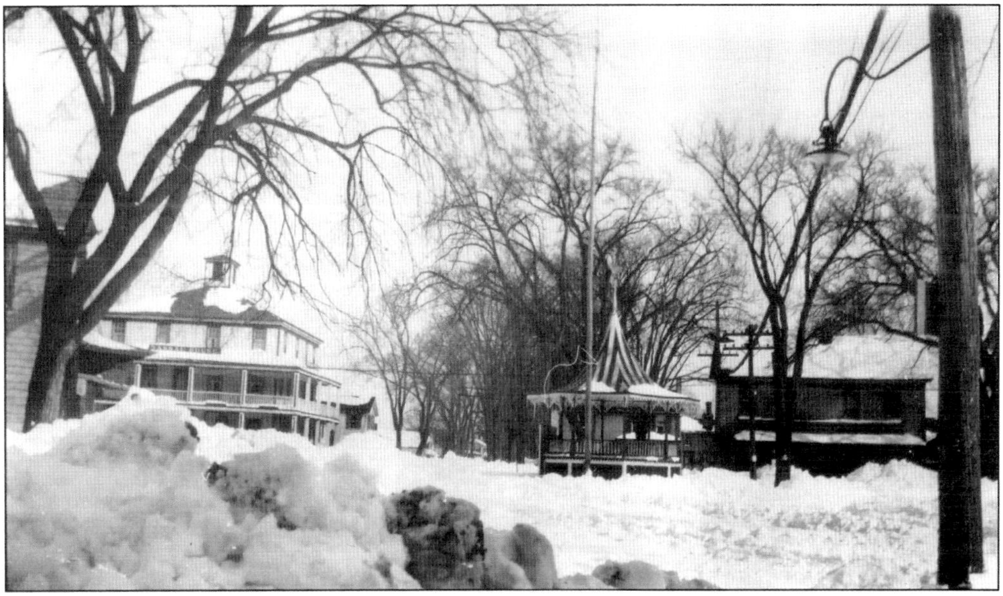

Looking north towards Elm Street on a snowy morning in the early 1930s, the view in this photograph, taken by Raymond Velie, shows the iconic bandstand in the center of the square. Beyond it to the left is the former Nassau House Hotel, which still had its old sign even though by then it was known as Kelly's Hotel, and to the right is Pitt's store. In 1907, the village bandstand was wired for electric lights. The Nassau Band performed weekly Saturday night concerts from the bandstand in the summers until the early 1930s. (Courtesy of Judith Marquette.)

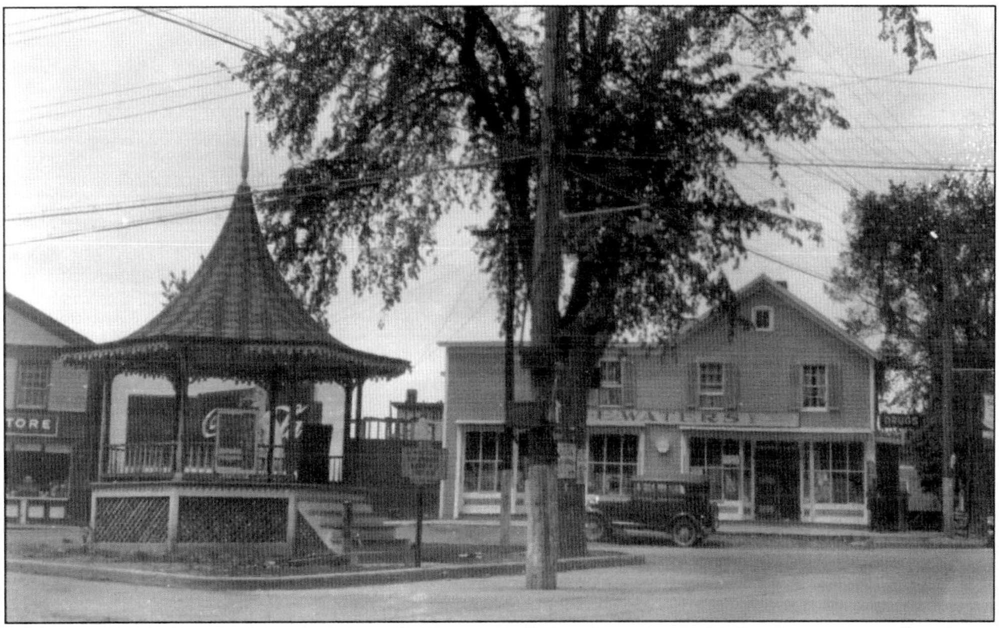

The area opposite the square, on the corner of Albany Avenue and Chatham Street, has been occupied by a commercial business since the 1700s. Waters Pharmacy, the third in the succession of four pharmacies located at or near the square, is seen here in the mid-1920s. To the far right, a Socony gas sign can just be made out. Fireworks were also sold around the Fourth of July. (Courtesy of Norman Rowe.)

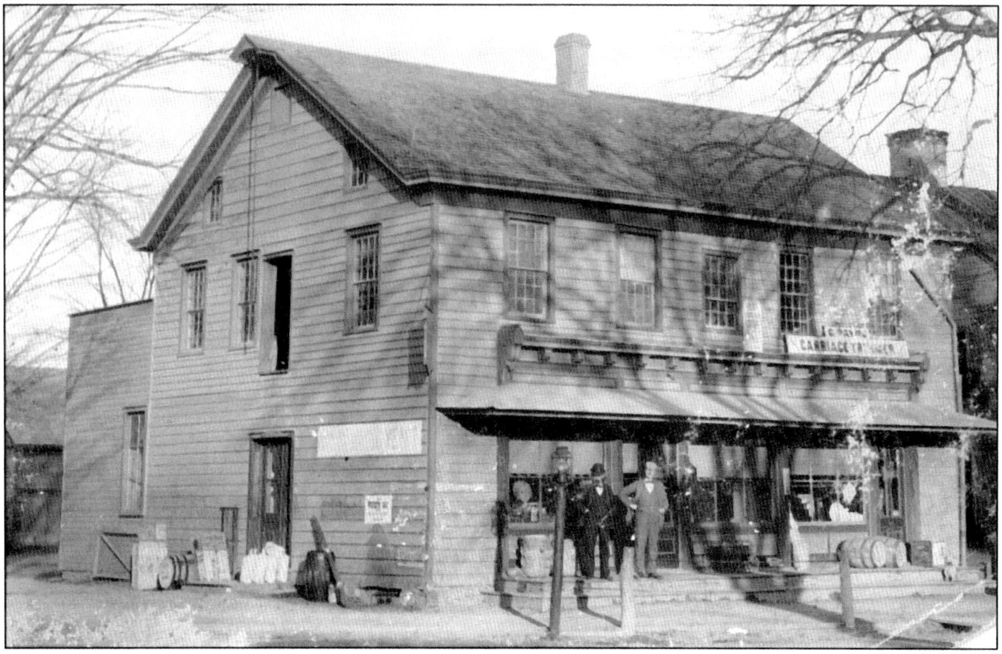

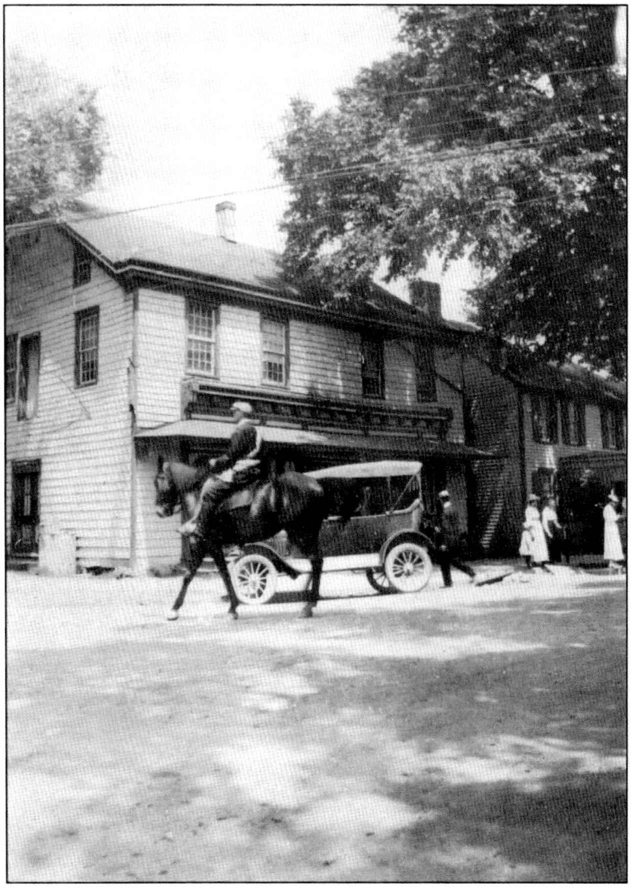

The building on the eastern side of the square, at the corner of Church and Elm Streets, has served as a commercial location continuously since it was first constructed in 1786. For many years in the late 1700s and into the early 1800s, a wagon factory was located on the second floor. At some point in the 1800s, the first floor was split to serve as the location for two storefronts. The photograph above shows a general store to the left and a harness shop to the right in the 1880s. Around the time motor vehicles replaced horsepower, the general store remained to the left of the building, with the smaller right side serving as the Nassau Post Office. The building is seen at left in 1918. (Above, courtesy of Nassau Free Library; left, courtesy of the Schodack Town Historian.)

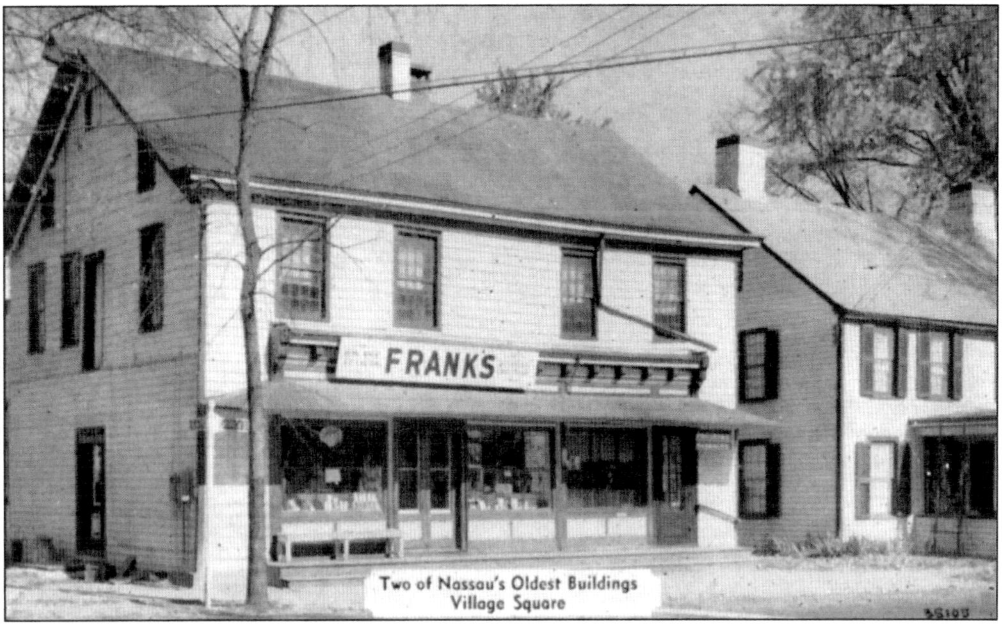

By the 1940s, much of the original building detail remained intact. The 12-over-12 windows—referring to the number of individual small panes of glass—the decorative wooden trim, and the narrow roof overhang were common in commercial buildings of the period. The photograph above shows that the name Frank's Store remained even after longtime owner Frank Pitts sold the business. By the late 1960s, the Soda Shack, an ice cream and snack bar, and Don McGill's barbershop occupied the building. At the somewhat sad point in the building's life below, the second-floor windows disappeared and the roof gutter drain spout was placed in a much more obvious location. Fortunately, later owners revealed the covered windows, and the building retains much of its original appearance today.

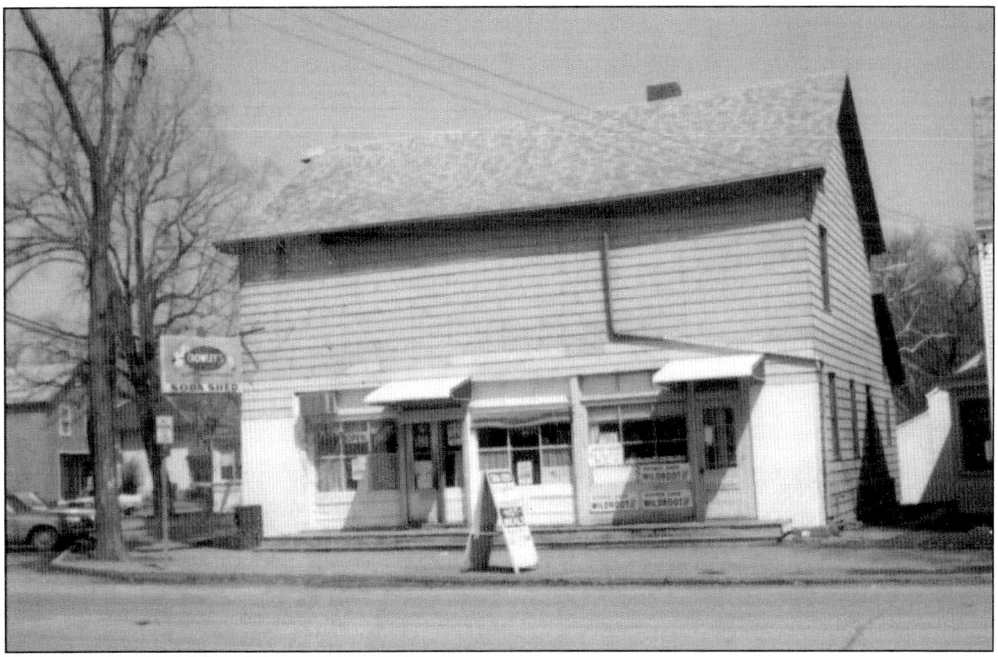

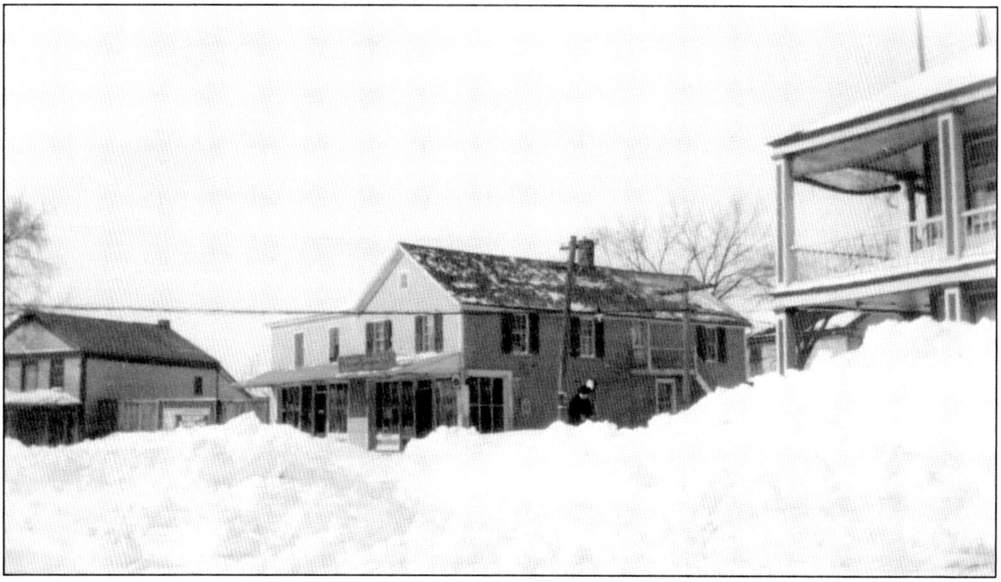

These commercial buildings, now long gone, faced the square on the corner of Chatham and Elm Streets. This image shows the Nassau pharmacy in the center and West's store to the left. The gap between the two was once S.J. Lennon's Confectionary. In the right corner are the porches of the Nassau House Hotel.

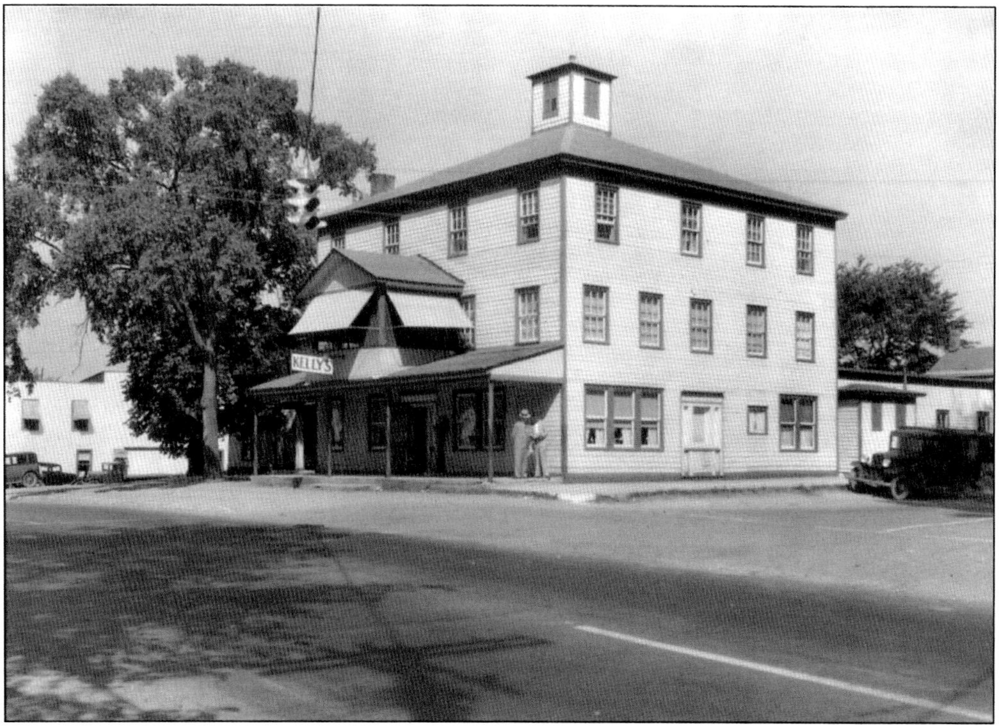

Kelly's Hotel, formerly the Nassau House Hotel, on the corner of Albany Avenue and Elm Street, is seen here in the early 1930s. William Kelly, a charismatic former boxer from Albany, bought the hotel in 1925 and named it after himself. In 1949, the business sold again, but the name remained until the building was demolished in the 1950s.

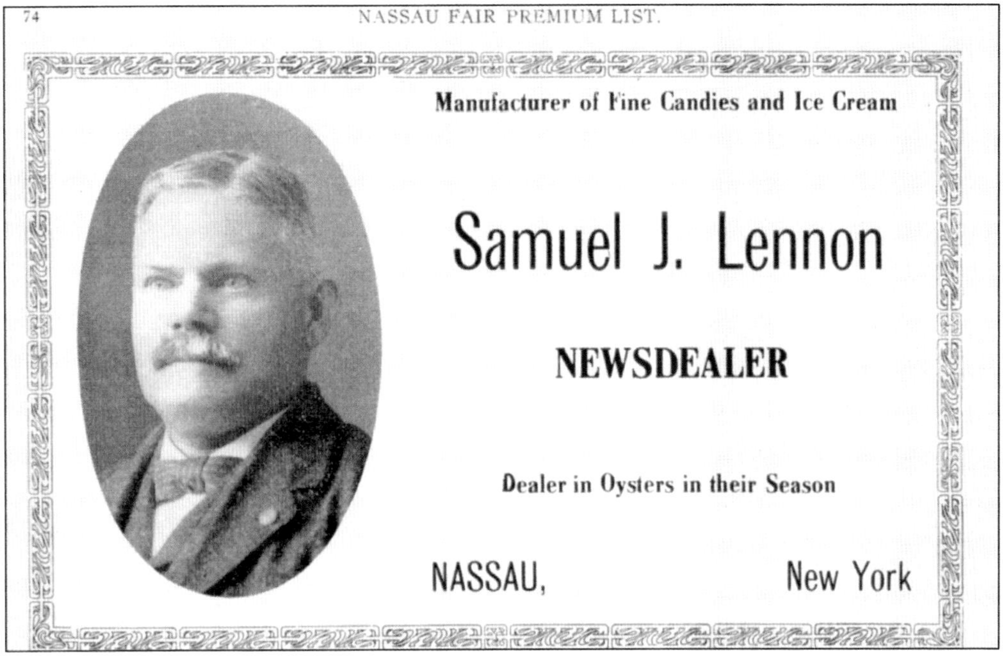

Samuel J. Lennon and his family operated a variety of businesses in Nassau, including a confectionary, a newsroom, and a lunchroom. In 1923, Lennon introduced ice cream sundaes, priced at 15¢, to Nassau. An Irish immigrant, he enlisted in the Union army at 18 as a drummer and fought in many of the most notable battles of the Civil War, including Bull Run, Antietam, and Gettysburg. When he was taken prisoner by the Confederates, he was the battalion color-bearer. He was often invited to Nassau School to tell about his exploits. The two-story portion of the building below was later moved farther down Chatham Street, turned sideways, and used as Kirk's and Spire's Store, and, later, Jake's Deli. The structure still stands today, as an apartment. (Both, courtesy of the Dan Smith collection.)

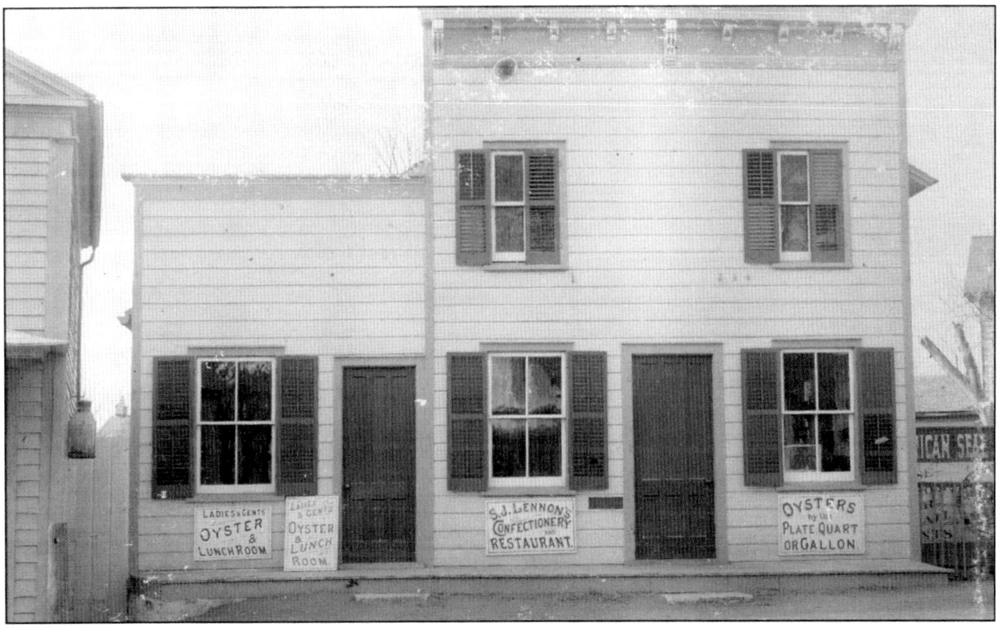

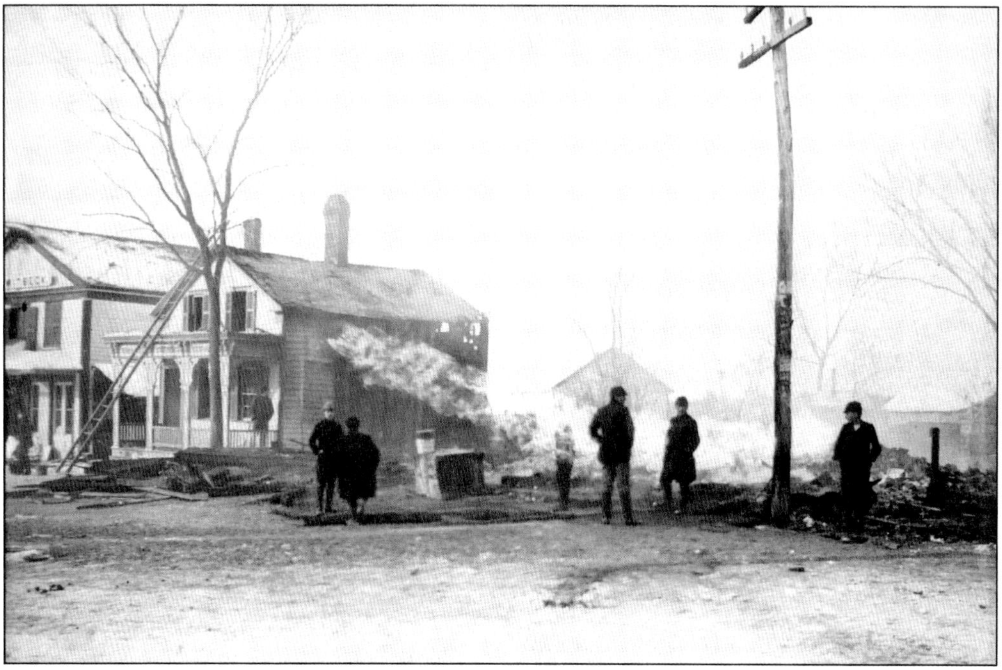

An 1890 fire destroyed the VanValkenburgh Inn, on the corner of Albany Avenue and Chatham Street. In two of Nassau's most notable events, the Marquis de Lafayette and later Joseph Bonaparte (Napoleon's brother and onetime king of Spain) stayed at the inn. Lafayette is remembered for planting an elm tree to note the occasion. The tree is featured on the village seal.

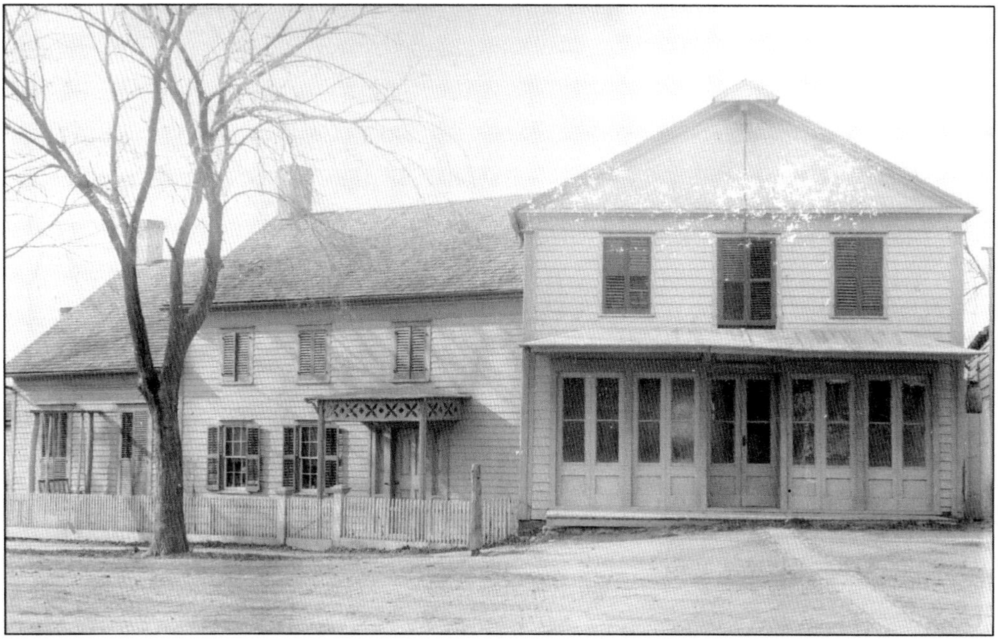

Nassau's businesses were constantly changing. This building on Chatham Street is a good example, as records show the following shop owners: Daniel Smith, P.N. Palmateer, Brownell & Mace, C.J. Mace, and Charles D. West. The building was last used as apartments before being torn down. (Courtesy of Nassau Free Library.)

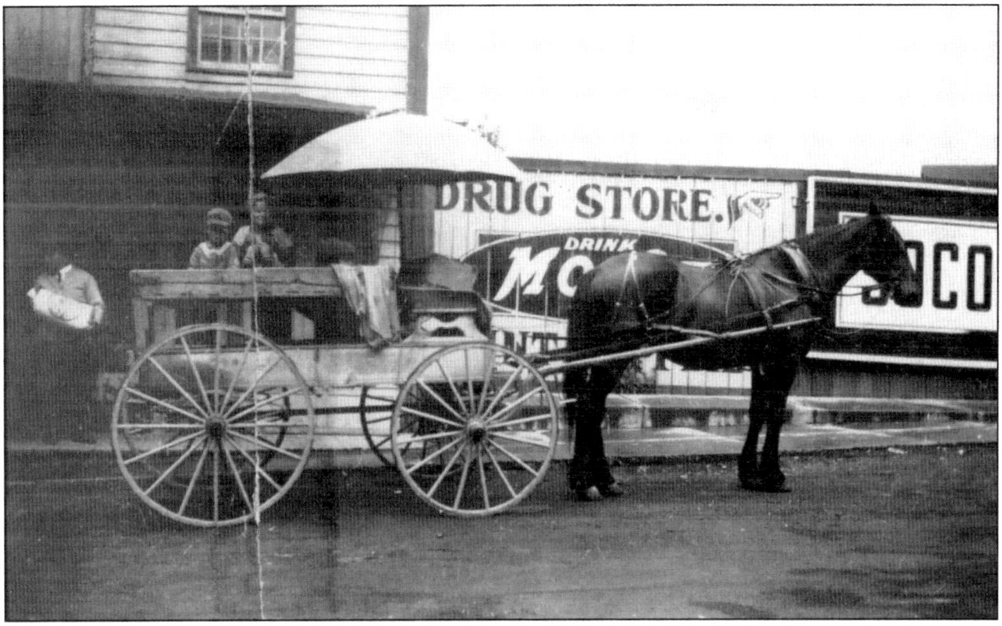

Charles D. West ran this grocery store in Nassau from the 1920s through the 1940s. He and his family lived adjacent to the store at 10 Chatham Street, and he was also the town clerk. Over the years, Nassau has had two Grand Unions, an A&P, an Arrowhead, and an IGA, in addition to many independent dealers. (Courtesy of Nassau Free Library.)

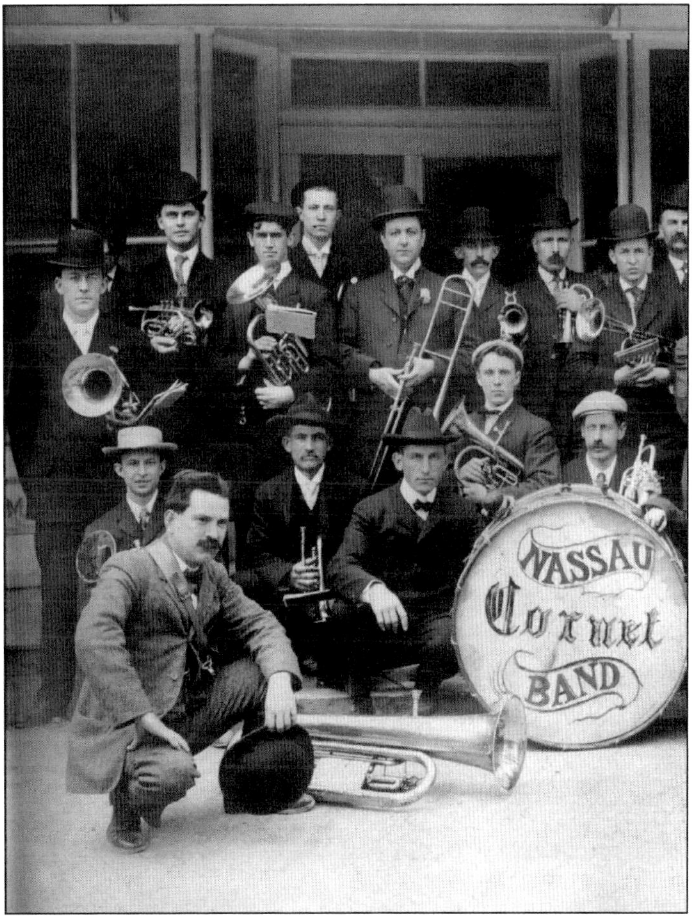

The entrance of the pharmacy serves as the backdrop for this photograph of the Nassau Cornet Band, taken around 1890. In addition to cornets—a type of trumpet—the group also features other brass instruments, as well as woodwinds and percussion. (Courtesy of Nassau Free Library.)

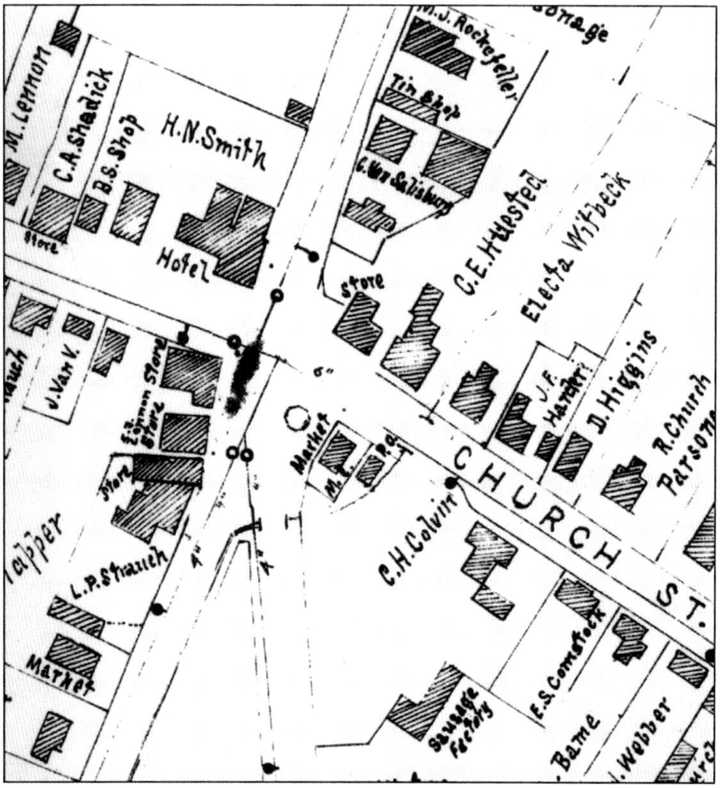

The central squares of most towns and villages have traditionally been places for shopping, socializing, and meeting others. At left, a 1905 plan shows the proximity of the hotel and the four commercial buildings at the square. Below, in the village square, are, from left to right, (first row) Clayton Roth, Otto Kosegarten, Timothy Bruck, Frank Roshirt, Charles Kosegarten, and Harry Bull; (second row) unidentified Methodist minister and unidentified; (third row) Oscar Winters, Matt Roshirt, Frank Kennedy, unidentified, and William Brown.

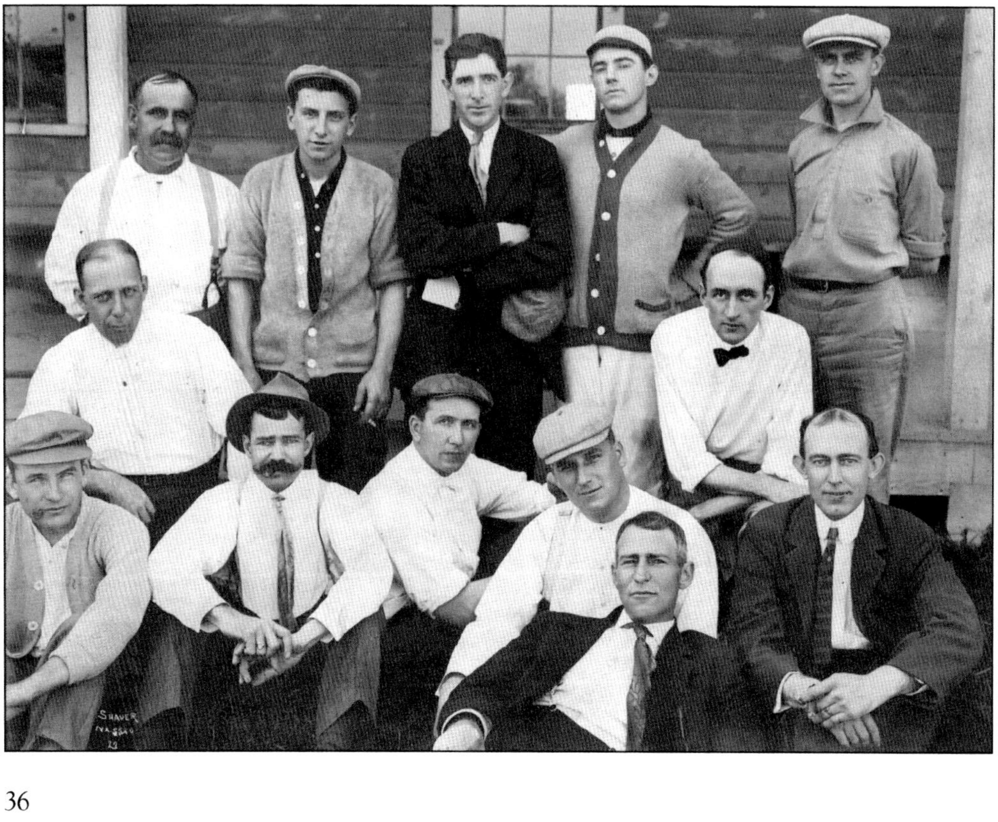

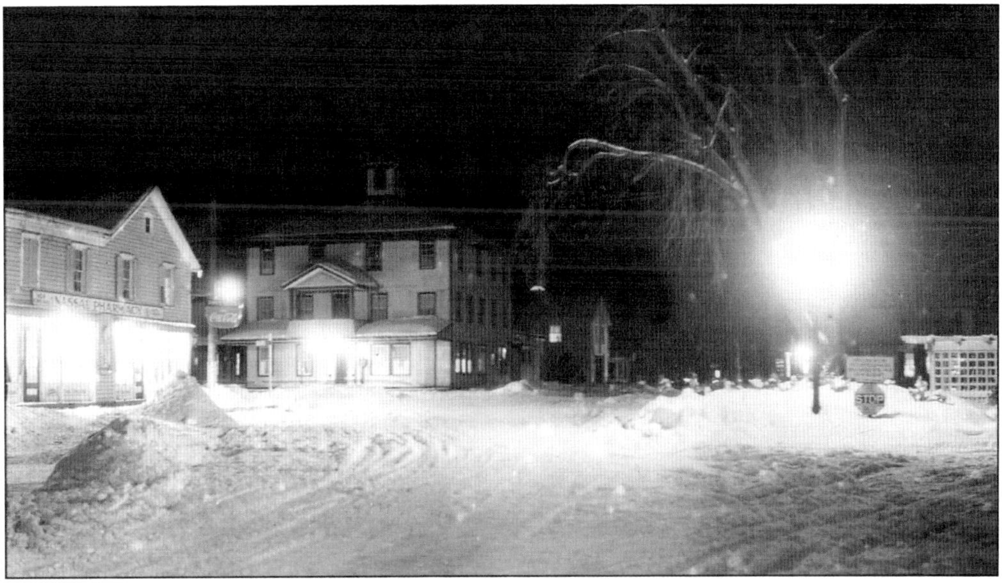

Talented photographer Raymond Velie captured this time-exposure nighttime photograph in the mid-1930s. The bright lights spill out of the pharmacy and the hotel, casting their reflections on the white snow. In a 1933 public vote, it was decided to remove the bandstand from the village square. (Courtesy of Judith Marquette.)

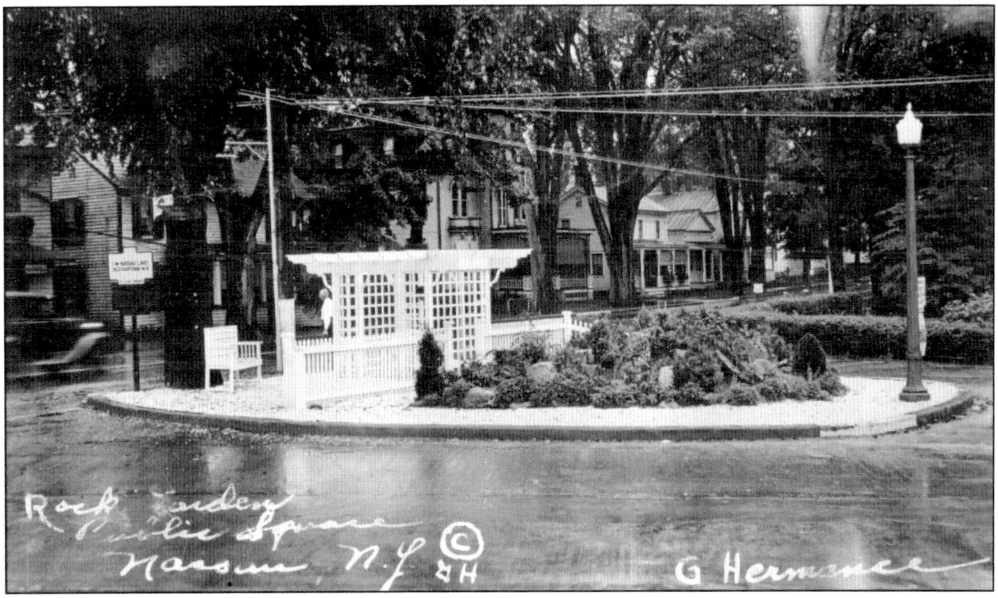

This photograph shows the ornamental rock garden that replaced the bandstand. Beyond the square to the right, a border hedge defines Nellie Lyon's formal garden, at 10 Church Street. (Courtesy of Nassau Free Library.)

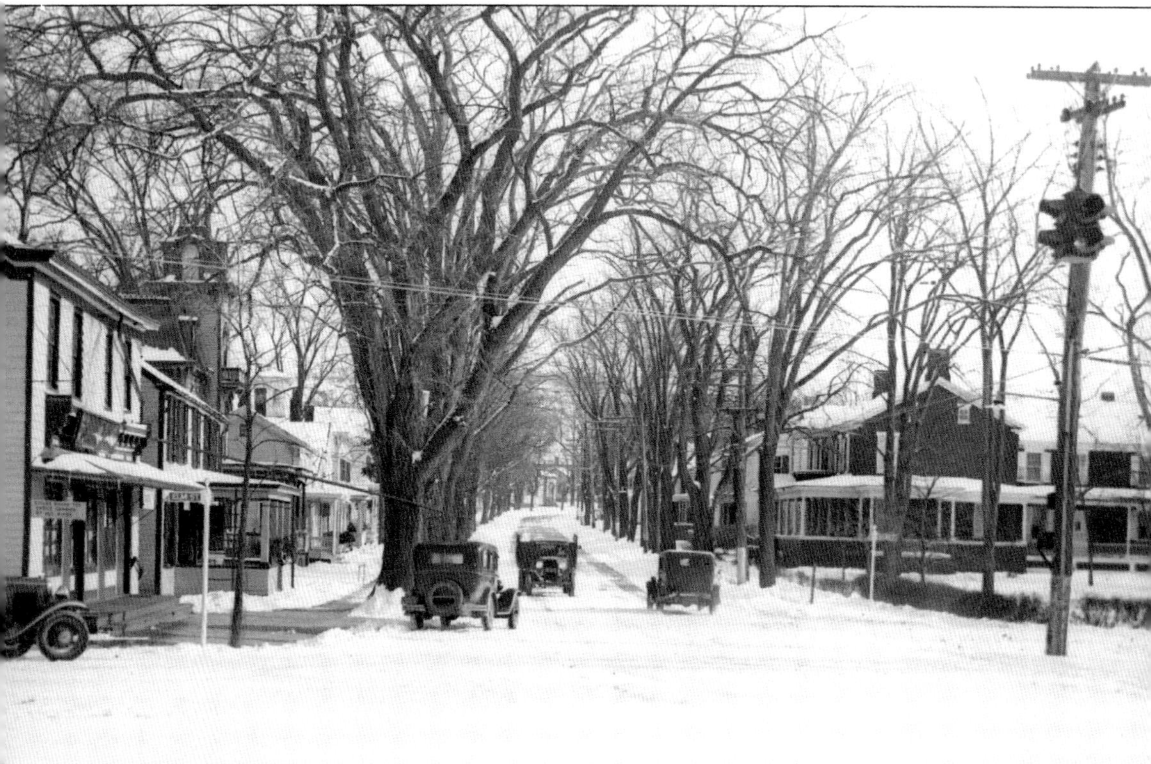

Cars make their way along Church Street on a snowy February day in 1937. Nassau's first stoplight, installed in 1933, is visible. Prior to the installation of the light, a large metal sign depicting a policeman holding a stop sign was used. Known as a "silent policeman," it had not proved effective in slowing the ever-increasing flow of traffic on what was referred to as the Albany-Pittsfield highway. (Courtesy of Nassau Free Library.)

Four

Nassau's Fair and Trolleys

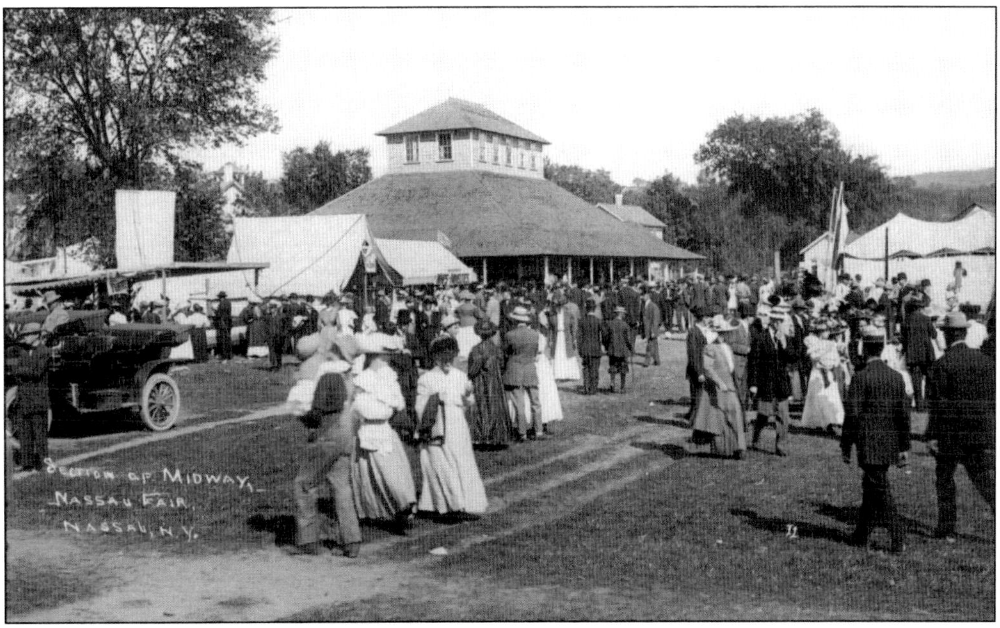

From 1873 until 1943, the Nassau fair, officially known as the Rensselaer County Agricultural and Liberal Arts Society, held its annual exposition at the 40-acre fairgrounds bordering Chatham Street and New York State Route 203. The Women's Arts and Crafts Building is seen here. Multiple exhibition halls featured commercial products, floral displays, vegetables, and cattle and sheep exhibits. The yearly county fair was a major event in Nassau and the surrounding communities. While fair week was a favorite time of year for Nassau residents, it was also the one time everyone remembered to lock his or her doors at night.

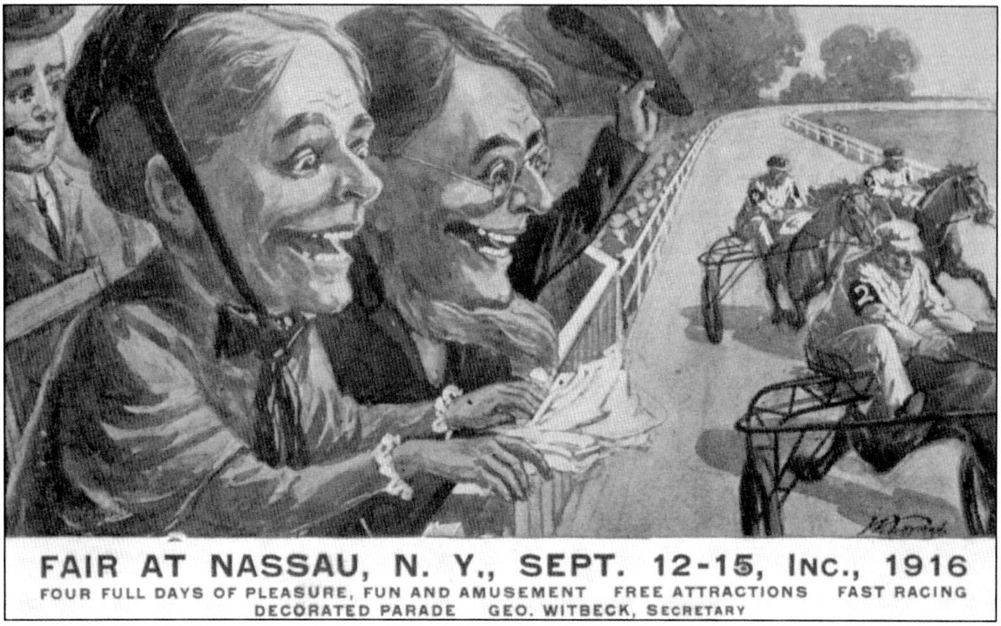

Harness racing was one of the major attractions at the fair. Trainers from throughout New York as well as from nearby locations in Massachusetts entered horses to run. It was not unusual, even in the 1890s, to have prize money in the thousands at stake. The rare promotional postcard above depicts a frenzied public at the fair. Below, spectators crowd the rail as horses come around the backstretch. Throughout the history of the fair, the grounds were year-round training quarters for horses competing at Saratoga and at other betting and county fair racetracks throughout the state. (Above, courtesy of the Dan Smith collection.)

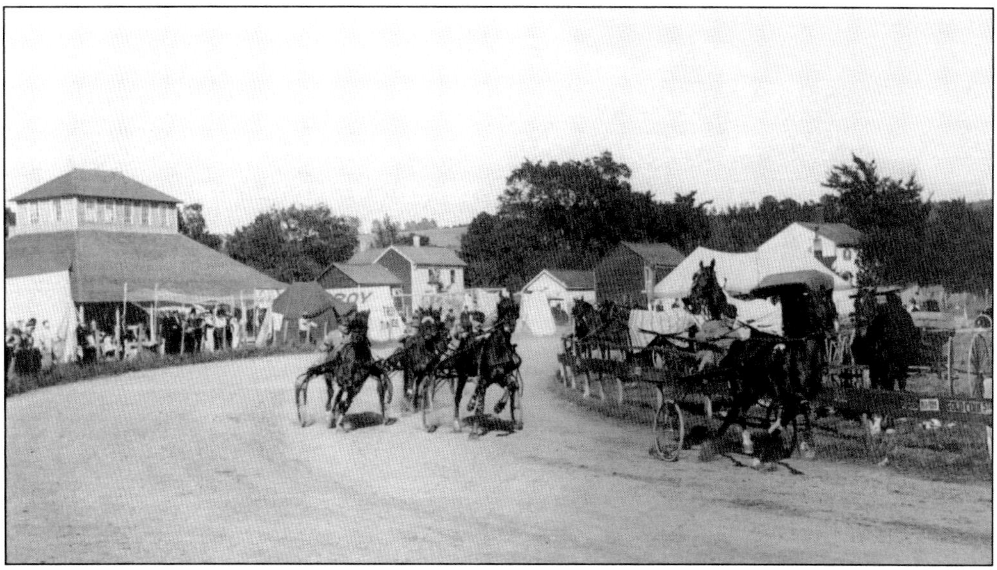

At right, the premium book for the 1910 fair lists all the categories in which judging took place, as well as complete racing information. Below, the Nassau Fair Committee poses for a photograph about 1890. Members, from left to right, are (first row) Charles Huested, Mr. Gardiner, Charles Kirby, and Will Kells; (second row) Jess Huested, Joel Morey, Thomas James, Delmar Lynd, John Messinger, and Jackie Grubb. The young boy in front is unidentified. The committee was composed of local farm owners, businessmen, and merchants. (Right, courtesy of the Dan Smith collection; below, courtesy of Nassau Free Library.)

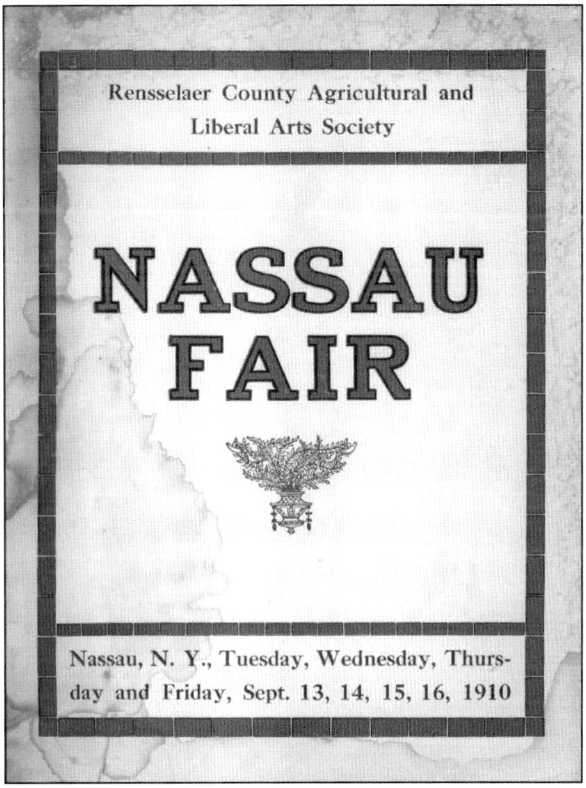

Rensselaer County Agricultural and Liberal Arts Society

NASSAU FAIR

Nassau, N. Y., Tuesday, Wednesday, Thursday and Friday, Sept. 13, 14, 15, 16, 1910

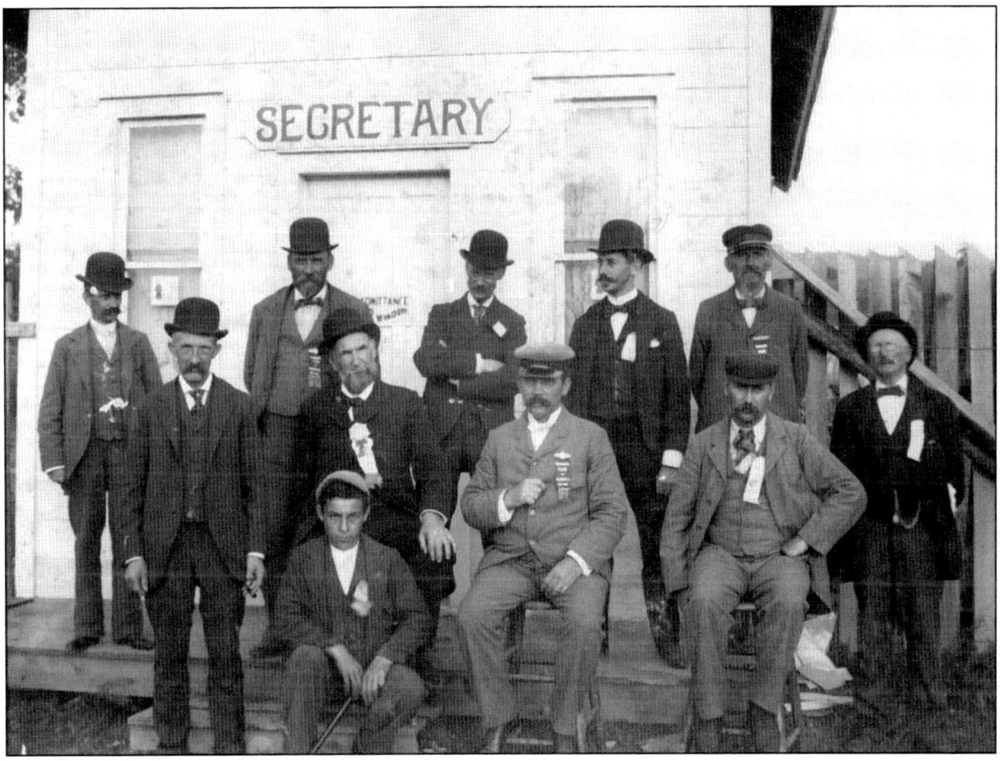

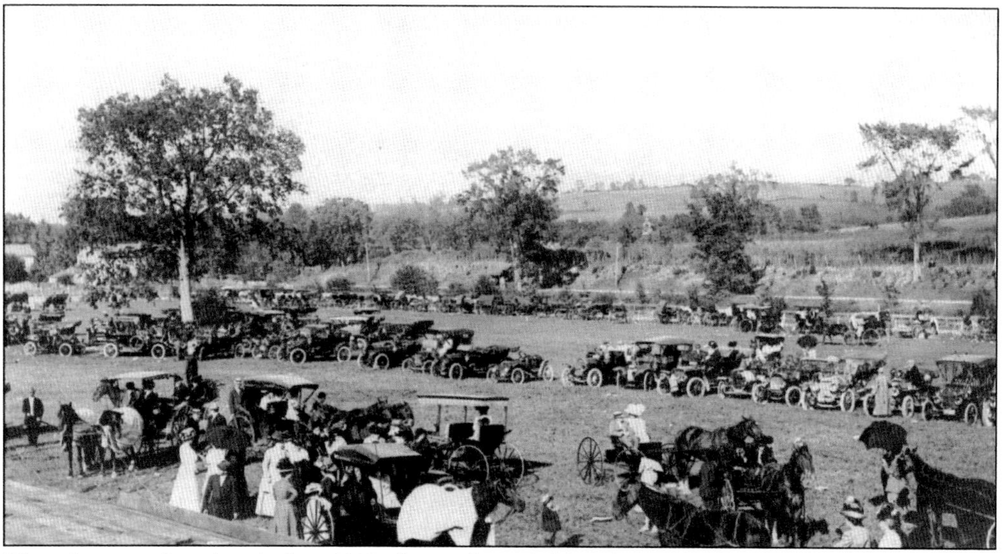

This photograph, taken before 1910, shows the infield parking area at the fair. To the rear are Chatham Street and the undeveloped area that would become Fairview Terrace. As with fairs of today, the Nassau fair offered a wide variety of attractions, including Wild West shows, oxen-pulling contests, and a carnival midway. Until the installation of lighting in 1925, the fair took place only during daylight hours.

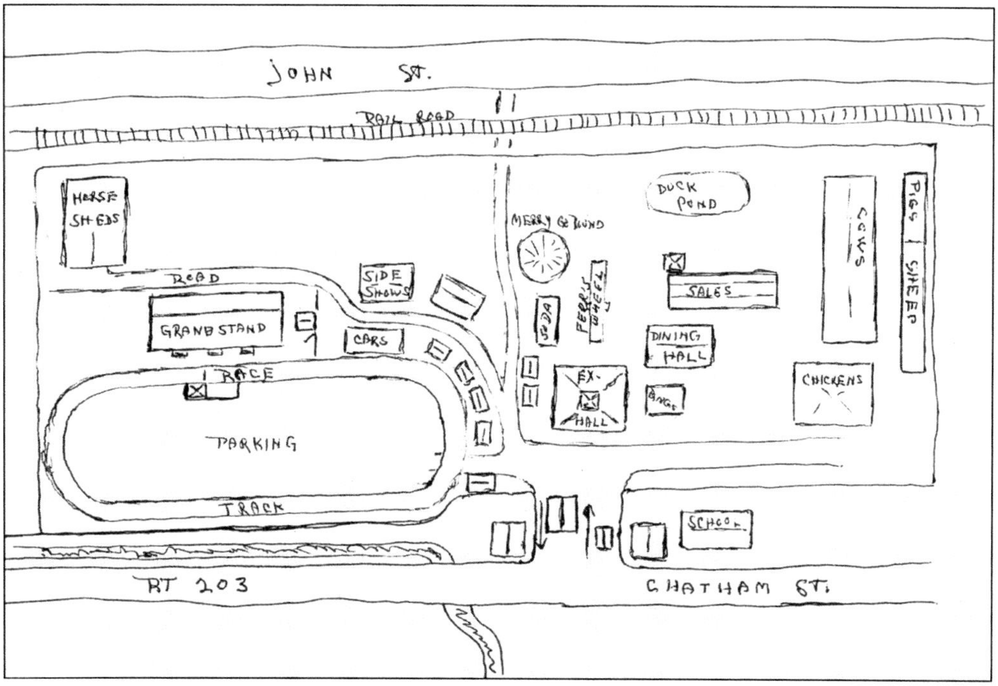

Lifelong Nassau resident Herman Kosegarten drew this map of the Nassau fairgrounds from memory in 1990. Growing up and living most of his adult life on John Street, opposite the property, and possessing a tremendous memory, Kosegarten offered a unique view of the fair operation and the scope of attractions and buildings. All except one fair building have long since disappeared.

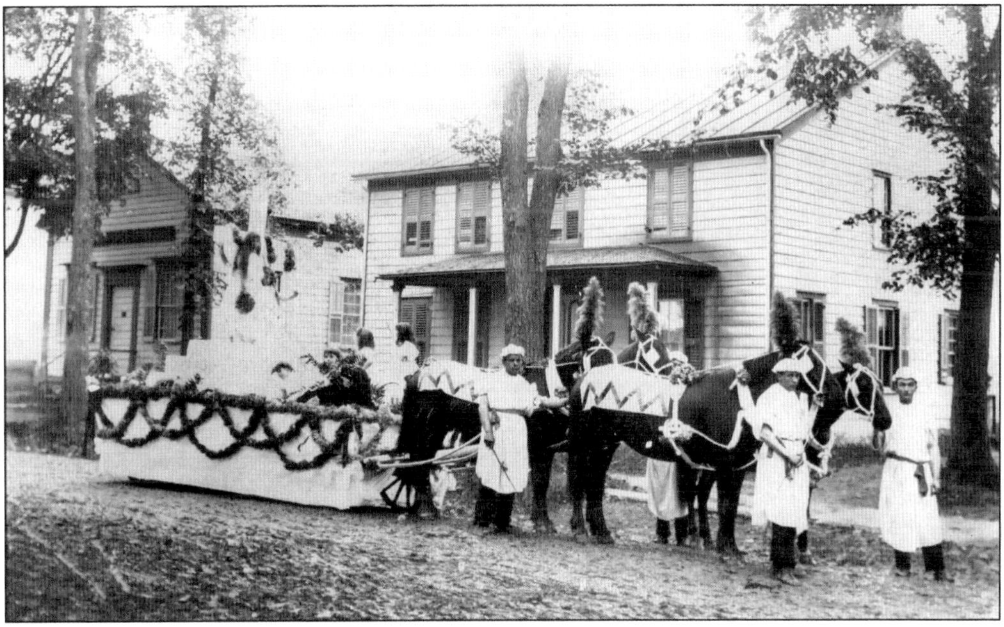

The floral parade was a popular annual feature of the fair around 1900. Community groups, individuals, and business competed to have the best-decorated displays. In 1901, prize categories included floats, chariots, double and single horse teams, men's and women's bicycles, babies and baby carriages, and business wagons. There were as many as six prizes in each category, with $50 awarded for first place. The tradition of floral parades goes back to ancient times, and continues today in Pasadena, California, with the Tournament of Roses Parade. (Both, courtesy of Nassau Free Library.)

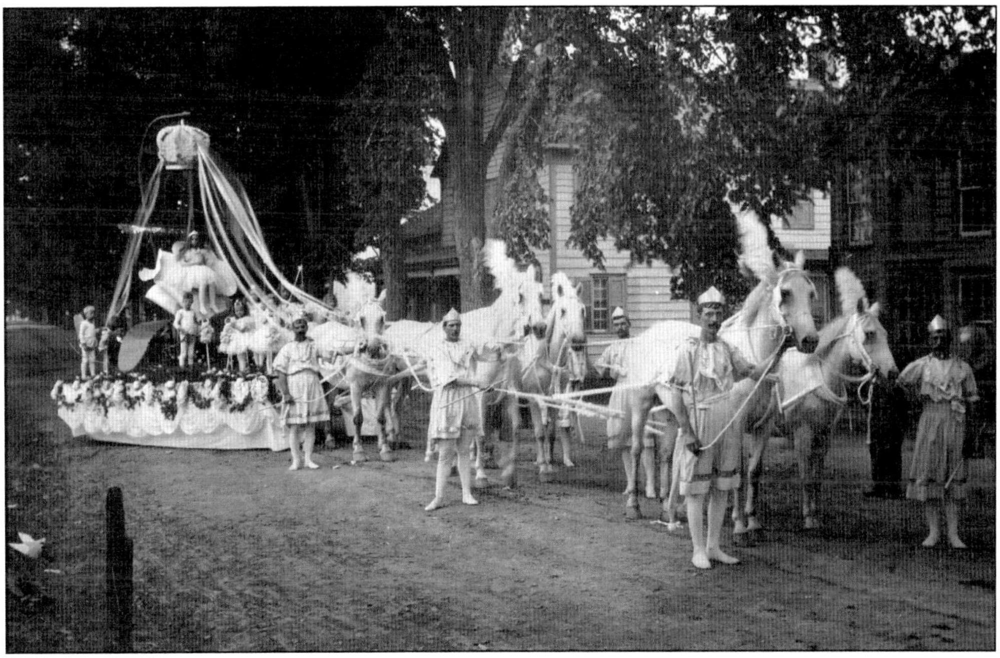

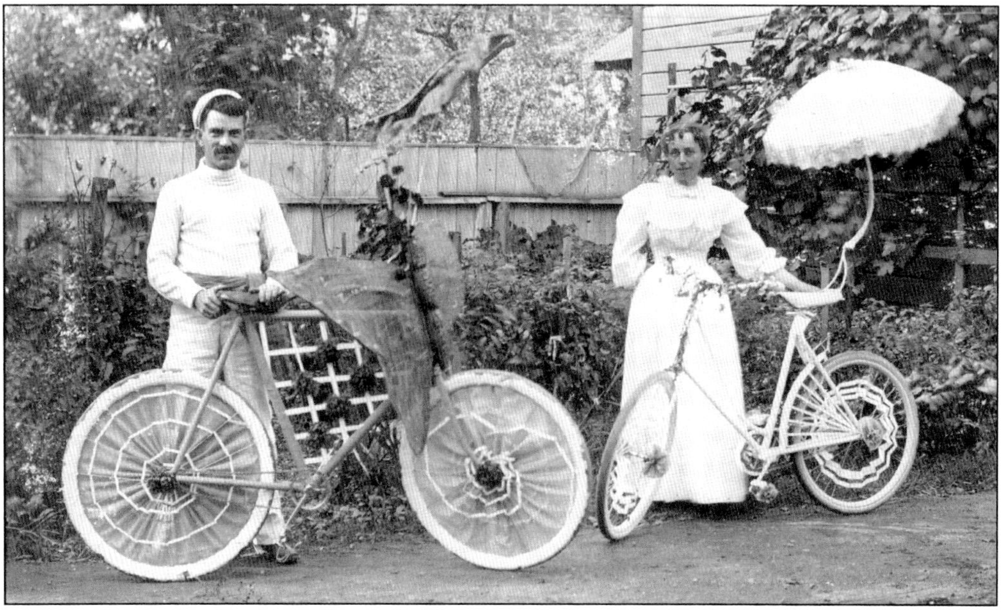

The photographer of many of the early images in this book, Elmer B. Shaver, is seen here with his wife, Minnie. The couple lived on Malden Street. Shaver is listed in a 1907 Albany business directory as a photographer, and many of his photographs were made into popular postcards. (Courtesy of Nassau Free Library.)

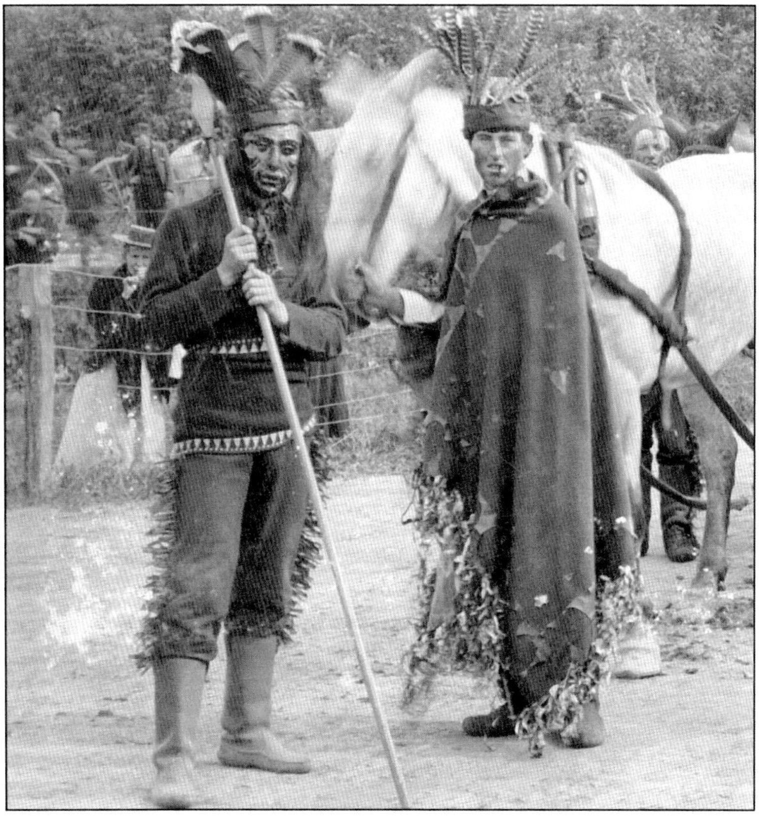

Floral parade floats often depicted scenes from local history. Here, the "Calico Indians" are remembered from the days of Big Thunder and the Anti-Rent Wars of the 1840s. Hoag's Corners was a hotbed of activity during the conflicts; one sheriff's deputy was even tarred and feathered in a rent dispute. (Courtesy of Nassau Free Library.)

Lilia Huested is seen here with her bicycle decorated for the floral parade. The daughter of storeowner George Huested, she later taught school at Nassau Union School, and, in June 1927, she was appointed the Nassau postmistress. (Courtesy of Nassau Free Library.)

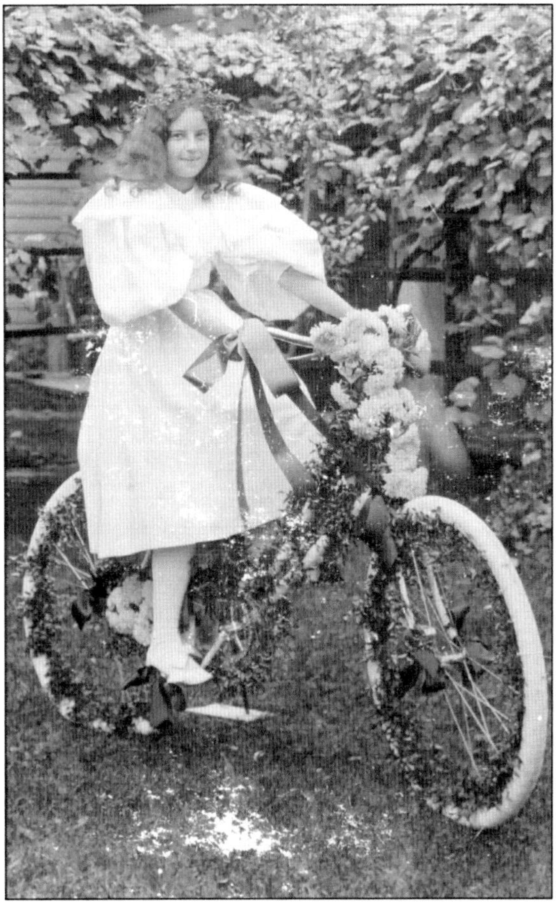

The 2,500-seat grandstand bordered John Street. Fair patrons paid extra to sit in the grandstand for the best view of the activities. In 1903, fair entry was 25¢, with an additional dime needed for a grandstand seat. The band concerts before the racetrack activities and during intermission featured Adam's Band, of Albany, and Cappallano's Band, of Rensselaer.

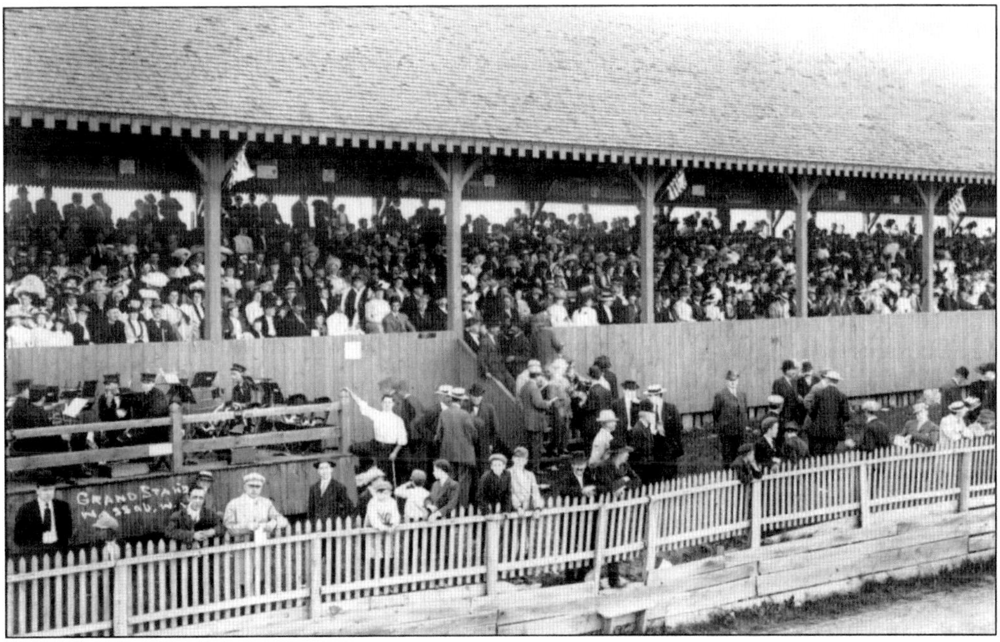

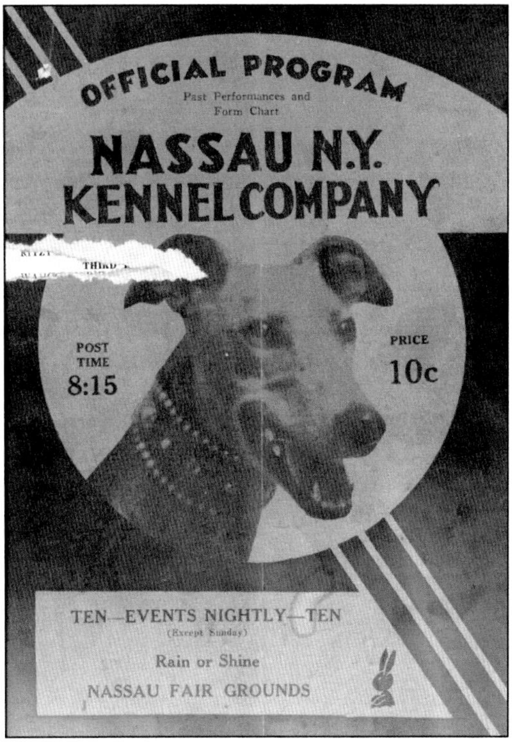

In the 1930s, greyhound racing was also held at the fairgrounds. Called the Sport of Queens because horse racing was known as the Sport of Kings, it attracted a mainly out-of-town audience and was generally disliked by Nassau residents. The announcer would call out, "Here comes the bunny, there goes your money," referring to the motorized rabbit the greyhounds chased, and the race would begin. (Both, courtesy of Nassau Free Library.)

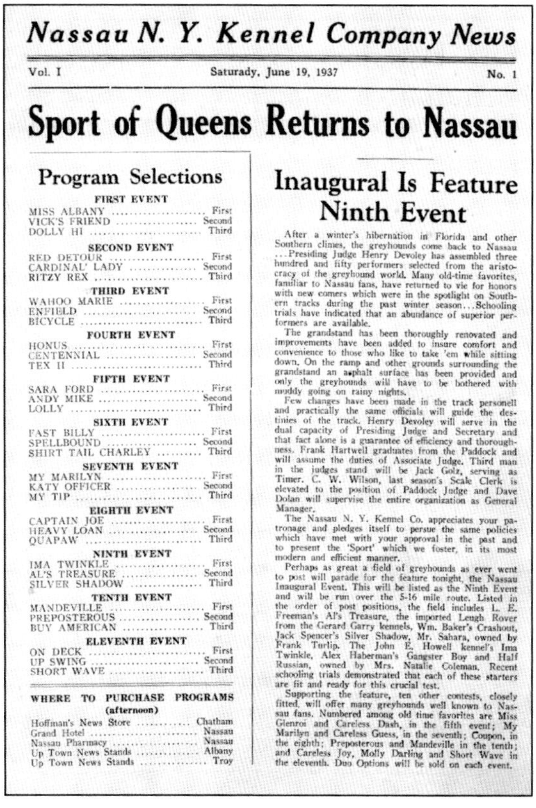

Nassau N. Y. Kennel Company News

Vol. I — Saturday, June 19, 1937 — No. 1

Sport of Queens Returns to Nassau

Program Selections

FIRST EVENT
MISS ALBANY .... First
VICK'S FRIEND .... Second
DOLLY HI .... Third

SECOND EVENT
RED DETOUR .... First
CARDINAL' LADY .... Second
RITZY REX .... Third

THIRD EVENT
WAHOO MARIE .... First
ENFIELD .... Second
BICYCLE .... Third

FOURTH EVENT
HONUS .... First
CENTENNIAL .... Second
TEX II .... Third

FIFTH EVENT
SARA FORD .... First
ANDY MIKE .... Second
LOLLY .... Third

SIXTH EVENT
FAST BILLY .... First
SPELLBOUND .... Second
SHIRT TAIL CHARLEY .... Third

SEVENTH EVENT
MY MARILYN .... First
KATY OFFICER .... Second
MY TIP .... Third

EIGHTH EVENT
CAPTAIN JOE .... First
HEAVY LOAN .... Second
QUAPAW .... Third

NINTH EVENT
IMA TWINKLE .... First
AL'S TREASURE .... Second
SILVER SHADOW .... Third

TENTH EVENT
MANDEVILLE .... First
PREPOSTEROUS .... Second
BUY AMERICAN .... Third

ELEVENTH EVENT
ON DECK .... First
UP SWING .... Second
SHORT WAVE .... Third

WHERE TO PURCHASE PROGRAMS
(afternoon)
Hoffman's News Store .... Chatham
Grand Hotel .... Nassau
Nassau Pharmacy .... Nassau
Up Town News Stands .... Albany
Up Town News Stands .... Troy

Inaugural Is Feature Ninth Event

After a winter's hibernation in Florida and other Southern climes, the greyhounds come back to Nassau ...Presiding Judge Henry Devoley has assembled three hundred and fifty performers selected from the aristocracy of the greyhound world. Many old-time favorites, familiar to Nassau fans, have returned to vie for honors with new comers which were in the spotlight on Southern tracks during the past winter season...Schooling trials have indicated that an abundance of superior performers are available.

The grandstand has been thoroughly renovated and improvements have been added to insure comfort and convenience to those who like to take 'em while sitting down. On the ramp and other grounds surrounding the grandstand an asphalt surface has been provided and only the greyhounds will have to be bothered with muddy going on rainy nights.

Few changes have been made in the track personell and practically the same officials will guide the destinies of the track. Henry Devoley will serve in the dual capacity of Presiding Judge and Secretary and that fact alone is a guarantee of efficiency and thoroughness. Frank Hartwell graduates from the Paddock and will assume the duties of Associate Judge. Third man in the judges stand will be Jack Golz, serving as Timer. C. W. Wilson, last season's Scale Clerk is elevated to the position of Paddock Judge and Dave Dolan will supervise the entire organization as General Manager.

The Nassau N. Y. Kennel Co. appreciates your patronage and pledges itself to persue the same policies which have met with your approval in the past and to present the 'Sport' which we foster, in its most modern and efficient manner.

Perhaps as great a field of greyhounds as ever went to post will parade for the feature tonight, the Nassau Inaugural Event. This will be listed as the Ninth Event and will be run over the 5-16 mile route. Listed in the order of post positions, the field includes L. E. Freeman's Al's Treasure, the imported Leugh Rover from the Gerard Garry kennels, Wm. Baker's Crashout, Jack Spencer's Silver Shadow, Mr. Sahara, owned by Frank Turlip. The John E. Howell kennel's Ima Twinkle, Alex Haberman's Gangster Boy and Half Russian, owned by Mrs. Natalie Coleman. Recent schooling trials demonstrated that each of these starters are fit and ready for this crucial test.

Supporting the feature, ten other contests, closely fitted, will offer many greyhounds well known to Nassau fans. Numbered among old time favorites are Miss Glenroi and Careless Dash, in the fifth event; My Marilyn and Careless Guess, in the seventh; Coupon, in the eighth; Preposterous and Mandeville in the tenth; and Careless Joy, Molly Darling and Short Wave in the eleventh. Duo Options will be sold on each event.

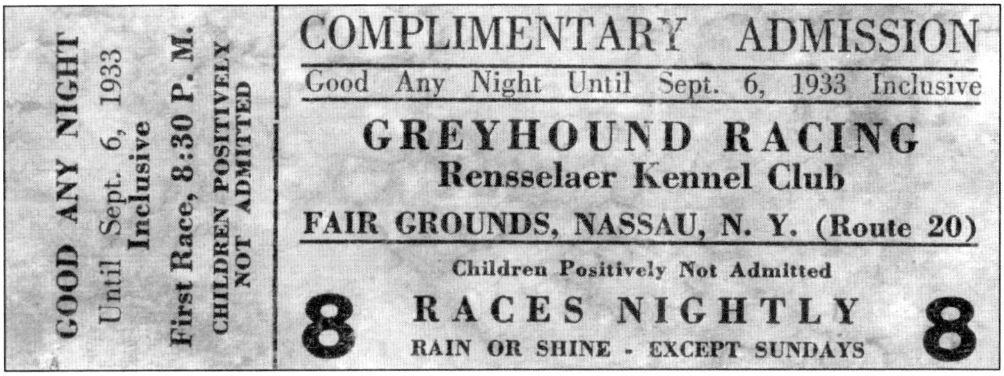

Greyhound racing was only held for a few years and ended with a dramatic raid by state police and sheriff's deputies on June 23, 1937, when the track was closed. While not exactly illegal in New York State, dog racing never received official sanction. Many suggested that the proximity to Saratoga Race Course was to blame. A complimentary ticket is seen above. The photograph below shows a well-maintained track and official's tower. During the early years of the Cold War, in the late 1940s and early 1950s, local civil defense volunteer units used the tower as an observation post. When a suspected enemy plane was sighted, a telephone call was made to headquarters with the call sign "Bravo Vector 23 Black." (Above, courtesy of the Dan Smith collection; below, courtesy of Nassau Free Library.)

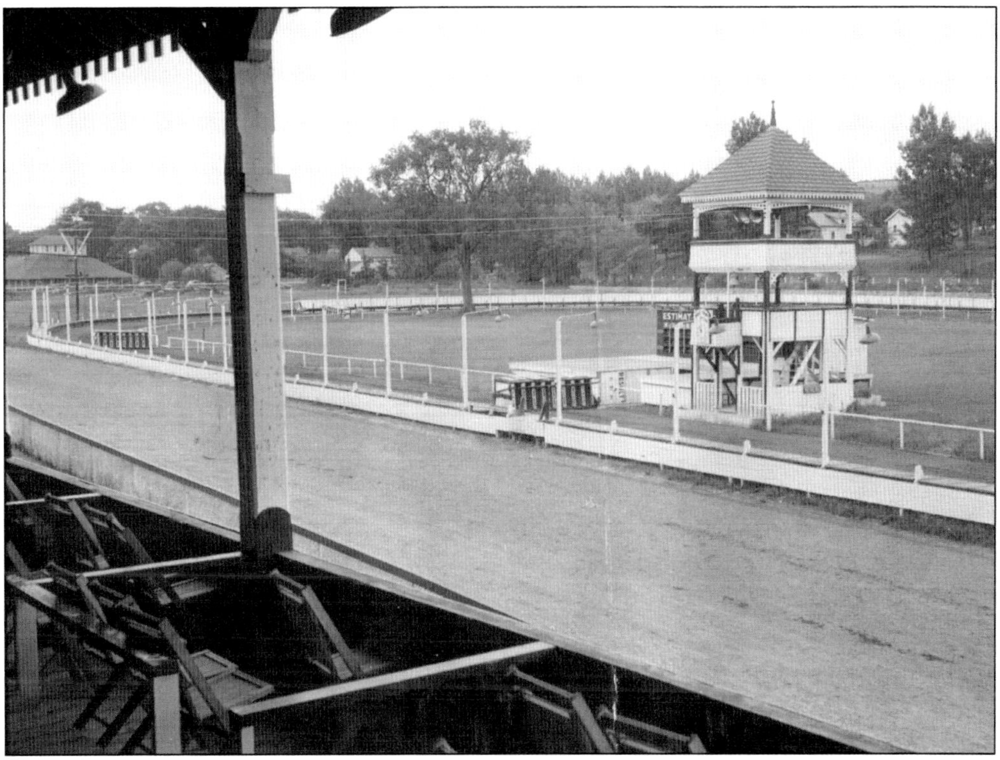

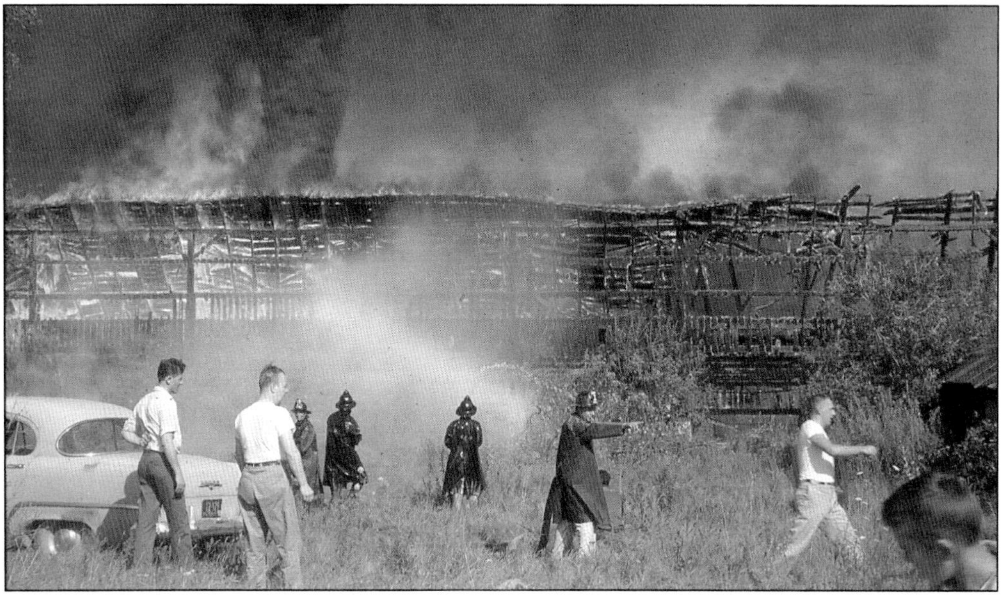

The last Nassau fair took place in 1943. The following year, Frank Feldman purchased the property for $8,500. In the years that followed, many proposals for the property were made, including a park and recreation center, but none ever came about. Horse training and storage continued, as did a retail store in one of the former exhibition halls; however, the grounds and wooden structures attracted unwanted attention from youths and fires and were a constant problem. It was said that every family in Nassau owned a set of the folding chairs that had previously been used in the grandstand. How they obtained the chairs was never determined. In the 1960s, portions of the grounds were used for summer field days held by the fire company. The 1961 grandstand fire is seen above. The fire below, in January 1968, destroyed the horse barns. (Above, courtesy of Robert Severance; below, courtesy of Nassau Hose Company.)

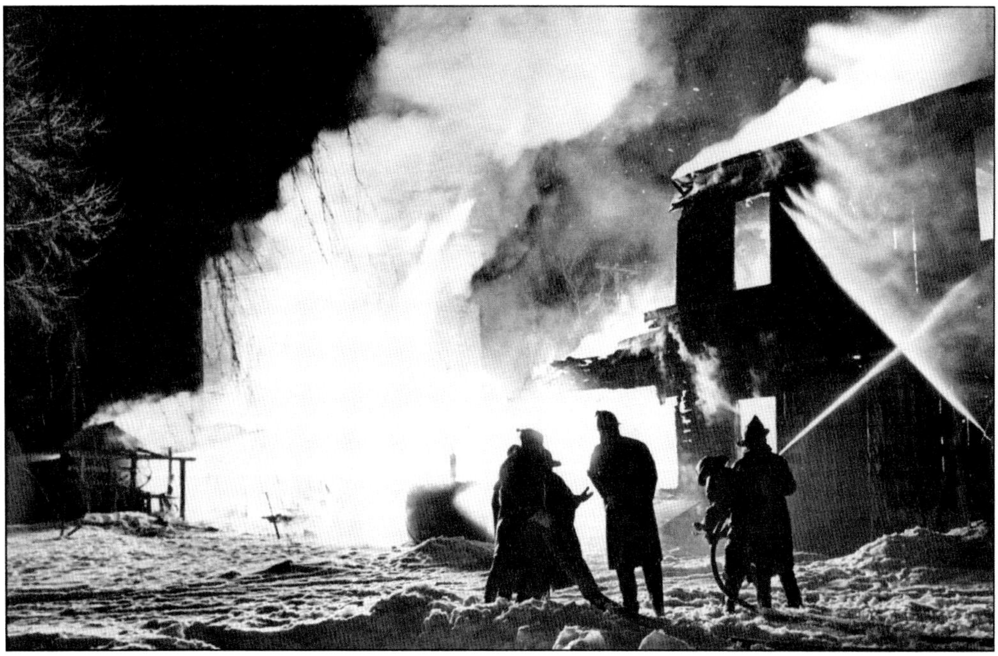

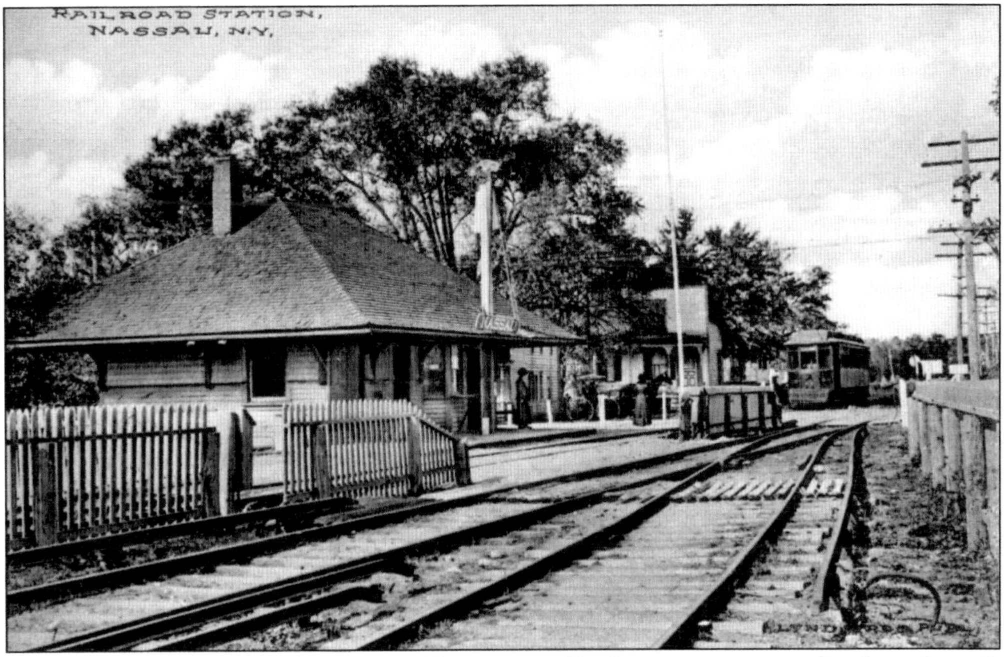

In what might be considered Nassau's golden age, a trolley line was constructed and ran through Nassau. The best-known operator was the Albany Southern Railroad, who ran the line between Albany and Hudson from 1909 to 1924. The introduction of rail service opened up Rensselaer and Columbia Counties to extensive development. In 1901, more than 300,000 passengers rode the line, and that number tripled the next year. In May 1900, the first engine passed through Nassau, and the station was completed in 1901. The railroad operated on a third-rail system, where one track was electrified and in contact with motors under the car. The electric current was generated by waterpower from Stockport Creek in Columbia County. In addition to providing rail service, the railroad company also sold electrical service to the communities along the route, including Nassau. (Below, courtesy of William Thomas.)

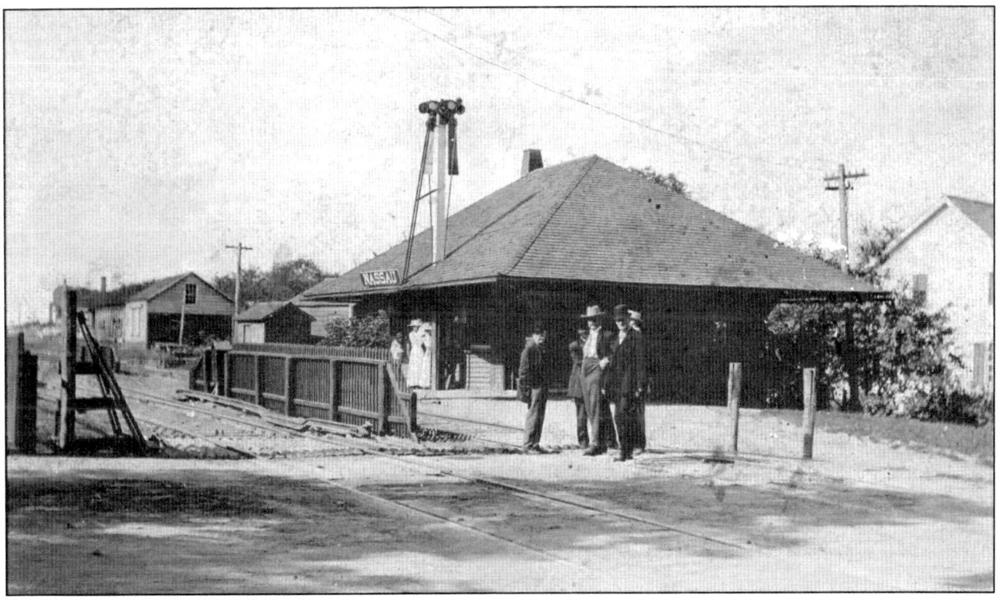

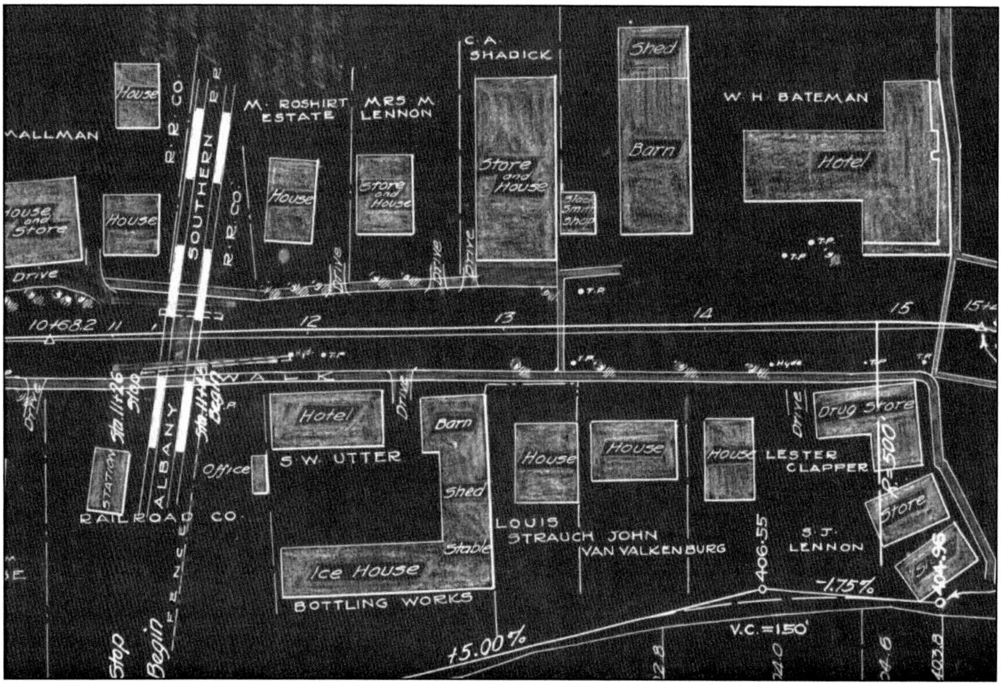

These construction blueprints, for the paving in 1913 of what later became US Route 20, clearly show Albany Avenue, the railroad crossing, the station, and adjacent buildings. Construction documents refer to the road as State Highway 5163. Popularly, it was known as the State Road or the Pittsfield Highway. Both passenger and freight service operated out of the Nassau station. There are still freight sheds on the former railroad property. (Courtesy of Village of Nassau.)

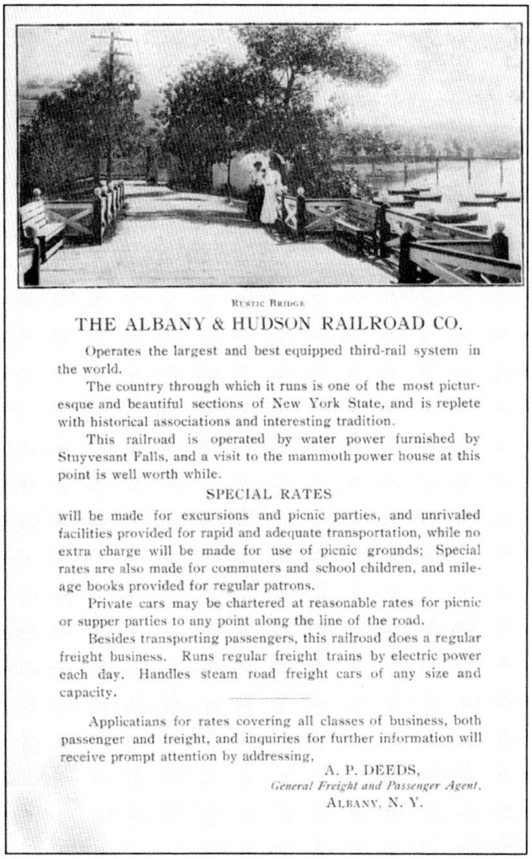

RUSTIC BRIDGE

THE ALBANY & HUDSON RAILROAD CO.

Operates the largest and best equipped third-rail system in the world.

The country through which it runs is one of the most picturesque and beautiful sections of New York State, and is replete with historical associations and interesting tradition.

This railroad is operated by water power furnished by Stuyvesant Falls, and a visit to the mammoth power house at this point is well worth while.

SPECIAL RATES

will be made for excursions and picnic parties, and unrivaled facilities provided for rapid and adequate transportation, while no extra charge will be made for use of picnic grounds; Special rates are also made for commuters and school children, and mileage books provided for regular patrons.

Private cars may be chartered at reasonable rates for picnic or supper parties to any point along the line of the road.

Besides transporting passengers, this railroad does a regular freight business. Runs regular freight trains by electric power each day. Handles steam road freight cars of any size and capacity.

Applicatians for rates covering all classes of business, both passenger and freight, and inquiries for further information will receive prompt attention by addressing,

A. P. DEEDS,
General Freight and Passenger Agent,
ALBANY, N. Y.

The predecessor of the Albany Southern was the Albany & Hudson Railroad. Initially stretching from Hudson to Niverville in Columbia County, the line absorbed the former Greenbush & Nassau Electric Railway Company to continue north, eventually ending in Rensselaer, with rights to continue on to Albany. (Courtesy of Nassau Free Library.)

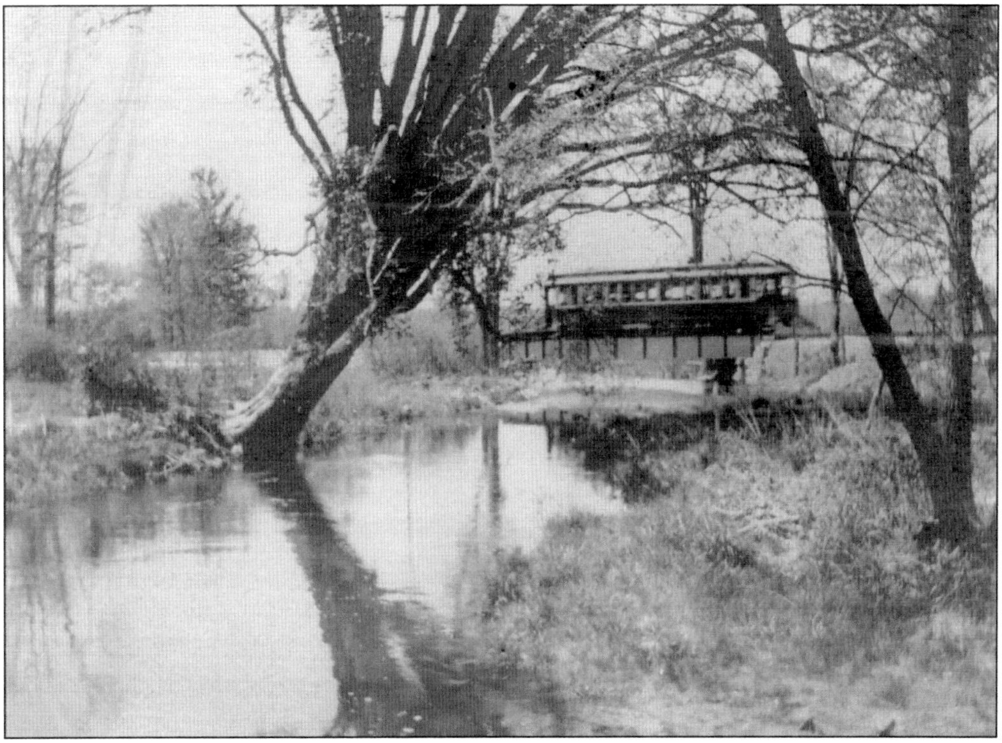

On what was promoted as "the Albany-Hudson fast line," travel from Nassau to downtown Albany took 40 minutes. Seen here crossing the Valatiekill just north of Nassau, this trolley would have just descended from the highest point on the line, Harris Hill, at 600 feet above sea level. (Courtesy of the Dan Smith collection.)

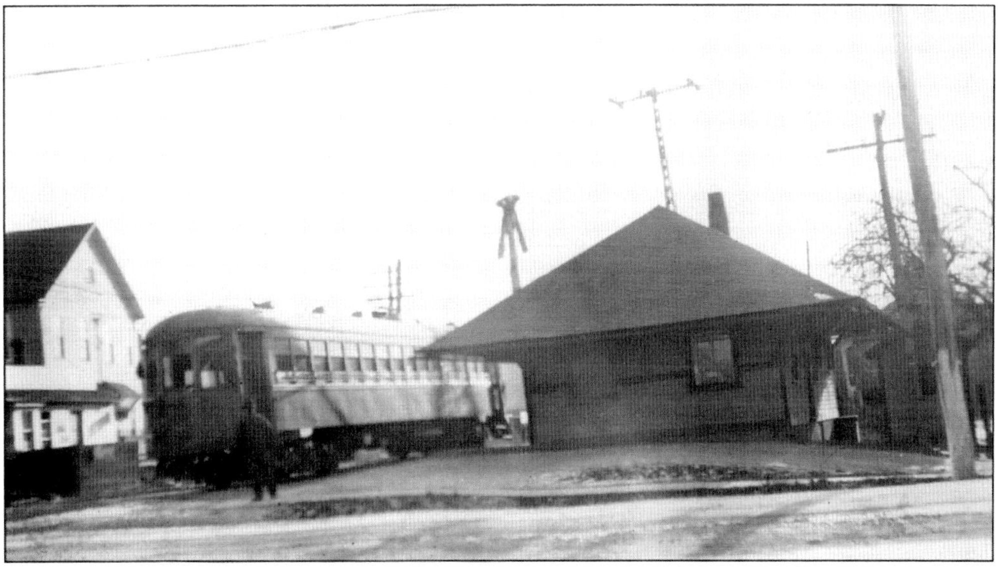

The Nassau station is seen here in the 1920s. To the left is a building that still stands and is now used by an antiques dealer, Antiques at Bailey's. In earlier years, the building served as a shirt factory, a soda bottling works, a firehouse with a fireman's hall upstairs, and again as a factory, for the manufacture of ballpoint pens. (Courtesy of Judith Marquette.)

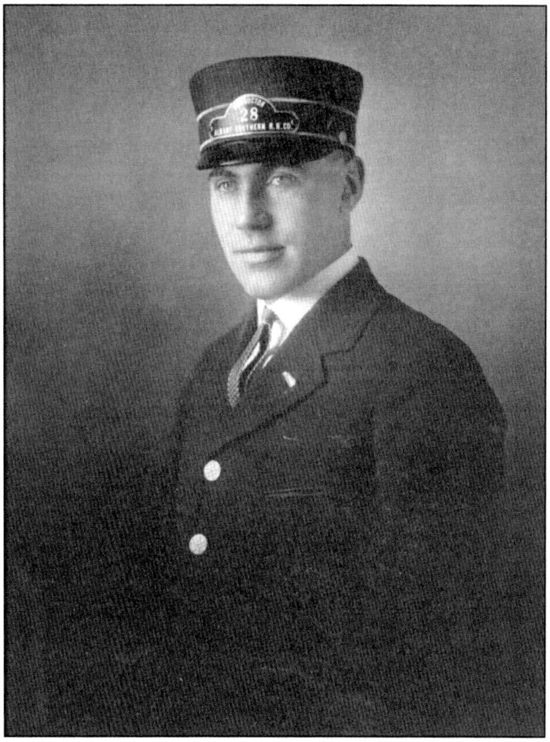

Raymond Velie served as a conductor on the Albany Southern Railroad. He is seen at left in his uniform and below standing at the Merchant's Crossing warning sign. The Velie family operated a wagon repair shop just below the crossing. During the period the railroad was in operation, single-car trains reached top speeds of 60 miles per hour. The entire distance between Hudson and Rensselaer ran on 37.25 miles of track and could be traveled in 90 minutes. Just before Christmas in 1929, the last train made its final run. The form of travel was inherently dangerous to man and animal alike, with live currents surging through the unprotected third rail, and the company could not withstand the economic pressures of the Depression. Much of the original railroad right-of-way is still owned by National Grid, and recent discussion has proposed creating "rail trail" paths under the wires. (Both, courtesy of Judith Marquette.)

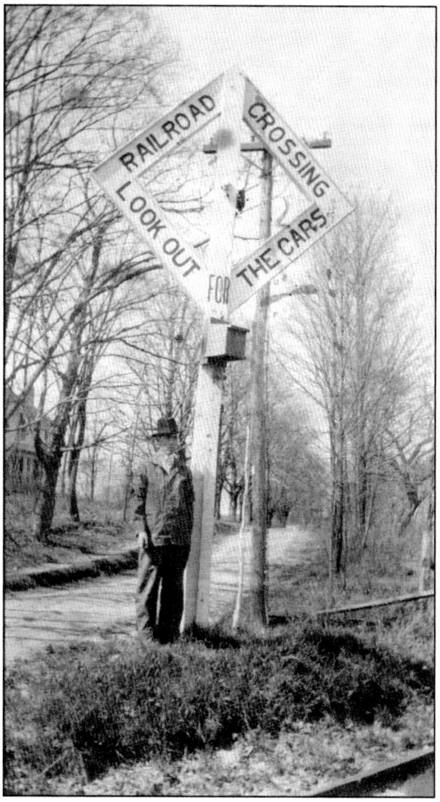

Five

Around the Village

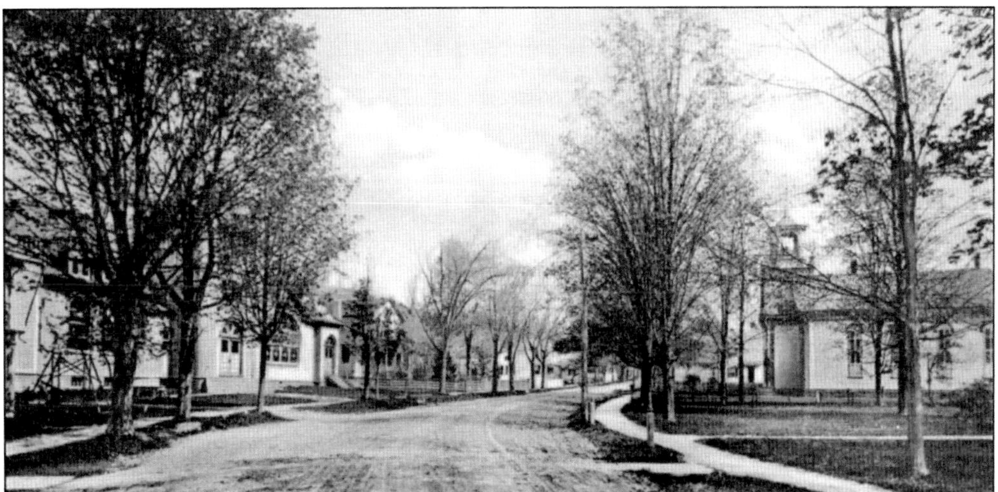

In the early 1900s, Nassau was a neat, tidy village. Still primarily self-sufficient from the outside world, most residents stayed close to home for their jobs, their commerce, and their entertainment. Among many other professions, Nassau boasts a vinegar manufactory, three blacksmiths, seven merchants, four dressmakers, three bartenders, eleven carpenters, nine farmers, "a gentleman," and one assemblyman in a census from that time. This photograph shows the bend on upper Church Street crowned by two houses of worship: the recently constructed third Nassau Reformed Church (left) and the Nassau Methodist Episcopal Church (right).

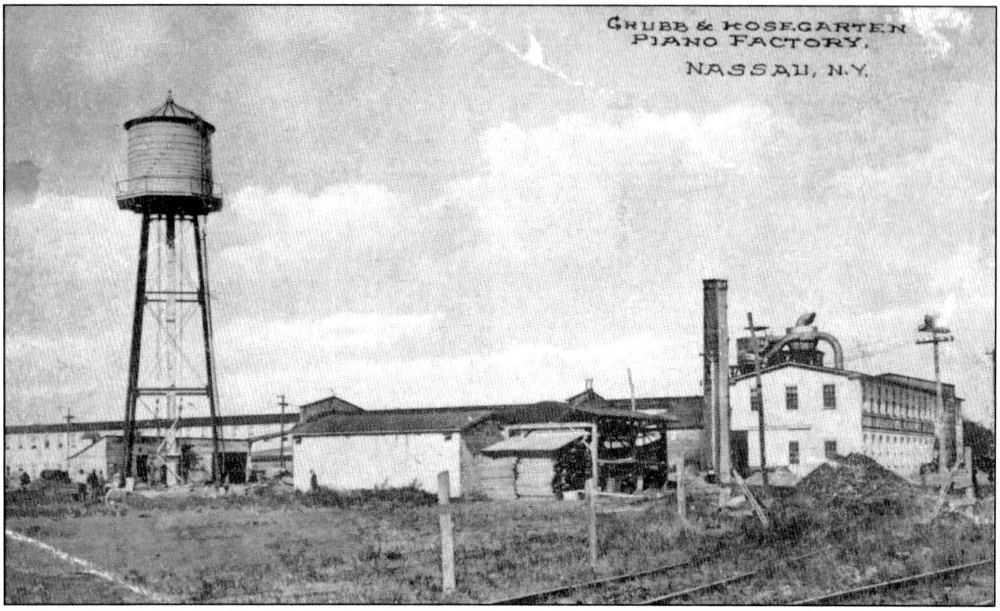

The Kosegarten Brothers Piano Action Factory, shown above, previously known as Grubb & Kosegarten, was Nassau's largest employer for many years. It was adjacent to the Albany Southern tracks and opposite the fairgrounds. The Kosegarten family held great respect in the community, and the origins of the firm date back to 1837, with production starting in Albany. The factory then moved to Bunker Hill, several miles west of Nassau, until it was destroyed by fire. The new factory was located on John Street in Nassau, where it prospered. By 1915, more than 30 percent of the working population of Nassau village was employed by the firm. The factory whistle signaled the start and end of shifts and also sounded the alarm for the fire department. The photograph below, taken about 1910, shows the factory. Pictured, from left to right, are Albrecht C. Kosegarten, secretary and treasurer; Otto F. Kosegarten, vice president; Cora Mensing Waterbury, bookkeeper; and Charles W. Kosegarten, president. (Both, courtesy of Nassau Free Library.)

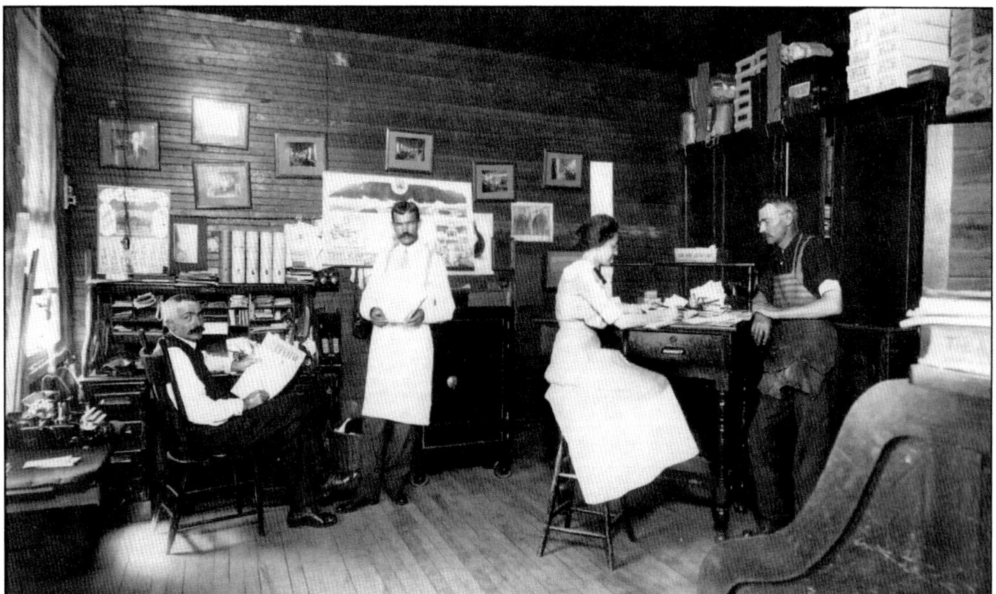

Seen here in the factory workrooms are, from left to right, Albrecht O. Kosegarten, Charles W. Kosegarten, and Timothy Bruck. The factory worked 10-hour days, from 7:00 a.m. to 12:00 p.m. and 1:00 p.m. to 6:00 p.m., with a one-hour lunch break. (Courtesy of Nassau Free Library.)

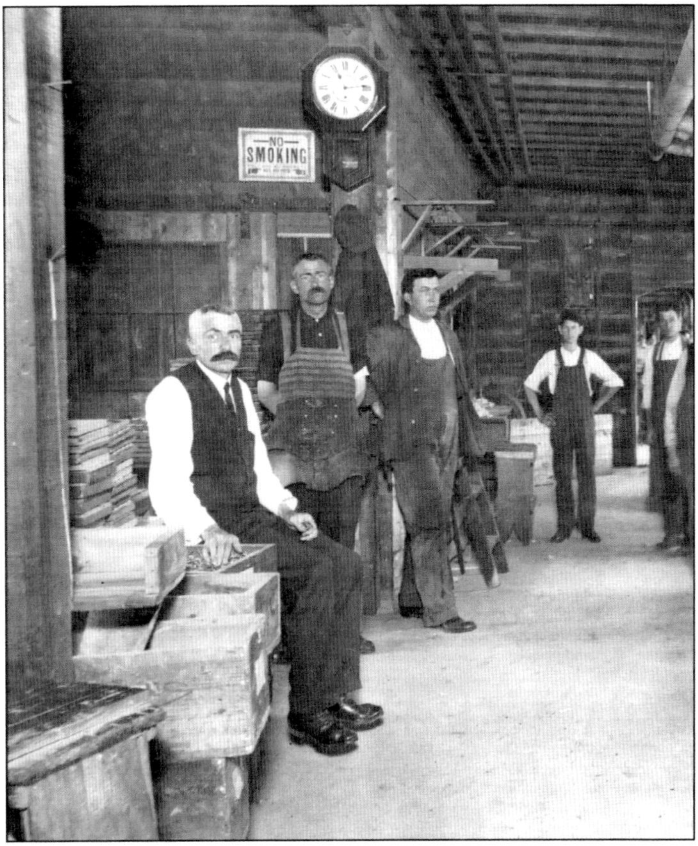

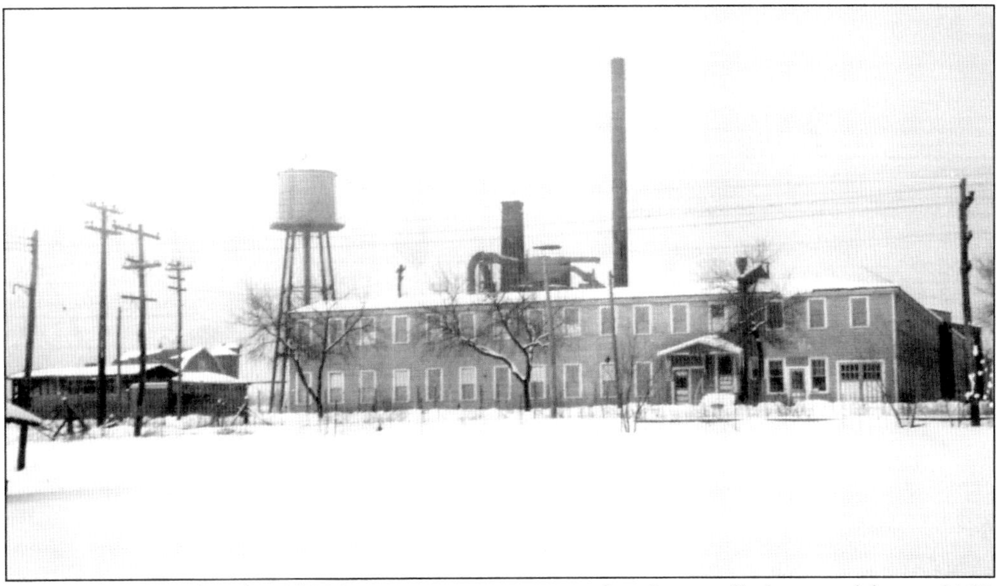

At the company's height, 35,000 piano actions were produced annually by a workforce of 160. In 1929, the business was liquidated, as more and more people began turning on their radio for family entertainment, rather than sitting down and playing the piano, as they had in years past. This photograph is from an early-1930s sales brochure attempting to sell the property.

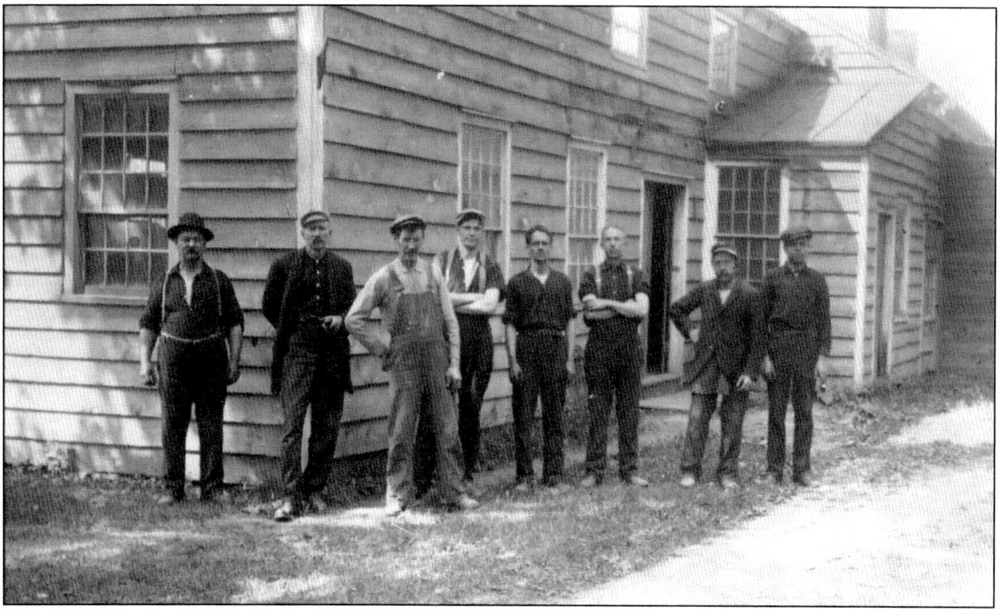

James Van Allen Sr. purchased an existing foundry on Church Street in 1858. For more than 50 years, he and his sons produced plows and other farm implements there, as well as fittings for the piano action company. Local legend holds that a burning ember from the foundry lodged into the steeple of the nearby Reformed church, causing a fire that burned the church to the ground on December 28, 1900. (Courtesy of Nassau Free Library.)

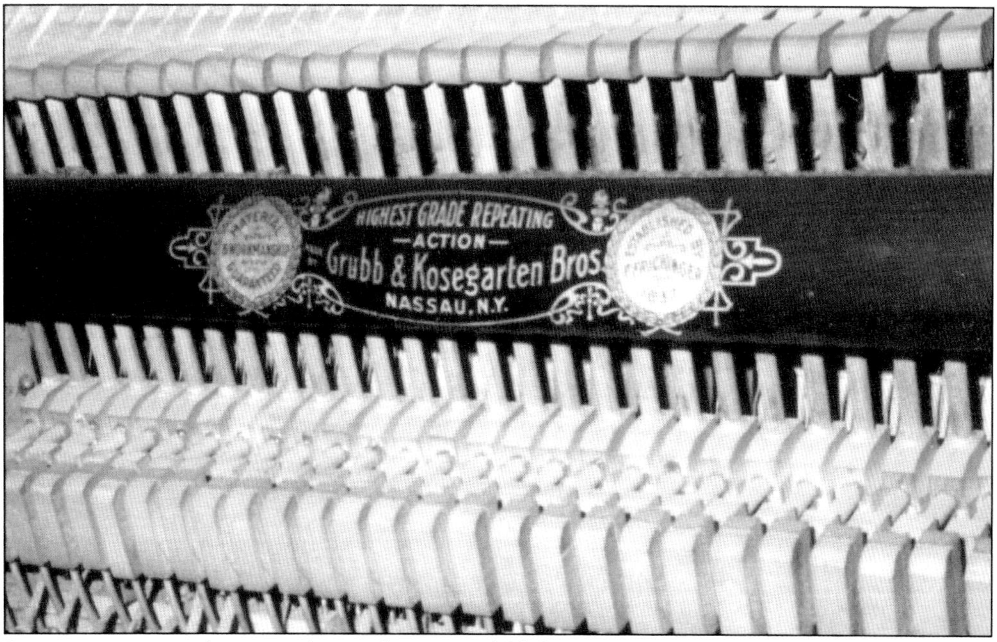

Piano actions, seen here, are the mechanisms of felt hammers that strike the piano strings when a key is depressed on the keyboard. Pianos were often built of subcomponents manufactured by a variety of specialist companies. Through a series of marriages and buyouts, the firm's name gradually evolved from Frickenger & Company to Frickenger & Grubb, Grubb & Kosegarten, and, finally, Kosegarten Brothers.

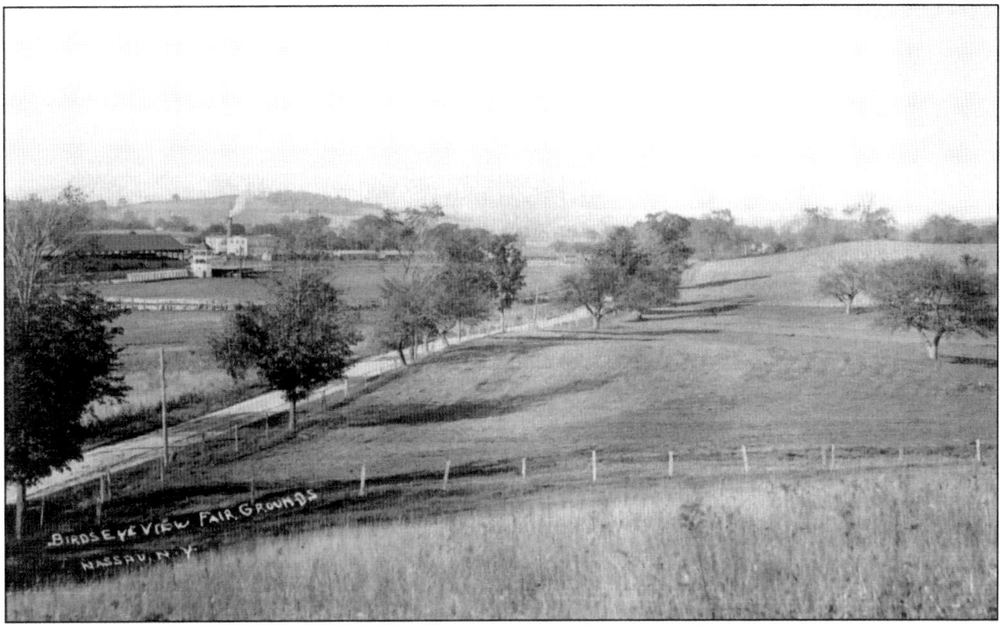

Many of the most frequently found photographic images of Nassau are postcards created for sale by the Nassau pharmacy. Starting with O.F. Burroughs around 1890, then the Lynd Brothers, and, until 1980, Waters Pharmacy, each pharmacy owner sold photograph cards under his name. Local photographers Elmer Shaver and George Harder are credited with capturing most of the images. In some cases, the same image was sold by succeeding owners. Here, the same photograph of the undeveloped Fairview Terrace sold by O.F. Burroughs (above) was again issued by the Lynd Brothers in the 1920s (below), this time with "colorized," whiter clouds. (Below, courtesy of the Dan Smith collection.)

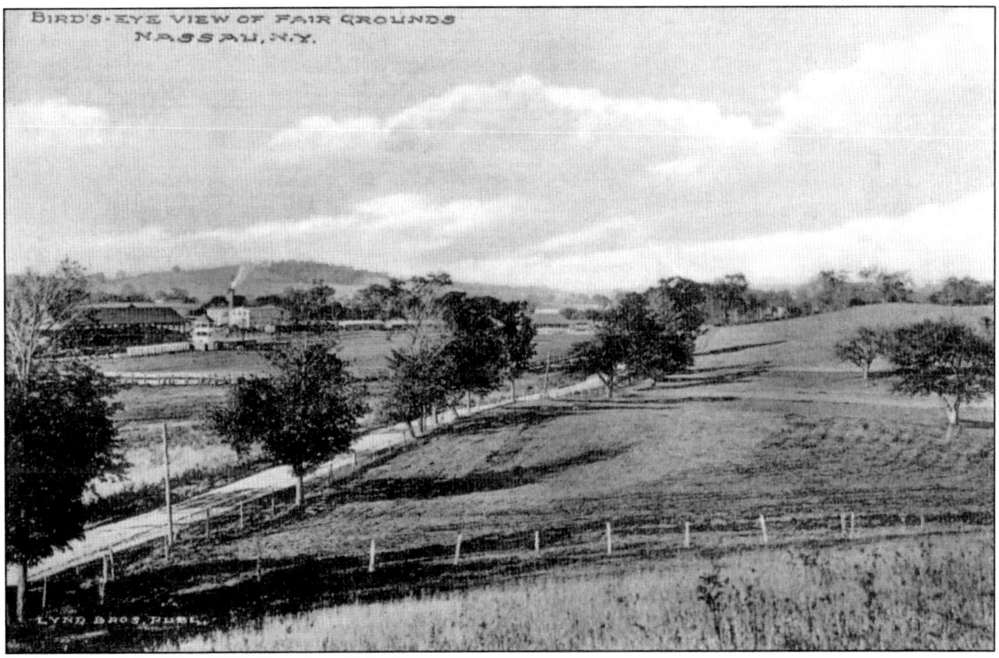

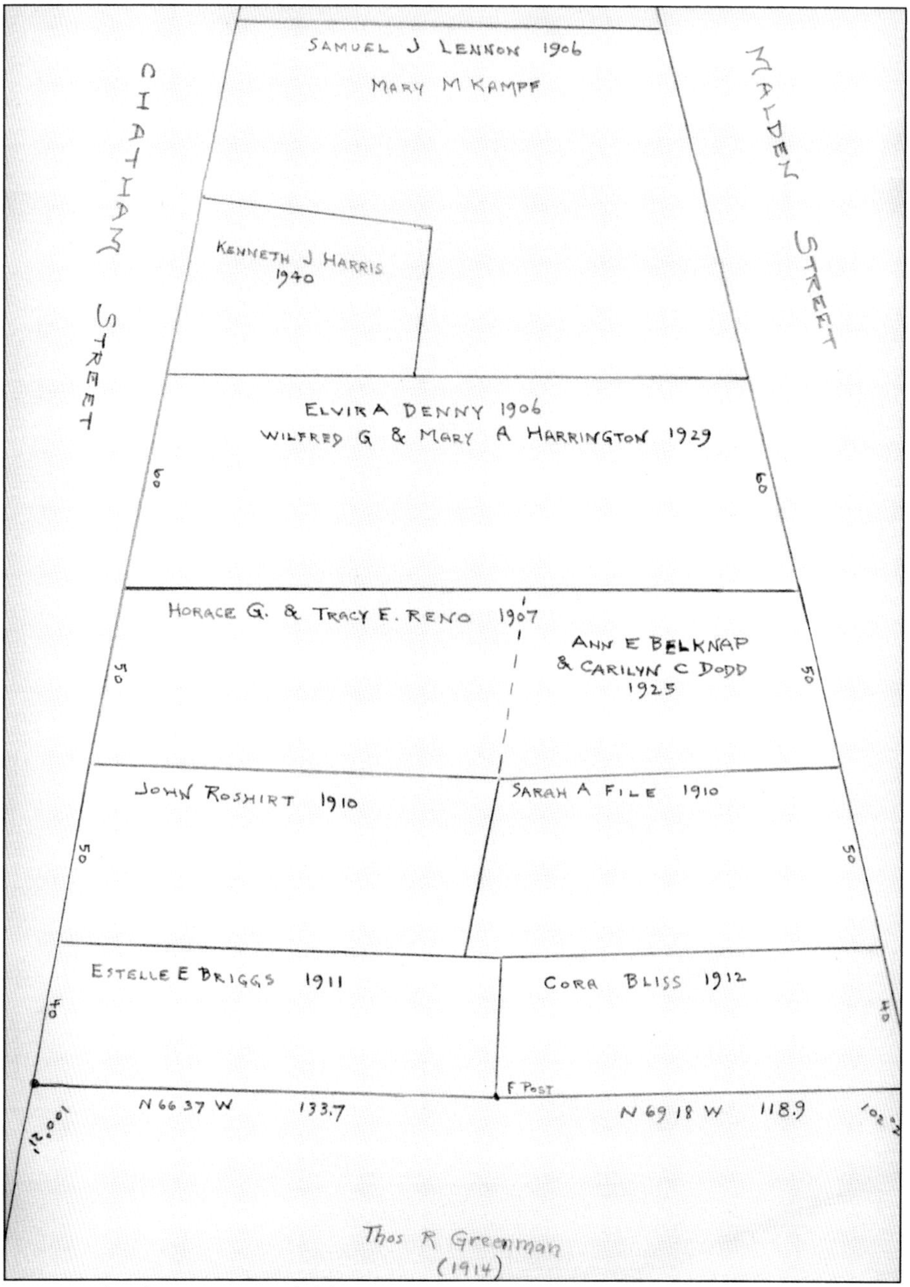

By 1900, much of Nassau's available room for development had been built on. Many of the structures built adjacent to the main streets and roads still stand today. However, the property between Chatham and Malden Streets continued undeveloped and was referred to as pastureland. The owner of the property, Carolyn Colvin, a descendant of early settler Jonathan Hoag, began selling lots around 1905. Thomas Greenman, a former undertaker turned property speculator, then developed Greenman Terrace, now called Fairview Terrace, starting in 1916. Greenman moved on to Florida and was fondly remembered for many years by Nassau schoolchildren for sending a case of oranges to the school at Christmastime. This hand-drawn 1943 map details the development. (Courtesy of Village of Nassau.)

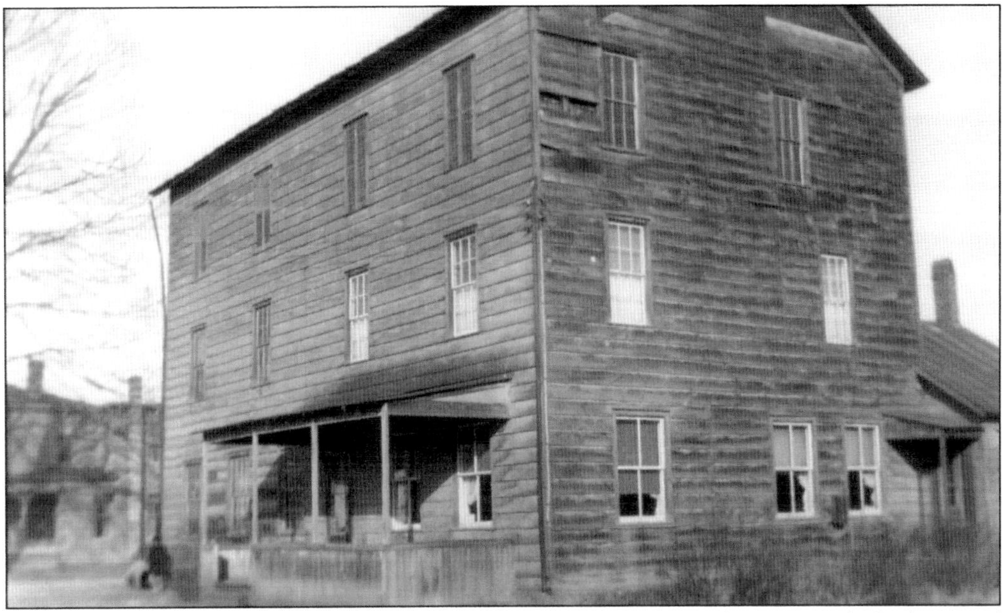

Opposite the developing tract was the Hermance Wagon Factory, at the corner of Chatham and Griswold Streets. Gilbert Hermance manufactured wagons and sleighs there from 1886 to 1926. The third floor of the building was used by the local Masonic order. The building was demolished in 1964 to make room for apartments. This photograph was taken in 1955. (Courtesy of Nassau Free Library.)

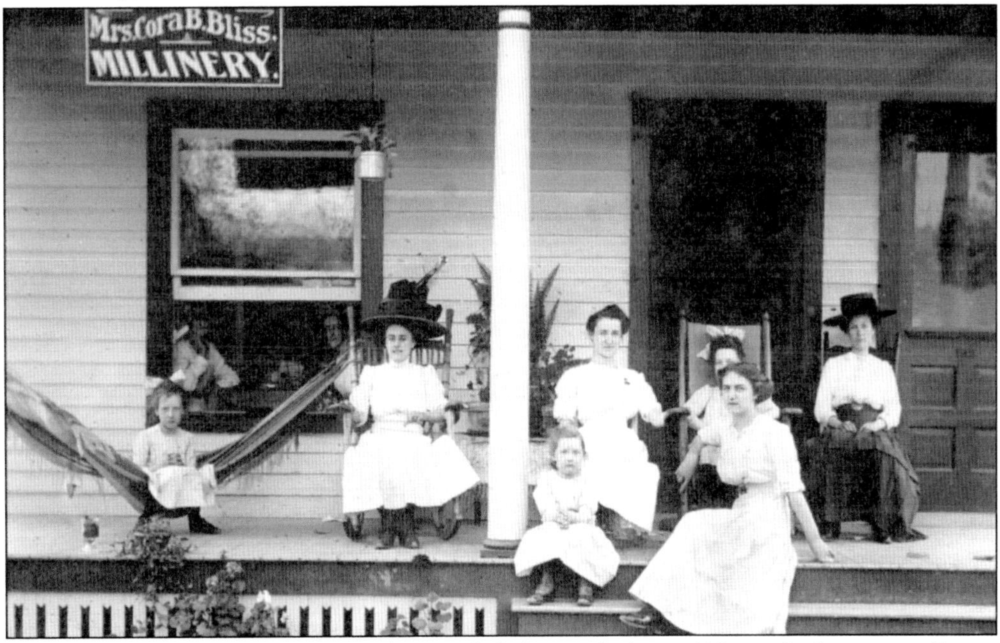

In the early 1900s, hats were very much part of a lady's wardrobe, and Nassau had its own millinery shop to provide fashionable women with suitable headgear. Cora Bliss made and sold hats at 18 Malden Street. Her least expensive hat was $5, and the business continued until 1919, when the spread of the so-called Spanish influenza epidemic affected both Bliss family members and customers. (Courtesy of Nassau Free Library.)

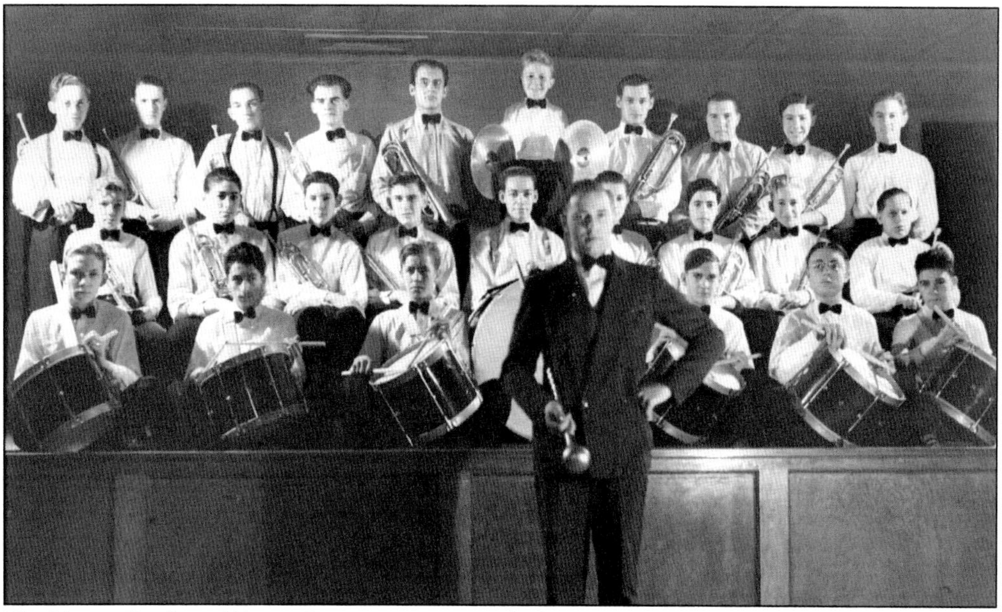

The Nassau Bugle and Drum Corps was active in the late 1930s and early 1940s. Here, on the stage of the firemen's hall, leader Raymond File poses with, from left to right, (first row) Frank Winters, Frank Spataro, Roy Wood, Leslie Hanson, Donald Chandler, and Russell Decker; (second row) Harry Winters, David Roth, Matthew Tierney, Edgar Cooper, Robert Baker, Robert Bushnell, Walter Schermerhorn, Sylvester Currier, and Kenneth Ashley; (third row) Jack West, Dudley Zusy, John Connolly, Milton Thompson, Cortland Hart, Sammy Schipps, Robert Bailey, Vernon Miller, Clayton Laraway, and Stanley Winters. (Courtesy of Nassau Free Library.)

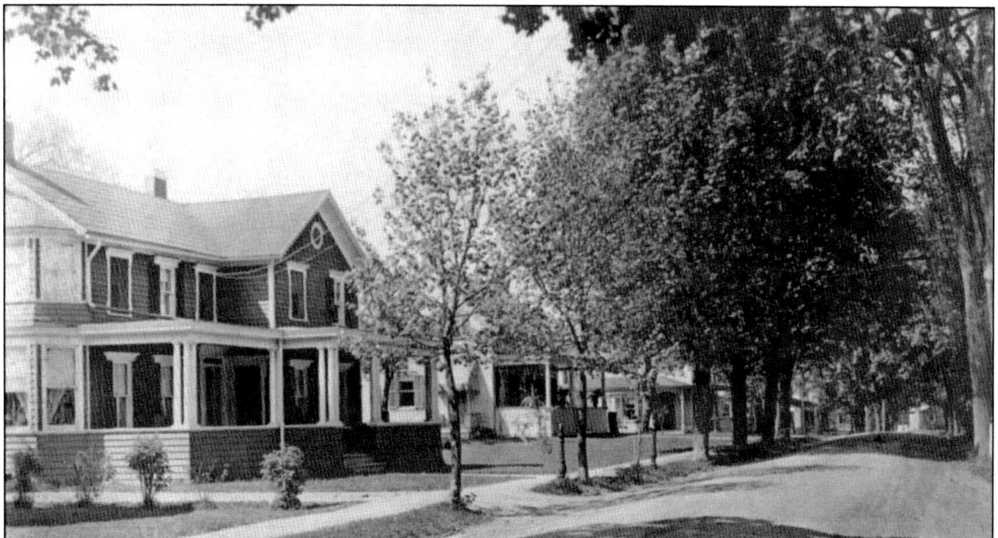

By around the time of the Civil War, most of the property on Elm Street had been developed with large homes. A popular entertainment establishment, Winter's Hall, was located in the former Presbyterian church, which was originally built on Albany Avenue as part of the Nassau Academy and then moved to Elm Street in 1846. In the 1920s, the building, seen here, was converted into a private residence.

Carrie "Grandma" Lout, seen here on her Chatham Street front porch in the 1930s, was the matriarch of a family that was typical of the times. The daughter-in-law of German immigrant farmers in Schodack, she and her husband, William, moved to Nassau and raised a family. William worked at the woolen mills in Brainard, and their son George worked at the piano factory. (Courtesy of the Lout family.)

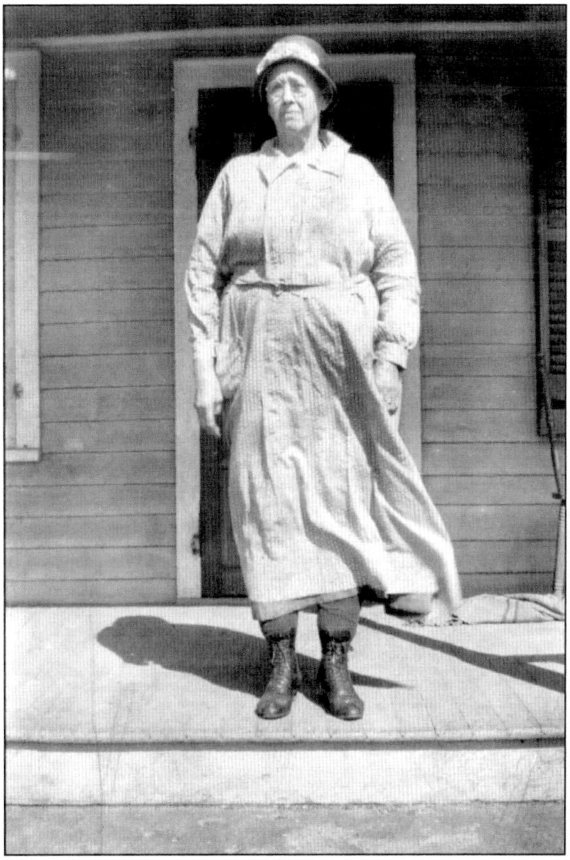

Entertainment in small towns was often local people performing amateur theatrics. The Nassau Hose Company is seen below performing a minstrel show at the Nassau Hose Company Hall, at the rear of Albany Avenue. Minstrel shows, which usually involved white performers wearing blackface and are generally thought of as racist today, continued in Nassau through the early 1940s. (Courtesy of the William Sturm family.)

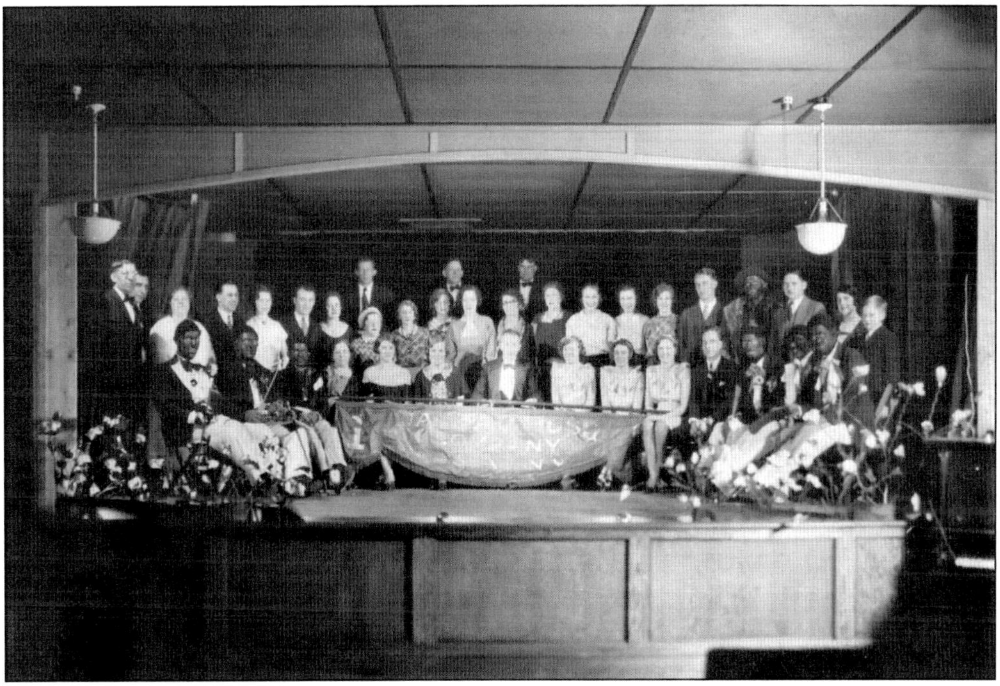

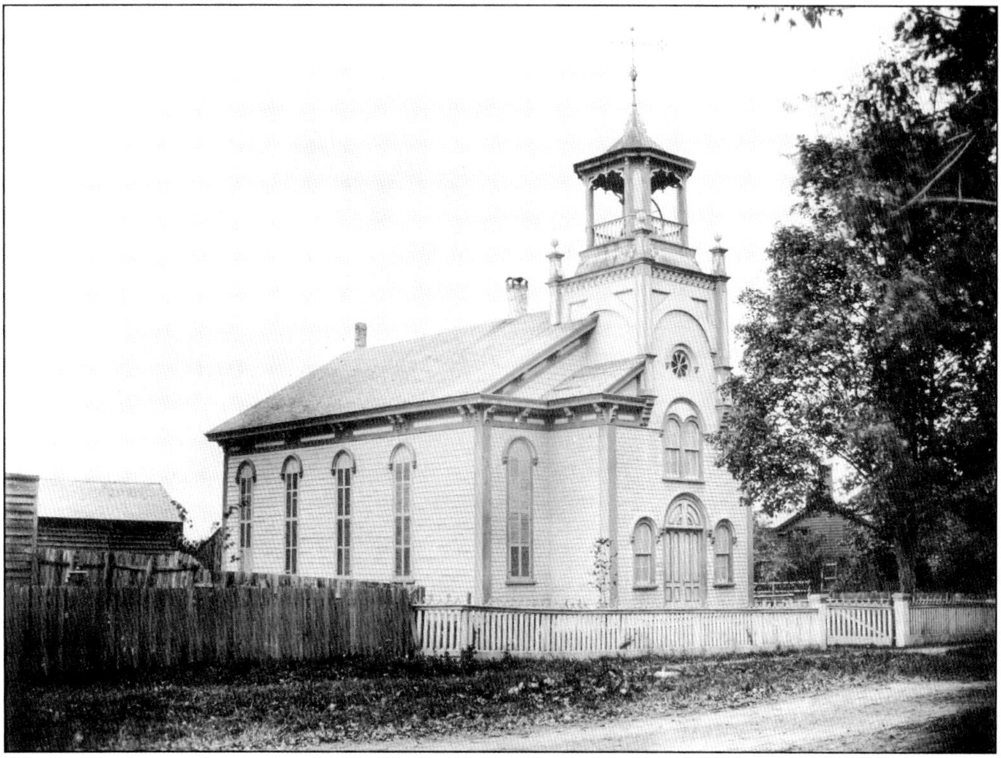

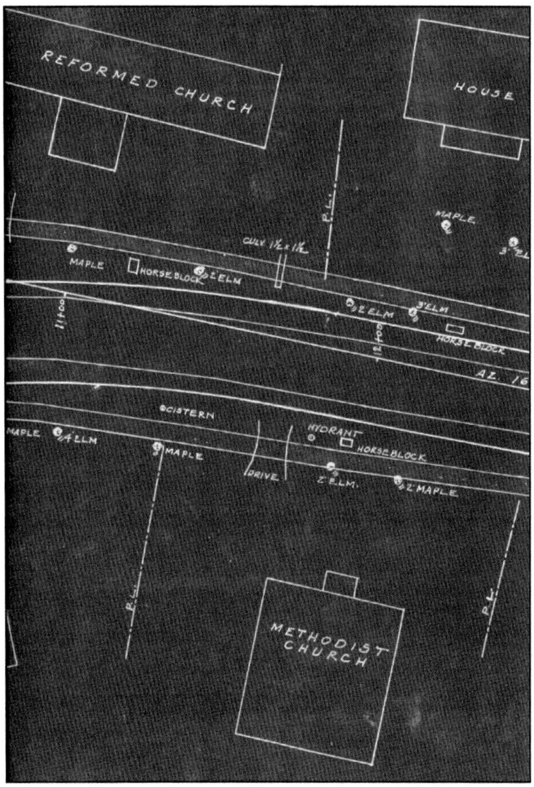

The photograph above, taken by Roscoe Velie in 1918, shows the Methodist Episcopal church prior to the addition of its second floor in 1923. The church structure dates to at least 1823, and is the oldest church building still in use in the village. At the rear of the photograph are sheds that were used to house horses during church services. The 1931 construction plan at left, for roadwork on Church Street, shows both the Methodist and Reformed churches along with vestiges of an earlier era: the horse blocks in front. A horse block is a raised platform, usually of stone, allowing for a comfortable step up or down for getting on a horse or into a carriage. Today, only 12 John Street retains its original horse block. (Above, courtesy of Judith Marquette; left, courtesy of Village of Nassau.)

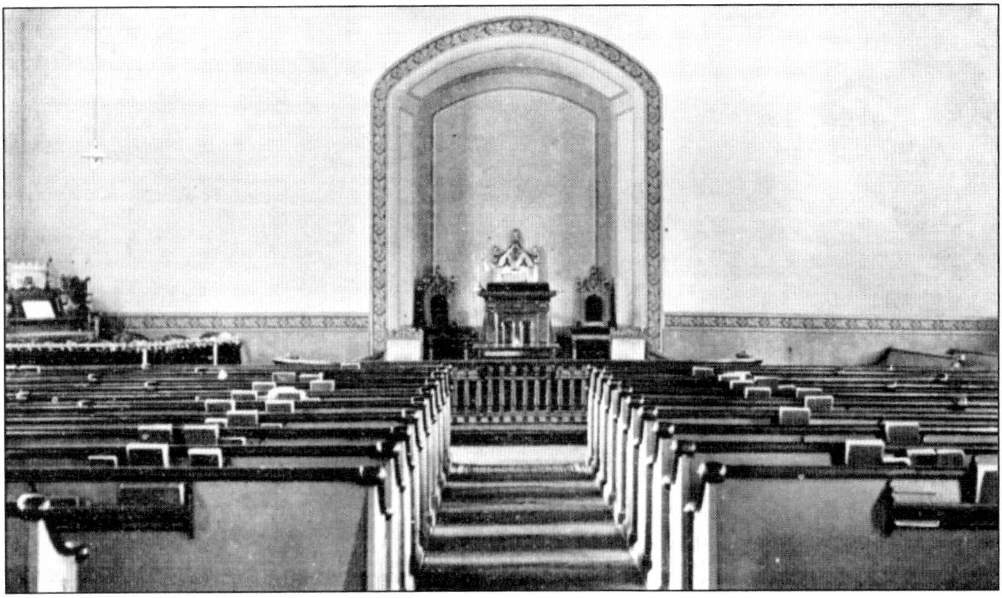

The interior of the Methodist church is seen here about 1900. In August 1948, national news was made at the church when guest speaker Rev. Ernst Bromley urged young men not to register for the military draft. A noted war resister and one of the original freedom riders from antisegregation efforts in the South, Reverend Bromley caused a brief but intense local uproar that summer.

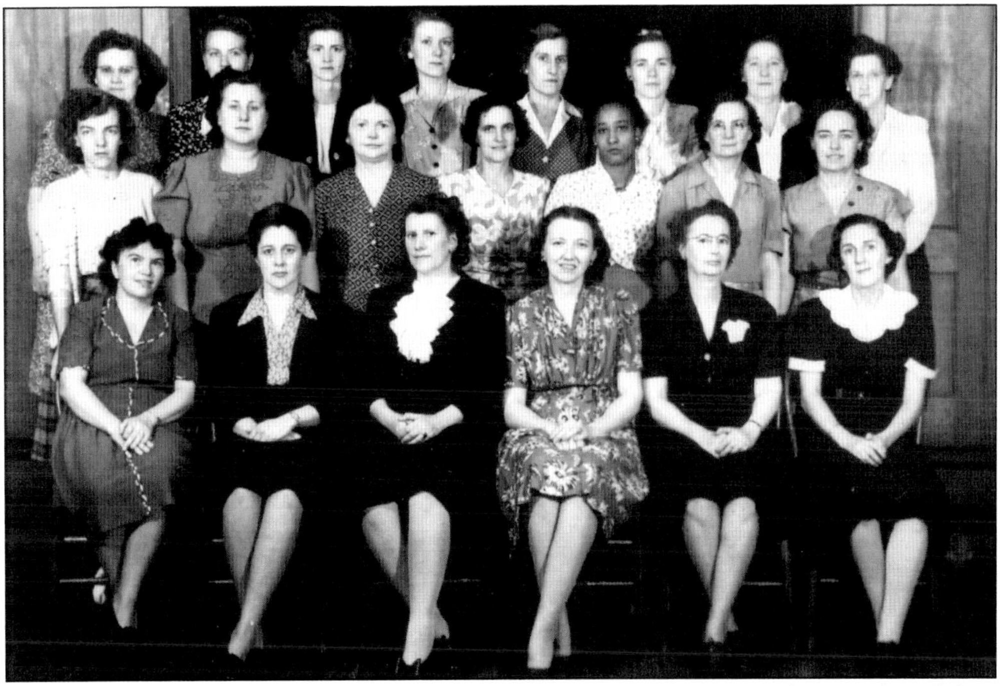

The Methodist church ladies pose for their photograph in 1941 or 1942. They are, from left to right, (first row) Bertha Prior, Ruth Thoma, unidentified, Elsie Morey, Ruth Holmes, and Jean Bulles; (second row) unidentified, Helen Chase, Gladys Crane, Marge Doolittle, Mildred Scott, unidentified, and Edna Stockman; (third row) Eunice Fuller (far left), Bea Weaver (fifth from left), and Mildred Young (far right). (Courtesy of Eleanor Bulles Coburn.)

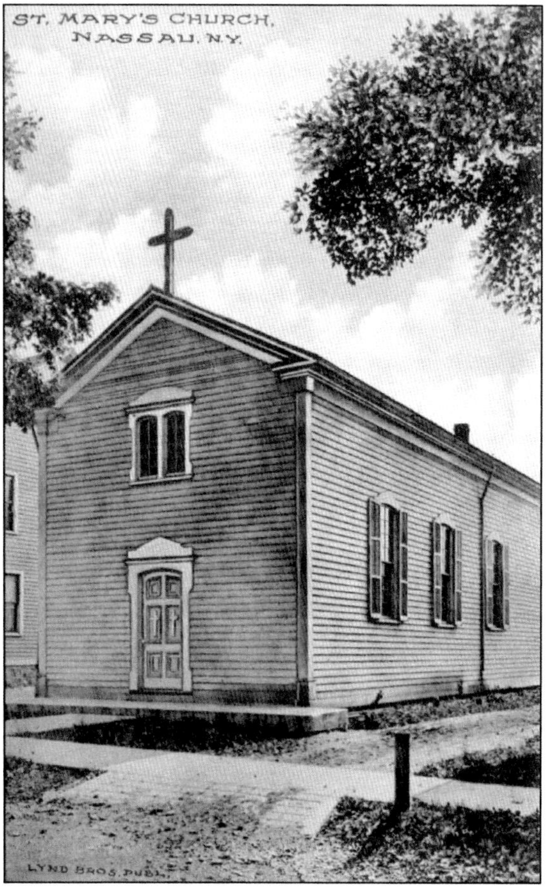

St. Mary's Roman Catholic Church was founded in the early 1850s. German Catholics formed the majority of parish members, and it was one of the earliest rural parishes east of the Hudson River. The image at left, from a period postcard, shows the first church, which was converted from a former residence on Church Street in 1852. This building served as the church until the 1920s, and later as the church hall. It was torn down in 1972 for the enlargement of the Nassau Free Library. The cornerstone for the present church, seen below, was laid on July 25, 1925, and it opened on May 30, 1926. Built with Tudor and Gothic influences, it could seat more than 300 people and featured Caen stone altars, Munich stained-glass windows, and a bell tower costing $50,000. (Left, courtesy of the Dan Smith collection.)

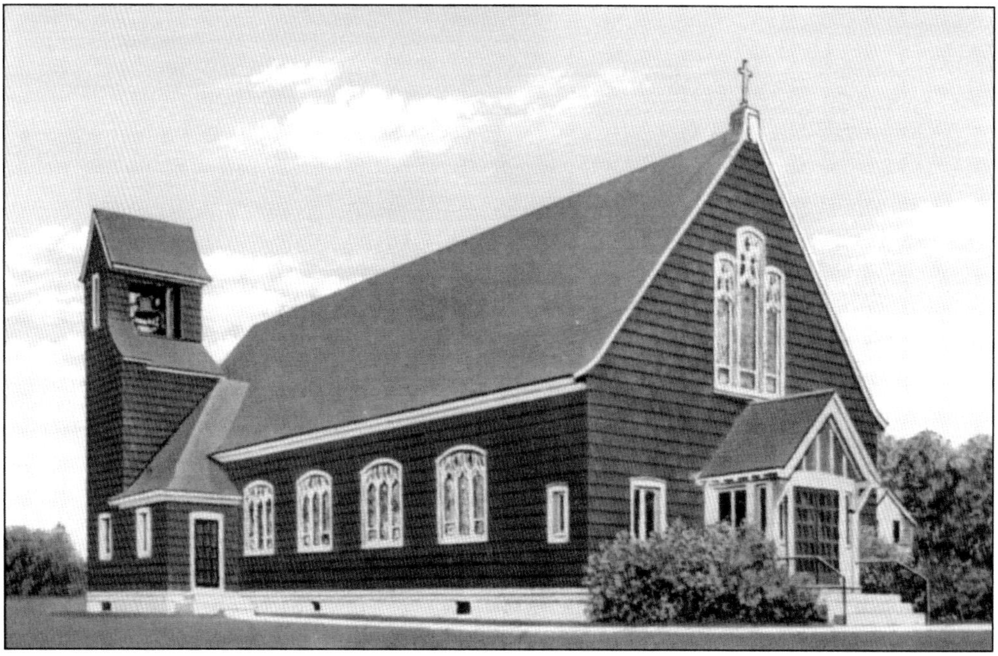

In 1902, the West Lebanon-based Columbia & Rensselaer Telephone & Telegraph Company extended its service to Nassau, with seven subscribers. By 1921, the number had risen to 175, including 15 in Hoag's Corners. Nassau operator Rita Velie is seen here about 1930. In 1951, direct dial ended local operator service. (Courtesy of Judith Marquette.)

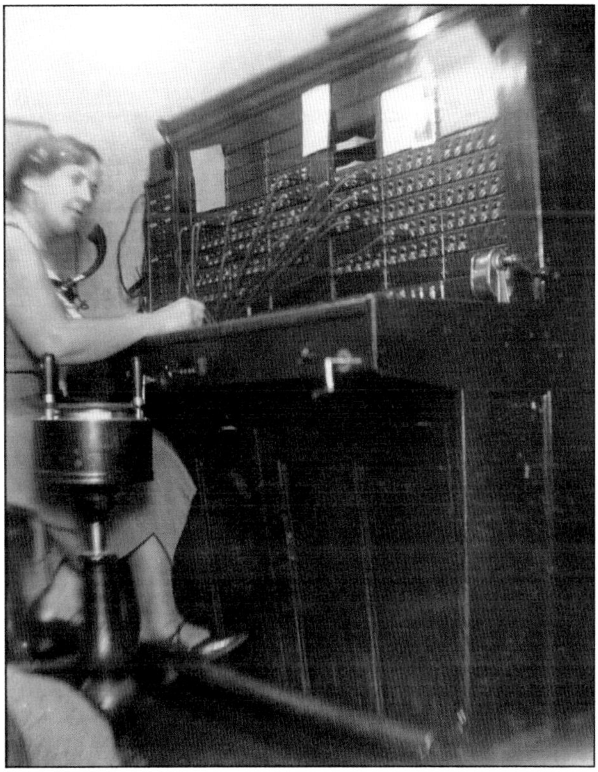

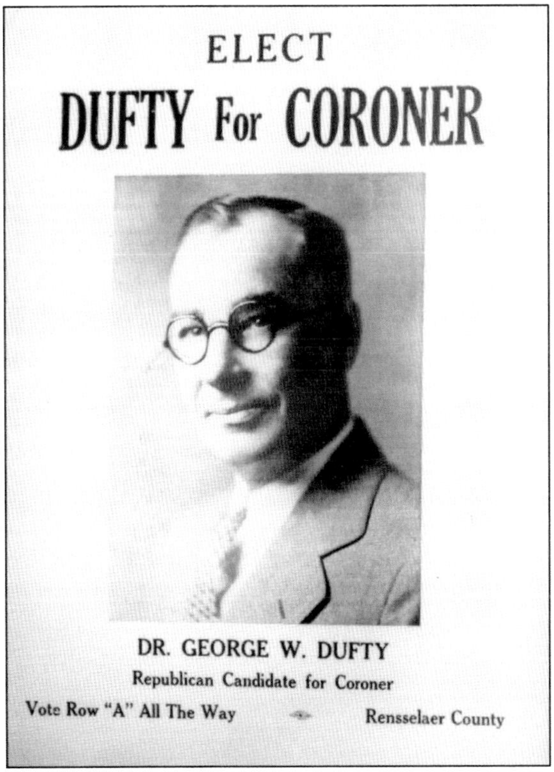

Dr. George Dufty, who won election as Rensselaer County coroner, practiced medicine in Nassau for more than 30 years. His former home and office, at 26 Church Street, later became St. Mary's friary in 1958. Other Nassau doctors over the years included Dr. Philip Neher, Dr. J.B. Southworth, Dr. E.P. Felt, Dr. Oscar Wilcox, Dr. Eli Denny, Dr. Boris Klasons, Dr. Velta Klasons, Dr. Vija Matisone, and Dr. Max Panitch.

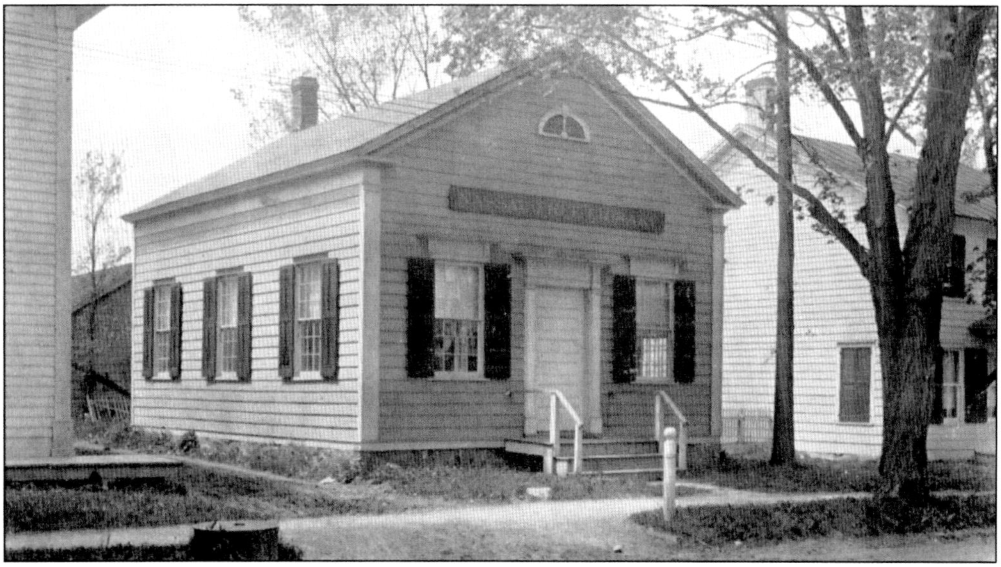

Located on Church Street, the Nassau Free Library was organized in 1881. The library has occupied the site above since 1893, when the one-room building was purchased from the Reformed church consistory. Started with a donation of 80 books at a time when the population was 356, the library has always been a cultural resource in the Nassau area. In the years after World War I, the library would open on Saturday nights to coincide with the summer band concerts at the square. Before the new Nassau School was built in 1939, students made weekly trips to the library, since the old school did not have its own. The original single room of the library is seen below in the 1970s. (Below, courtesy of Nassau Free Library.)

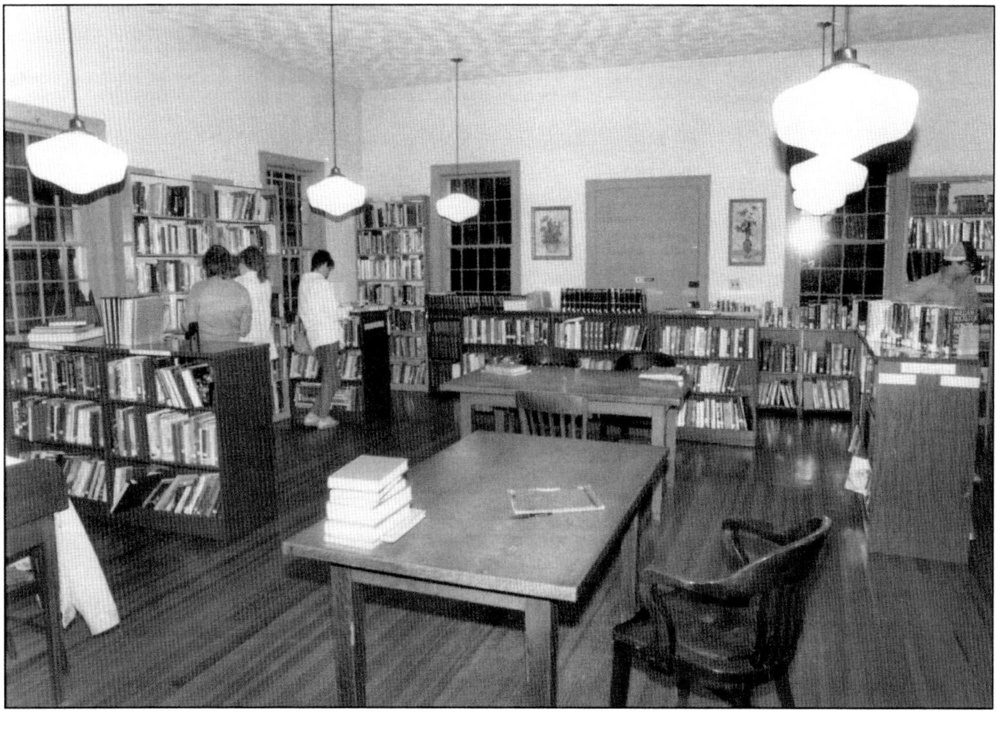

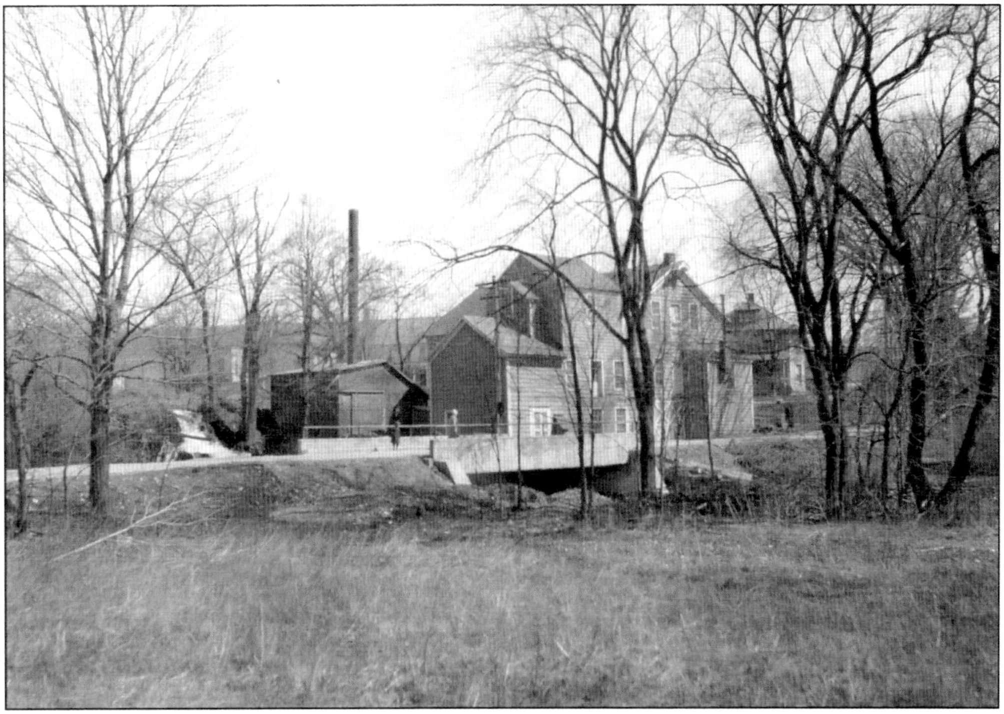

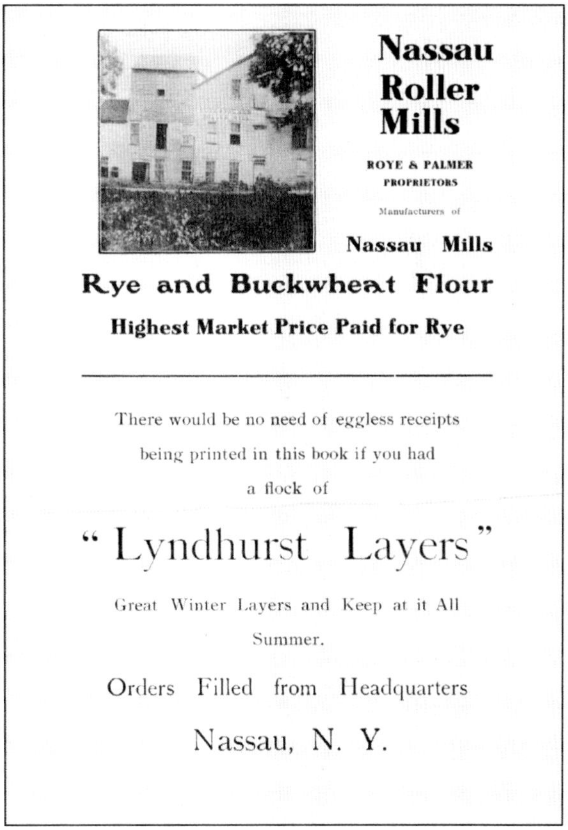

Many of the farmers in the area grew rye and buckwheat as cash crops. In 1874, with over 251,000 bushels harvested, Rensselaer County was second in New York State for rye production. From the early 1900s until 1924, Roye & Palmer's Nassau Roller Mills operated at the corner of Elm Street and Lake Avenue. Near the site of Jonathon Hoag's first mill from more than 100 years earlier, the mill property included water rights to Nassau Lake and a raceway system to divert the flow of water to the mill. Originally called Mill Street, Lake Avenue, in addition to having the gristmill, was also the site of a sawmill, a cider press, a machine shop, and a shirt factory. (Above, courtesy of Judith Marquette; right, courtesy of Nassau Free Library.)

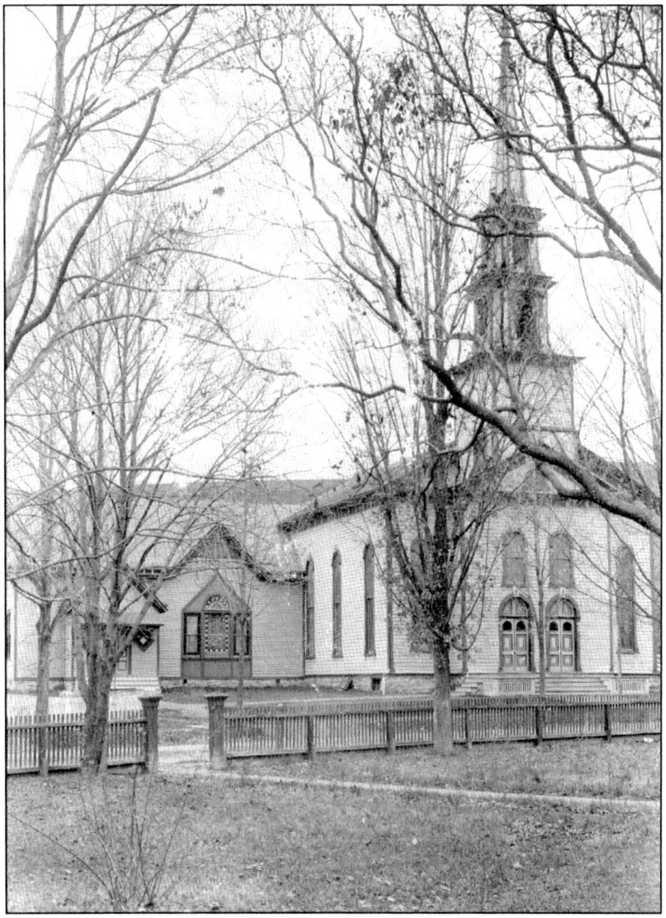

This image shows the second Reformed church building in Nassau village. Situated at the bend in upper Church Street, the building, with its commanding steeple, is visible in many of the earliest photographs of the era. The church was built in 1821, and the chapel (left) was donated by the Frickinger family and added in 1891. (Courtesy of Nassau Free Library.)

The third Reformed church structure was built in the same location as the second after it burned in 1901. The postcard below, from 1906, shows the front entry without its roof. There are deep culverts on either side of the street to aid in water runoff, a single kerosene streetlamp, and, on the right side, a horse block. Architect Samuel E. Kingman designed the building. (Courtesy of the Dan Smith collection.)

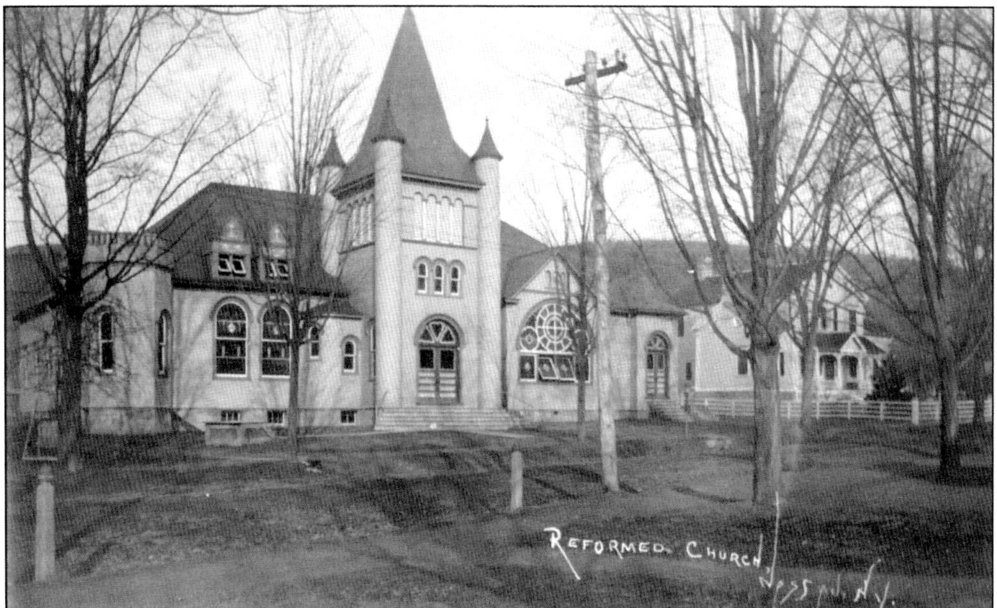

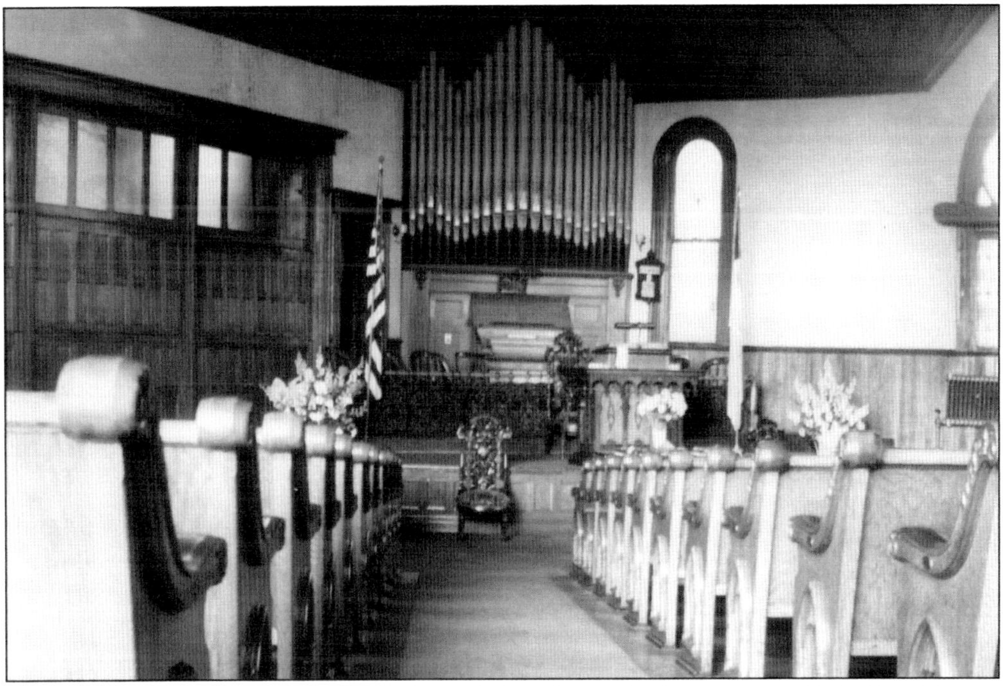

At the time of its completion, the Reformed church was the largest assembly hall in Nassau, seating 350. It was built in what was called the auditorium style, and an unobstructed view of the pulpit was available from every pew. In addition to church use, the Nassau Union School held graduations there and the Nassau Choral Society gave concerts there. The structure was added to both the National Register and the New York State Register of Historic Places in 1974. In the nomination document, the church building is cited as a "highly eclectic combination of Queen Anne, Moorish and Romanesque elements."

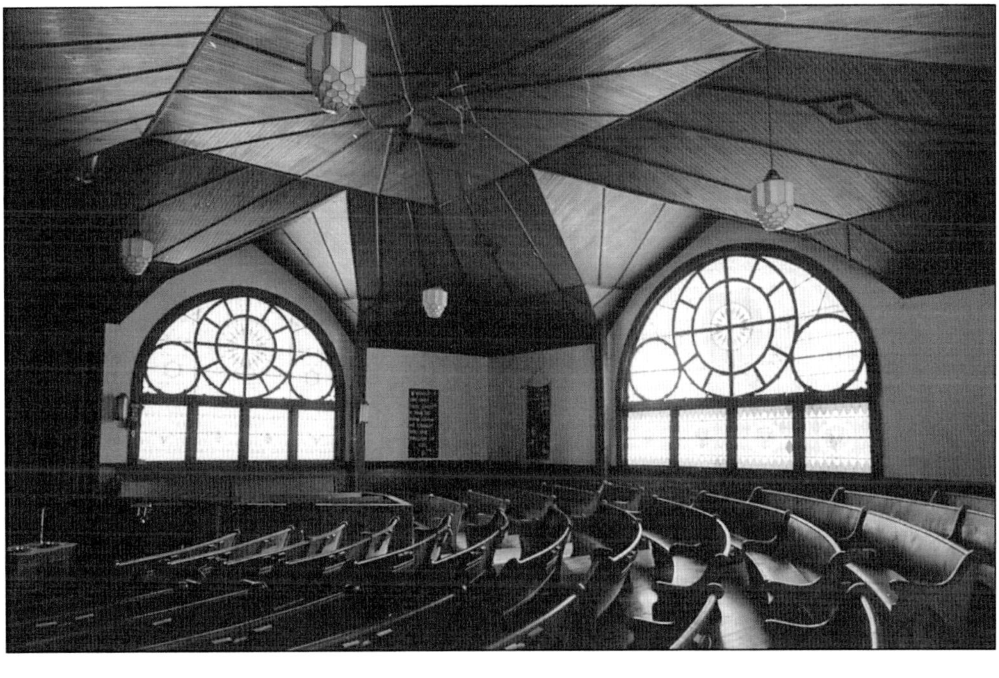

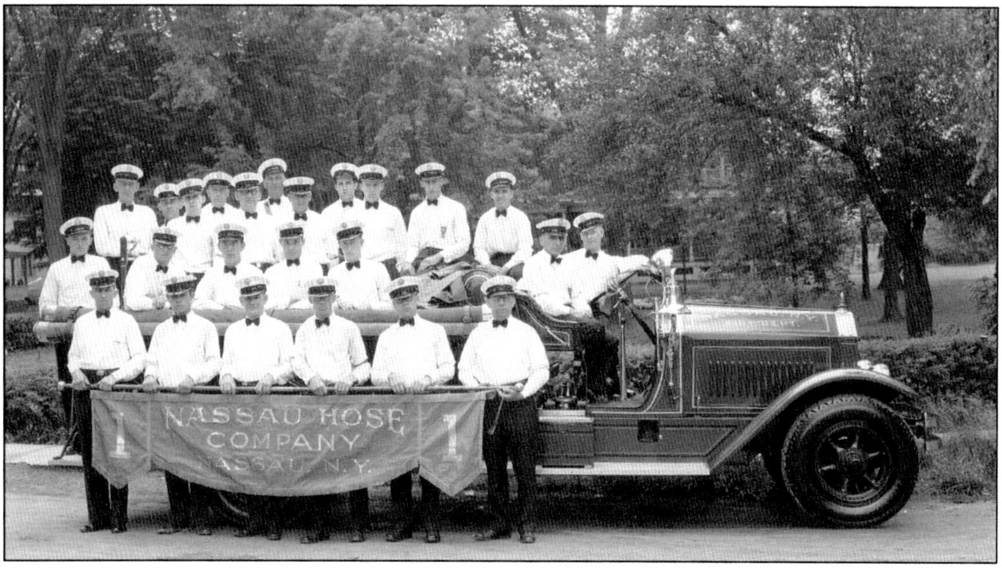

Purchased used, this 1926 American LaFrance fire engine served Nassau for many years. Seen here with it are, from left to right, (first row) Roy Allendorph, Ralph Lappias, Willfred Harrington, two unidentified men, and Joseph Roshirt; (second row) Charles Connelly, Ralph Mensing, Robert Hunter, Stillman Pitts, and Robert Schlegel; (front seat) Matthew Roshirt and Frank Pitts; (third row) Ralph Hyde, Norman Waters, Edson Currier, Robert Waters, unidentified, Clarence Germond, unidentified, Lloyd Welch, unidentified, Robert VanAlstyne, and Harold Currier. (Courtesy of Nassau Free Library.)

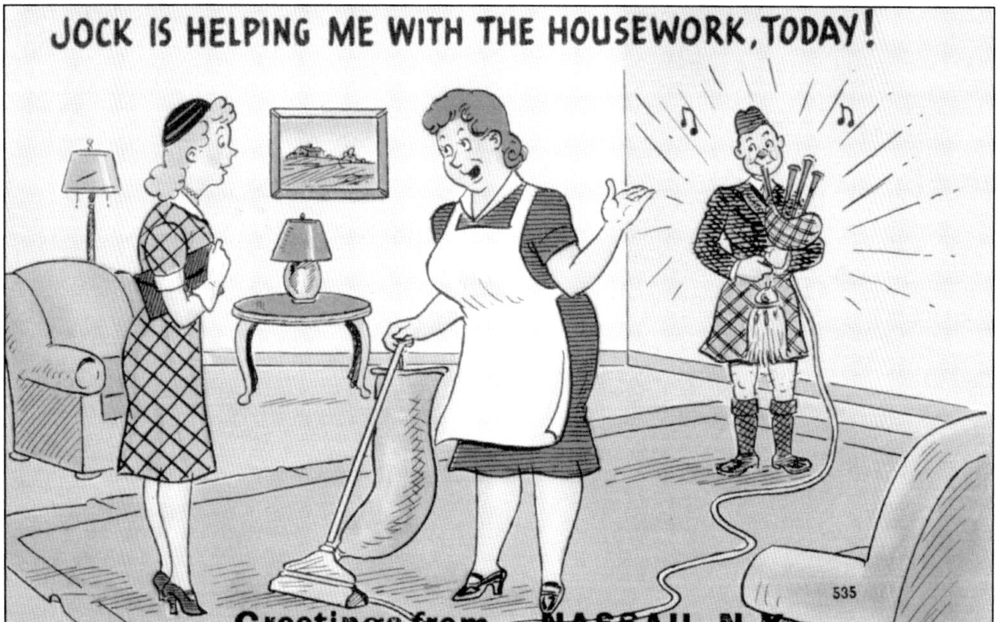

While George Eastman's invention of the Kodak box camera may have led to the demise in popularity of picture postcards, merchants in Nassau continued to sell "Greetings from Nassau, N.Y." cards. Obviously designed to be imprinted with the name of the locality of choice, several of these 1940-era cards remain as curiosities. (Courtesy of Village of Nassau.)

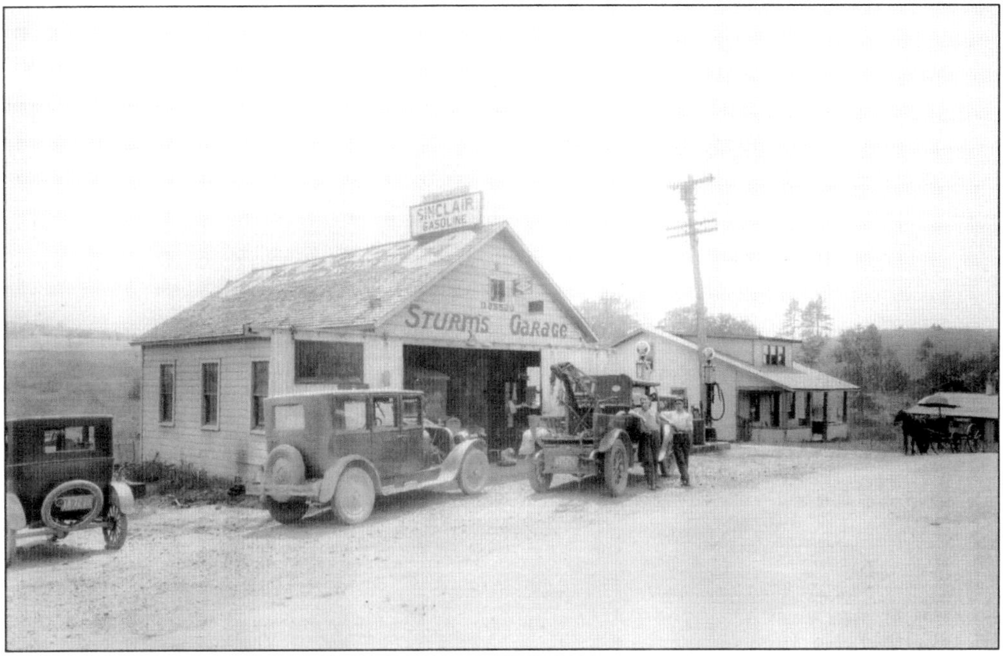

Sturm's Garage is seen above in the late 1920s. One of only a few garages on busy US Route 20 between East Greenbush and Lebanon, it was a popular place. Below, when a unique Ner-A-Car motorcycle stopped at the garage, it merited a photograph. Designed by Carl Neracher, these unusual machines were built in Syracuse. (Both, courtesy of the Sturm family.)

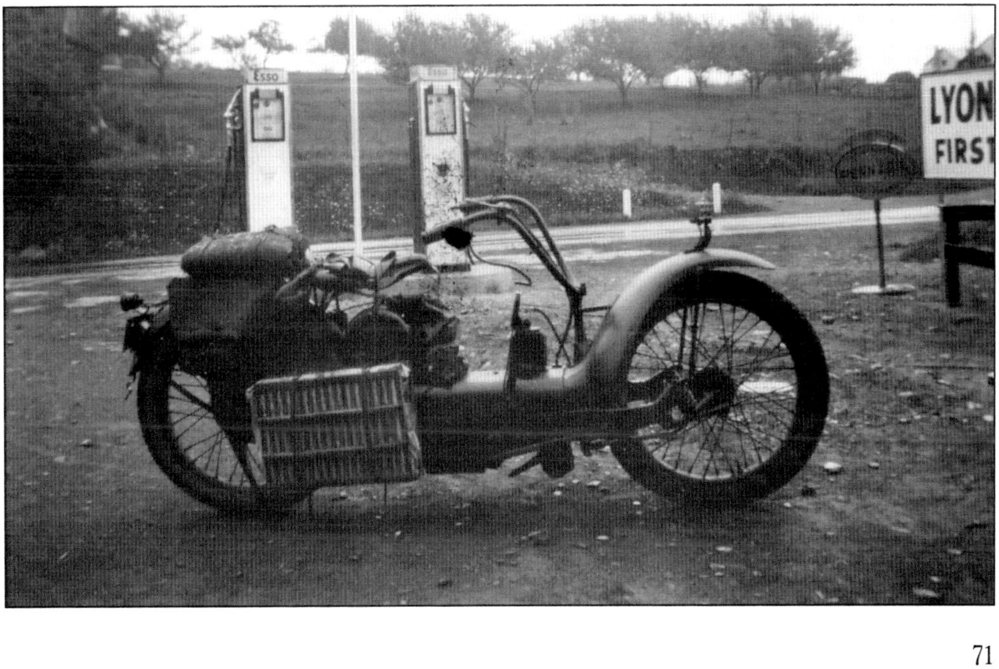

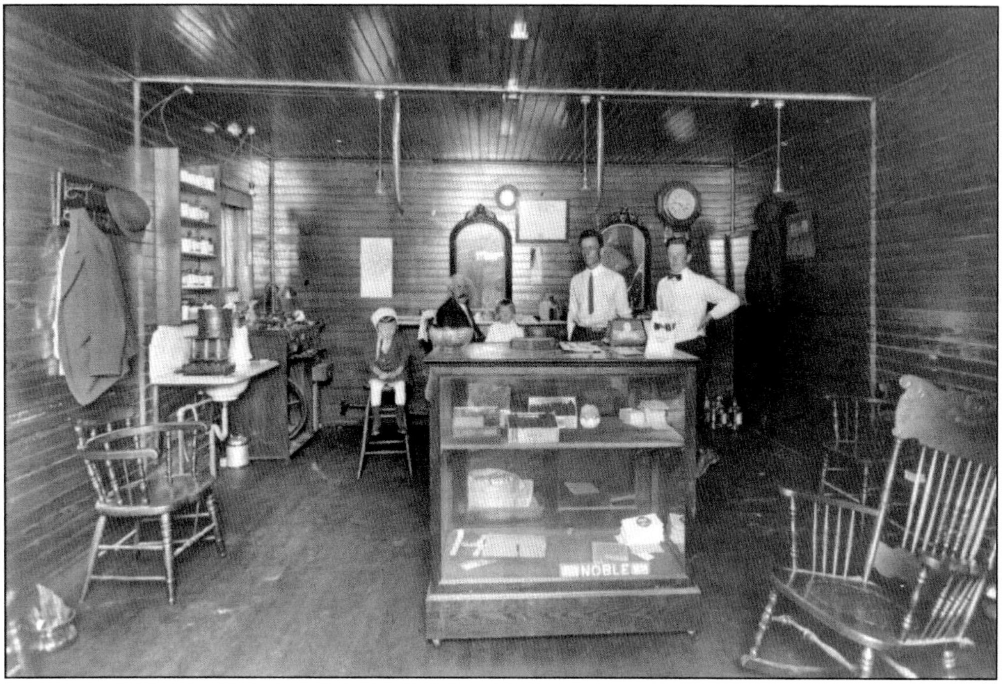

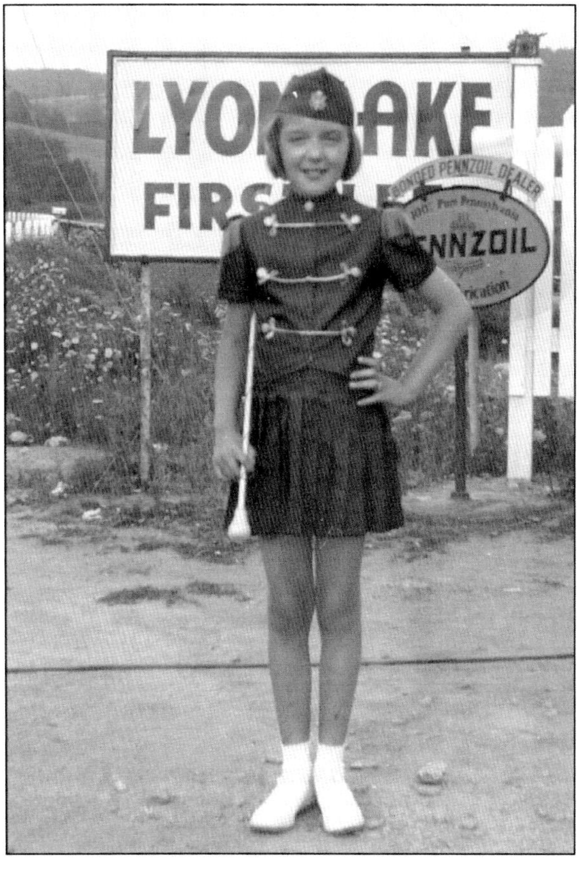

The inside of Grave's barbershop is seen around 1915. Pictured, from left to right, are daughter Mary Kosegarten, father Albrecht Kosegarten, son Herman Kosegarten, and barbers Howard Rowe and Colonel Graves. Both Rowe and Graves had short stays in Nassau. In much later years, Charles Saucca and Donald McGill had shops in Nassau. Stephan Zido also had a shop at Morey Park. (Courtesy of the Schodack Town Historian.)

Janice Amelia Vickery was the four-year-old mascot of the Nassau Hose Company Junior Drum and Bugle Corp in 1939. Her entertainment career began two years earlier, when she was awarded the blue ribbon in the Lebanon Valley Baby Show. Her father, Elmer L. Vickery, was on the World War I Nassau town honor roll, and the family name goes back in Nassau as far as the 1700s. (Courtesy of the Sturm family.)

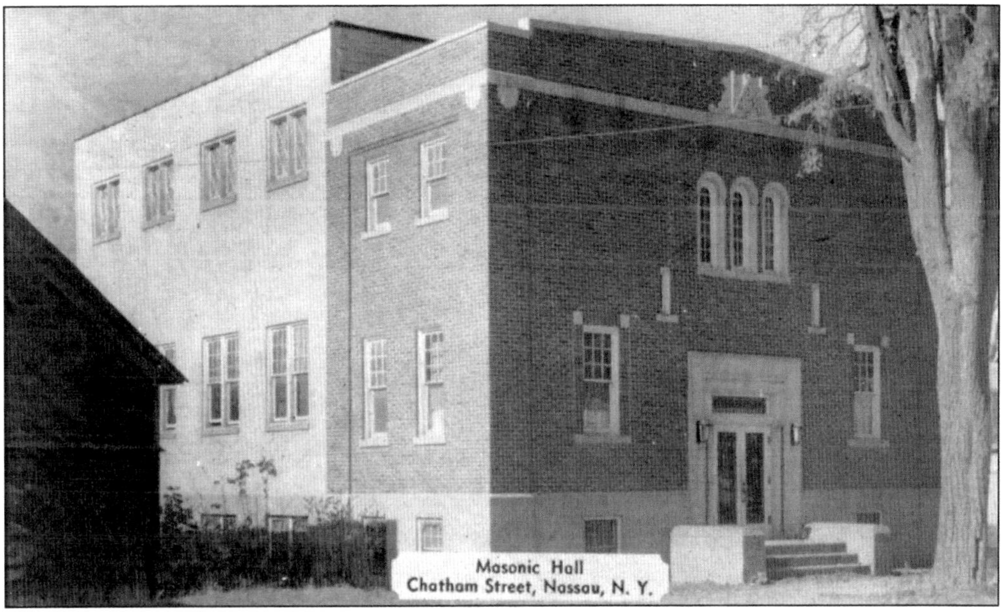

The Masons were active in Nassau from late 1800s until the 1980s. In 1930, they built this structure on Chatham Street. The upper floor was reserved for Masonic ceremonial purposes, while a large meeting room occupied the ground floor, which was used by the community for many purposes, including entertainment events, dinners, and public meetings. The basement housed a small bowling alley that was very popular.

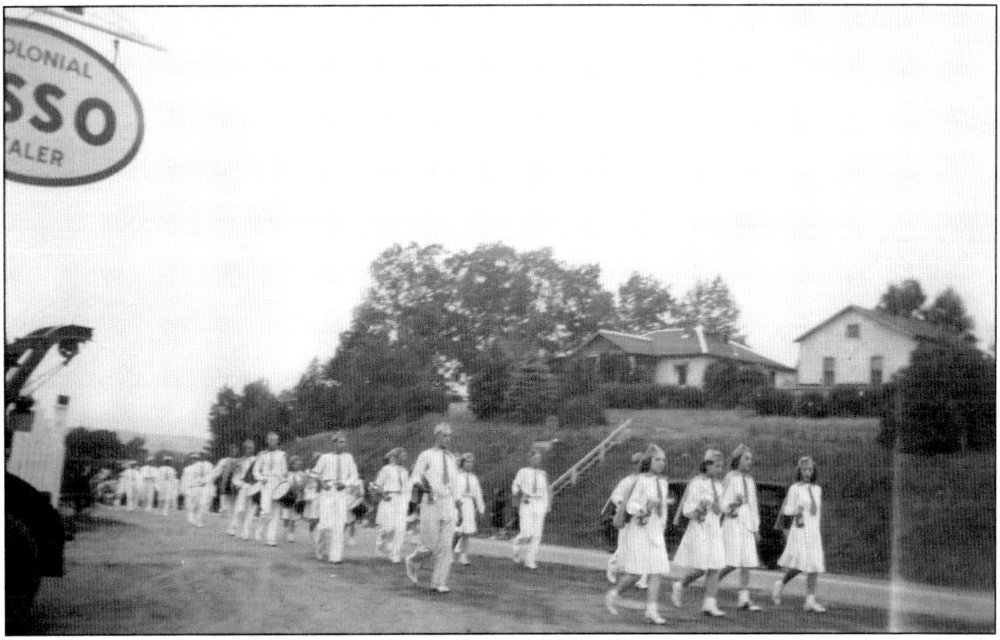

Between world wars, most parades in Nassau took place on Memorial Day and on the Fourth of July. Typically, and the route was planned around the village, for maximum exposure, and ended at the fairgrounds. After marching up Church Street from the village square, parade-goers would then loop back down the hill. The Nassau Drum and Bugle Corps is seen here during a parade. (Courtesy of the Sturm family.)

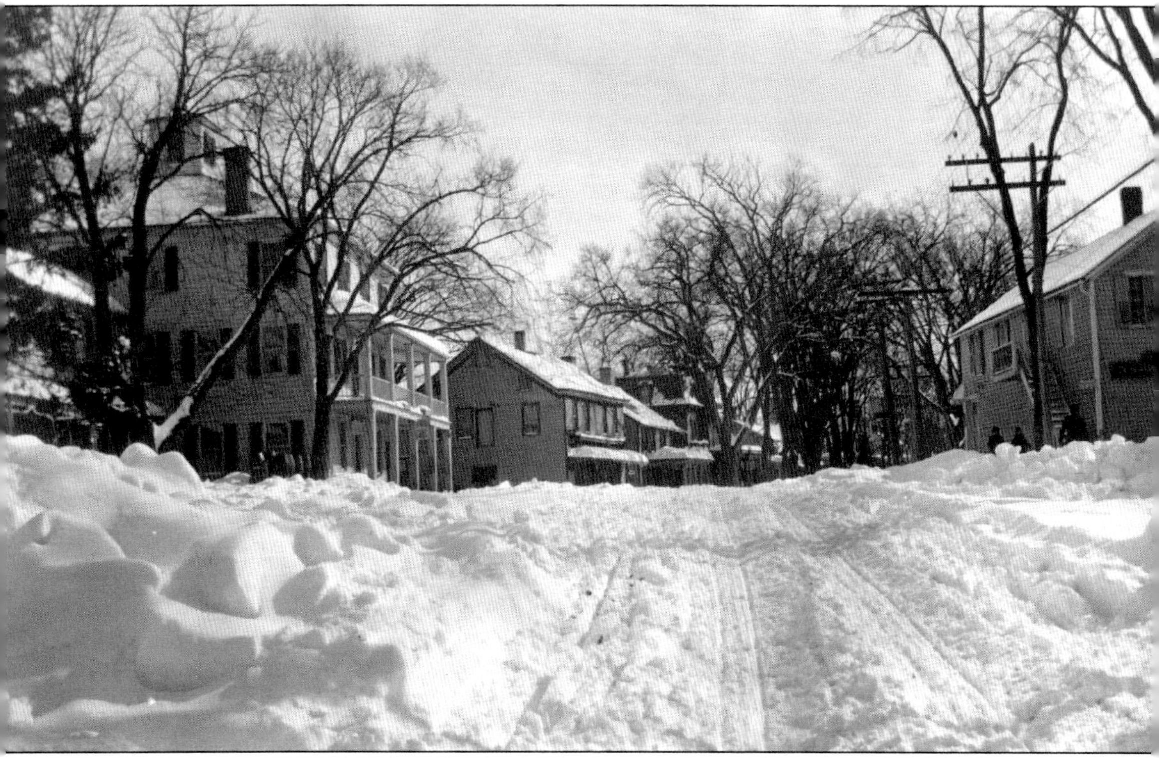

It was well into the 1920s before plowing roads after a snowfall was considered. Those who still owned a horse team used sleighs often up until that time. The view in this photograph, looking up Albany Avenue with the hotel on the left and the pharmacy on the right, shows Nassau as a cozy, well-maintained little village. In 1925, the village population was 757, a sizable increase from just 20 years earlier, when it had 455 residents. The town also grew during that period, with 1,991 residents in 1905 and 2,380 in 1925. (Courtesy of Nassau Free Library.)

Six

The Town

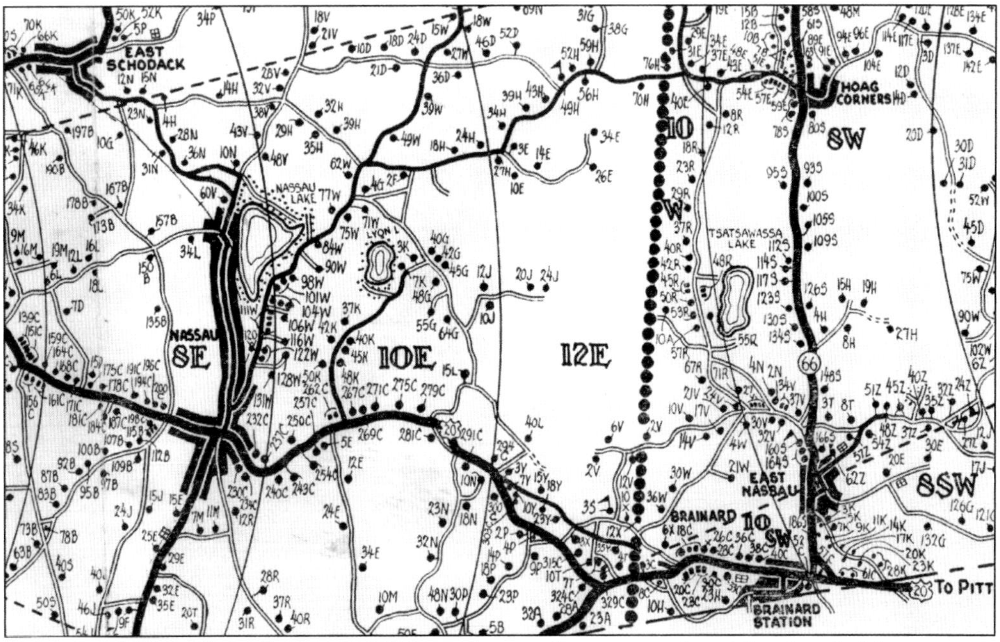

Once outside the village, the long tradition of farming becomes evident. This detail of the mapping system from the 1939 *Rural Guide to Rensselaer County* shows the locations of farms. Following US Route 20 east from Nassau village to the junction of Lyons Lake Road, a distance of about a half mile, travelers passed the properties of Charles Winters, Royal McIntyre, Meyer Sovitsky, Harold Loss, Abraham Balfoort, Joseph Lederman, William Baldwin, and Morris Schwartz. By the end of the 1890s, as more and more farmers were leaving agriculture, Jewish philanthropic groups were seeking to resettle Eastern European Jews in the United States. Nathan Naum, a Russian immigrant with an education in agriculture, represented the New York City–based Jewish Agricultural and Industrial Society and acquired many farm properties. By 1909, there were at least 62 Jewish farms in the area, and, by the 1920s, there were more than 200 Jewish families. The area between Nassau, East Nassau, and East Schodack is unique in its rich history of Jewish American growth, assimilation, and heritage.

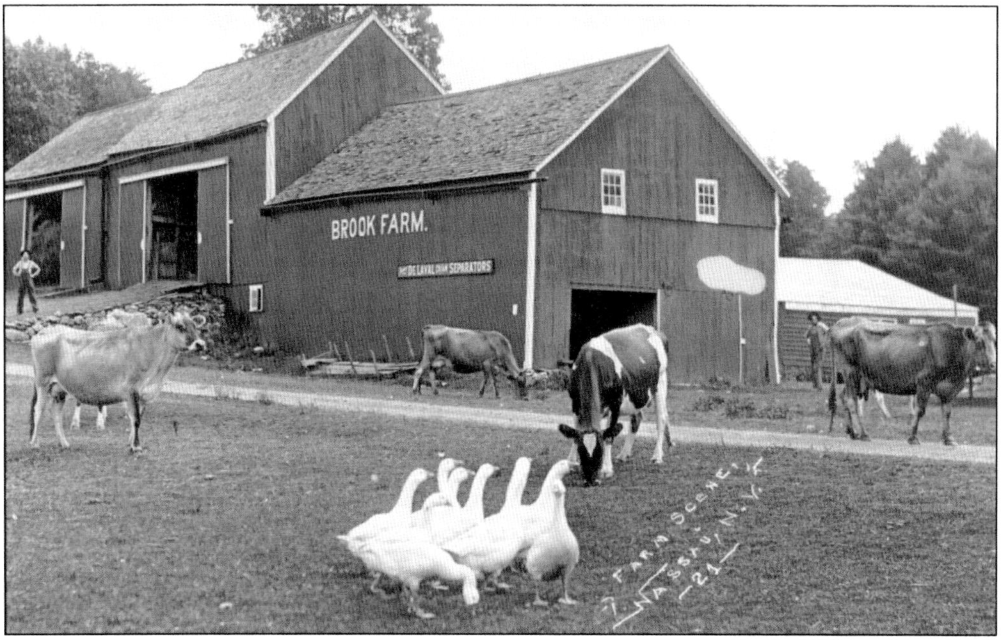

These two postcard scenes show the rural nature of Nassau around 1900. With more developed Nassau village only occupying about one square mile out of the total 45.2 square miles of the township, the majority of residents made their livelihoods through agriculture or by supporting agriculture. Gristmills, blacksmiths, and wagon builders all helped move crops to market. Grass, rye, potatoes, corn, oats, and buckwheat were the main field crops, with much of that being used to feed livestock. (Below, courtesy of Wally Stock.)

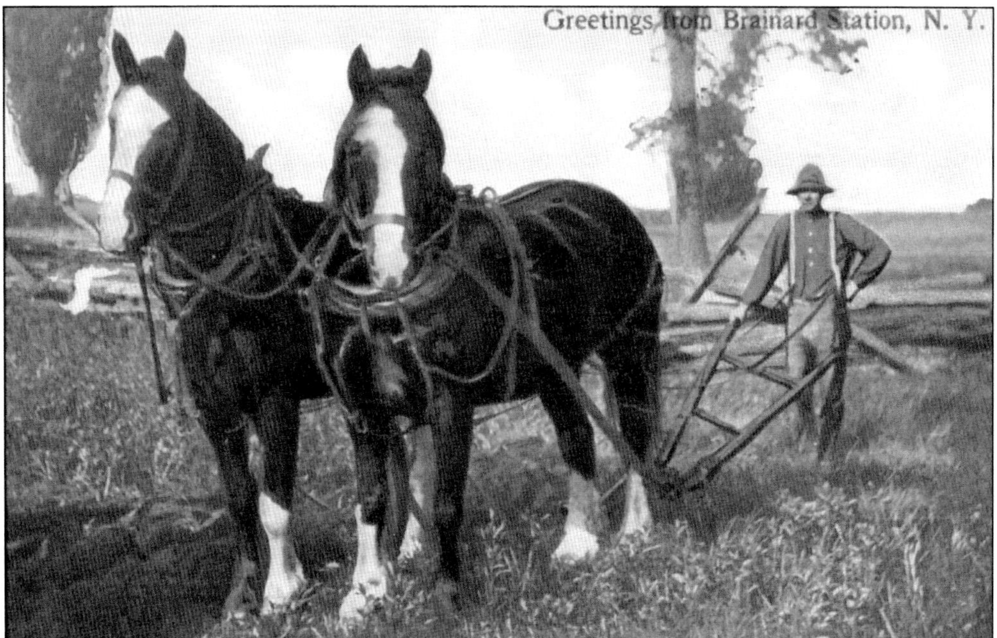

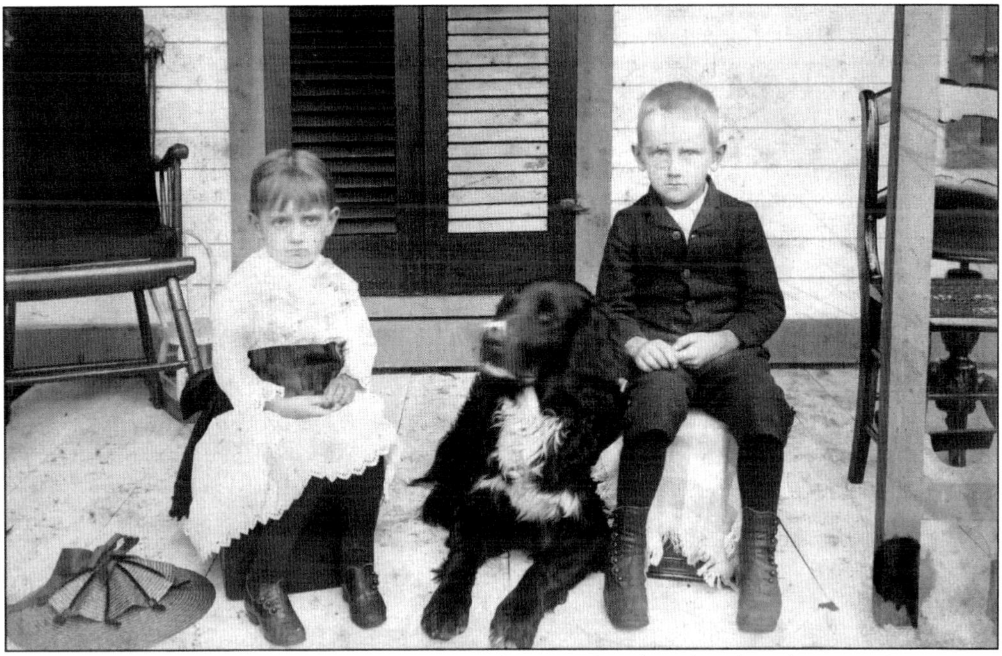

Little remains today except private homes in the once-bustling hamlet of Hoag's Corners. In his 1880 *History of Rensselaer County*, Nathanial Bartlett Sylvester writes that Hoag's Corners contains "two stores, a hotel, a union and Baptist church, a number of places devoted to various branches of manufacturer and a number of dwelling-houses." Above, Jennie Vincent and her brother Merton pose with their dog Blackie on the front porch of their house in Hoag's Corners in 1899. Today, their home is identified as being the location of anti-rent activities in the 1820s. Below, an 1876 F.W. Beers map of Hoag's Corners shows what is now New York State Route 66 running roughly north-south on the left. (Above, courtesy of Diane McGrath; below, courtesy of Village of Nassau.)

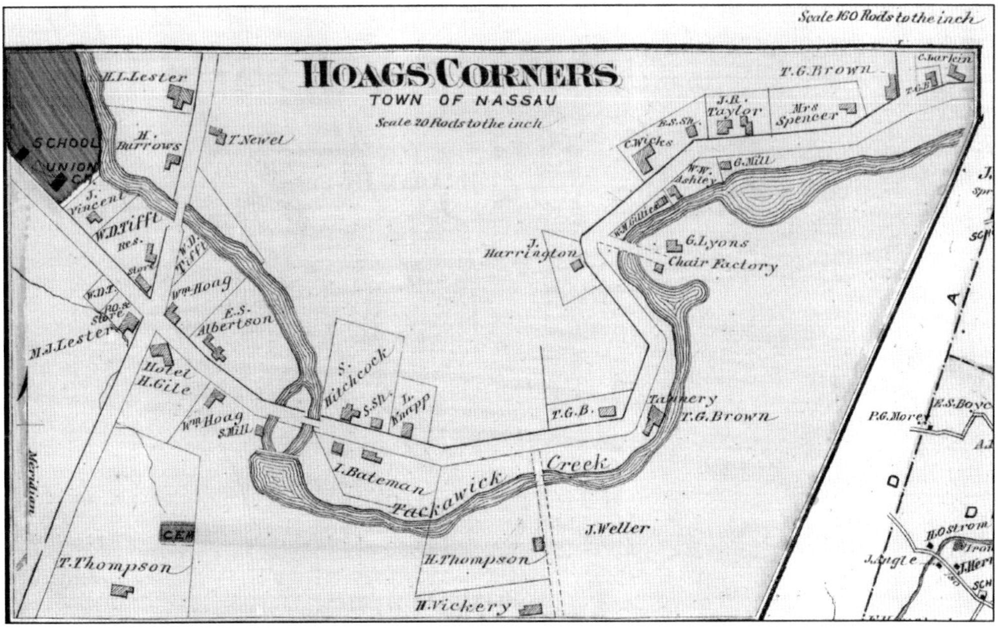

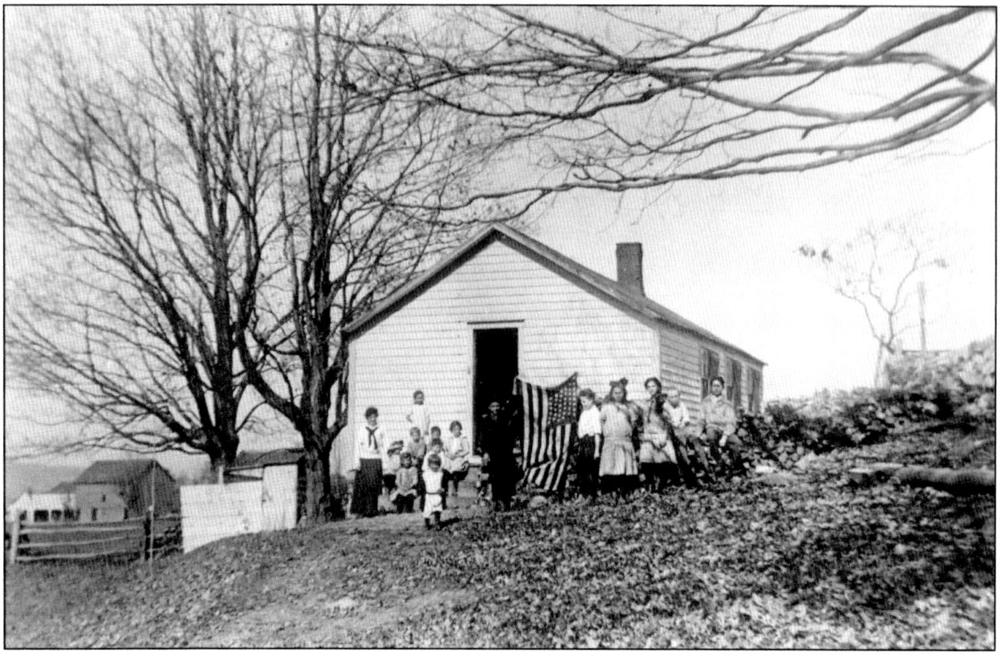

As the population of the town grew, the need for schools was recognized. While the New York State Legislature supported public education starting in the early 1800s, funding was slow to follow. By 1867, students ages 5–15 could attend school regardless of family wealth, and common school districts, and, later, union school districts were formed. Seen here is District No. 12 School, north of Millers Corners on Burden Lake Road. (Courtesy of the Schodack Town Historian.)

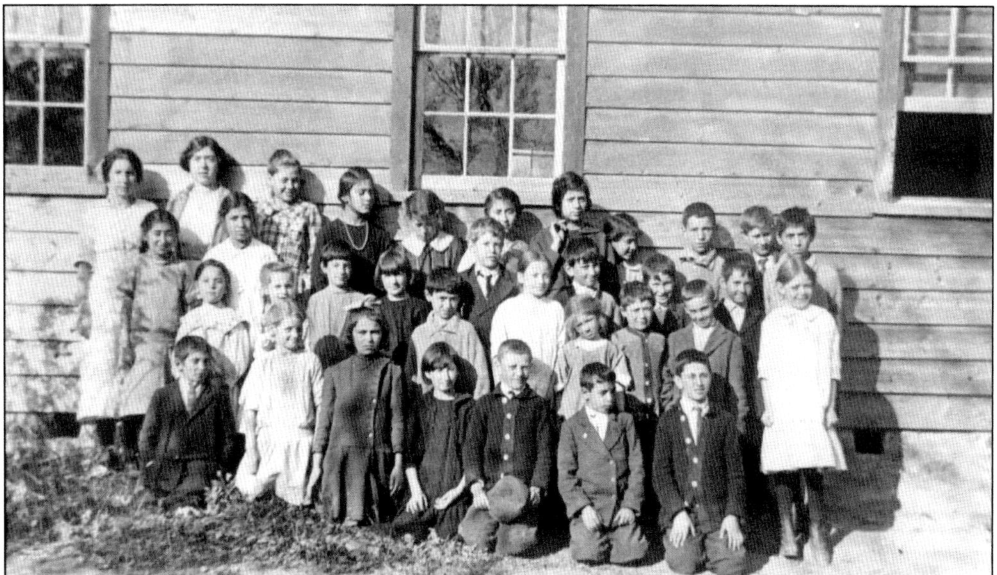

District No. 4 School was on Central Nassau Road, also known as Hoag's Corner Road and Route 16. The one-room schoolhouse was near the corner of Mud Pond Road. In this photograph from around 1900, family resemblances can easily be seen among the 30 students. (Courtesy of Nassau Free Library.)

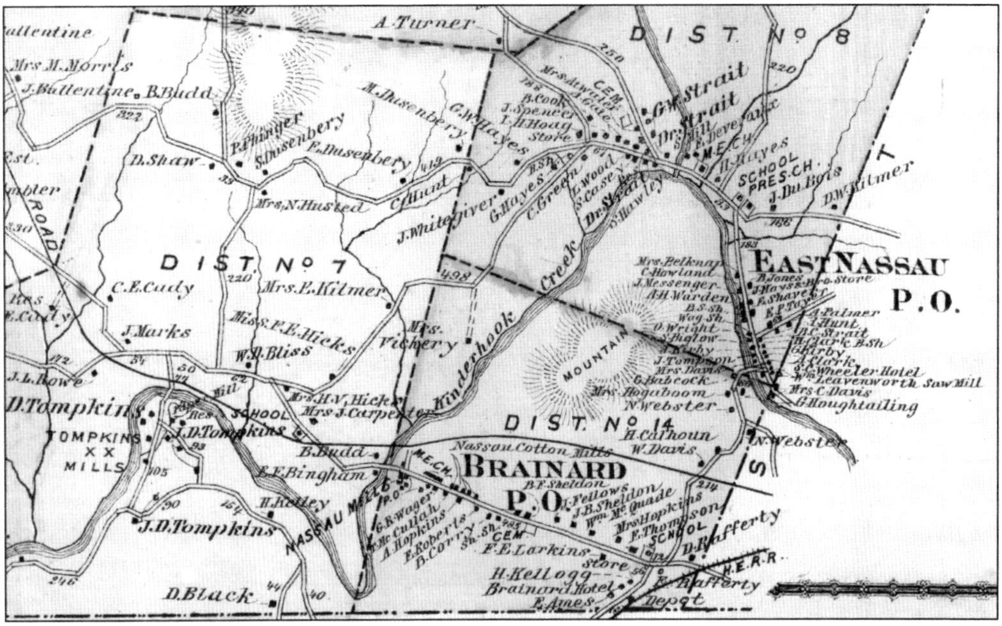

The hamlet of Brainard takes its name from an early settler family named Brainard, not to be confused with earlier missionary David Brainerd. The Brainards built the first two bridges over Kinderhook Creek. The available waterpower in the area spurred the construction of mills, and the Lebanon Springs Railway constructed a rail line linking Lebanon to Chatham in 1851. The hamlet was then known as Brainard Station. (Courtesy of Village of Nassau.)

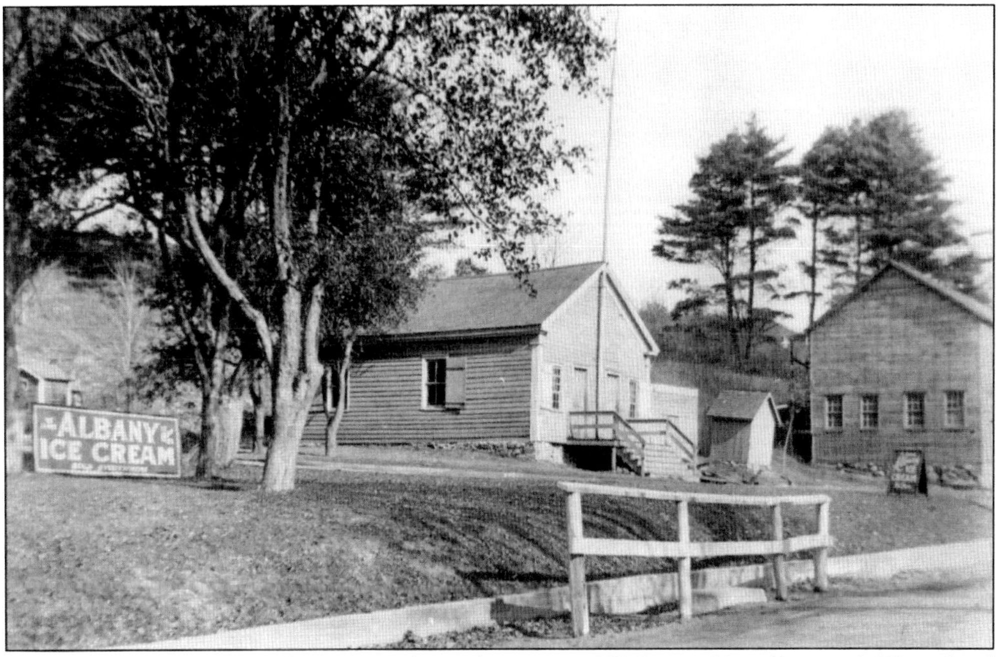

The District No. 14 schoolhouse stood on what is now US Route 20 in Brainard. The school served students living east of Brainard Bridge. Today, the bridge still separates the New Lebanon School District, to the east, and the East Greenbush School District, to the west. (Courtesy of the Schodack Town Historian.)

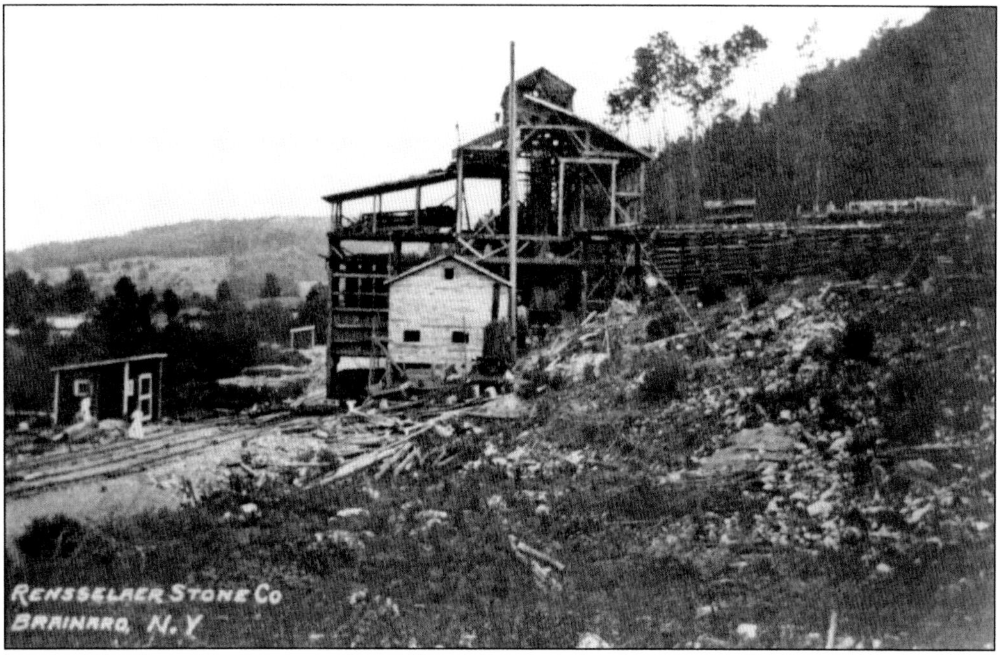

Brainard's industrial history runs deep. The early use of the waterpower offered by the Kinderhook Creek included the extensive paper mills of the Tompkins Company, starting in 1847. In the 1850s, when the mills were enlarged, they were rivaled only by Troy's factories. The mining of stone, particularly greywacke, seen here being mined, was prized in early road construction. (Courtesy of the Schodack Town Historian.)

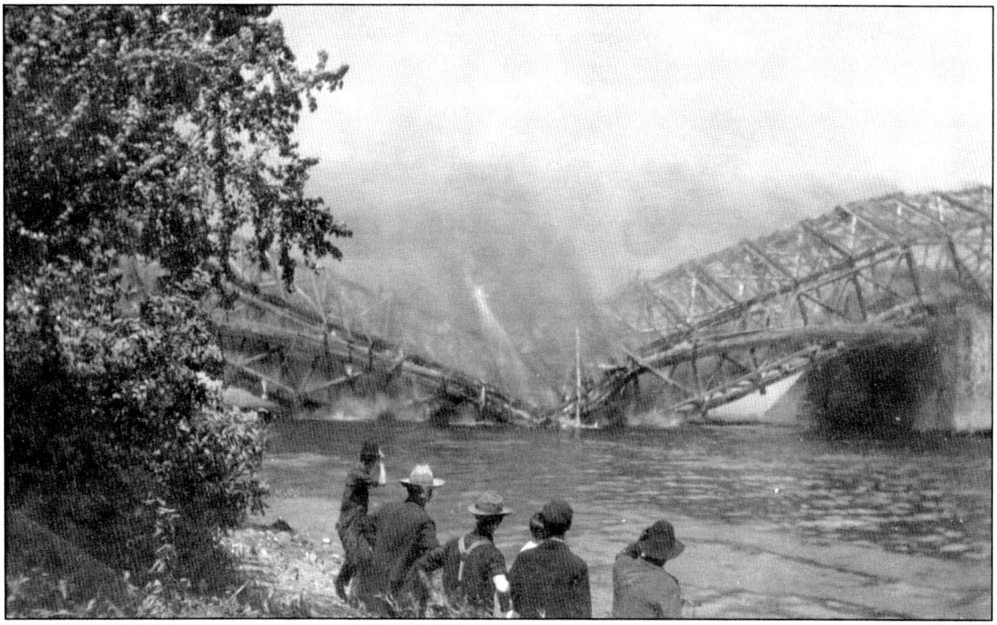

While much of rural Nassau's prosperity was based on abundant waterpower, those forces could also cause great destruction. In this 1930s-era photograph, Brainard Bridge is seen collapsing into Kinderhook Creek. Brainard's extensive mills were eventually done in by flooding. (Courtesy of the Dan Smith collection.)

Brainard was the only place in Nassau where steam and then diesel rail service operated. Initiated by the Lebanon Springs Railroad in 1852, the line ran from Chatham into Brainard, then to Lebanon Springs, and then on to Bennington, Vermont. The company consolidated with the Rutland Railroad in 1901 and continued operating until 1953. This photograph shows a double steam locomotive coming into Brainard in 1950. (Courtesy of Wally Stock.)

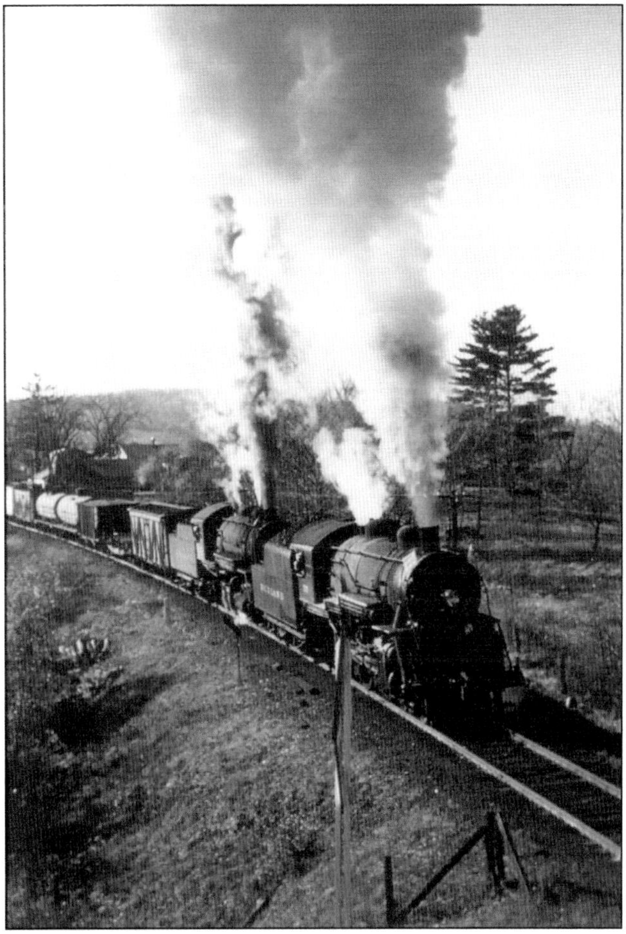

The photograph below was taken just east of the Kinderhook Creek bridge on what is now US Route 20, before it was paved about 1915. Stone for much of the road construction project on to the state line was mined in Brainard by skilled Italian immigrants employed by the Lane Construction Company. During the years-long duration of the project, workers lived in quarters adjacent to the mine. (Courtesy of Wally Stock.)

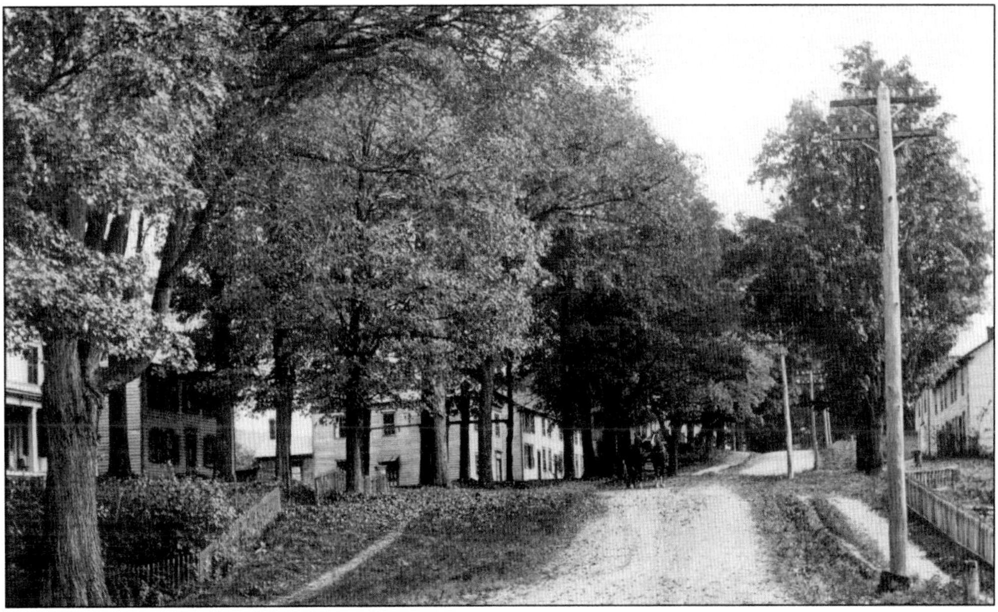

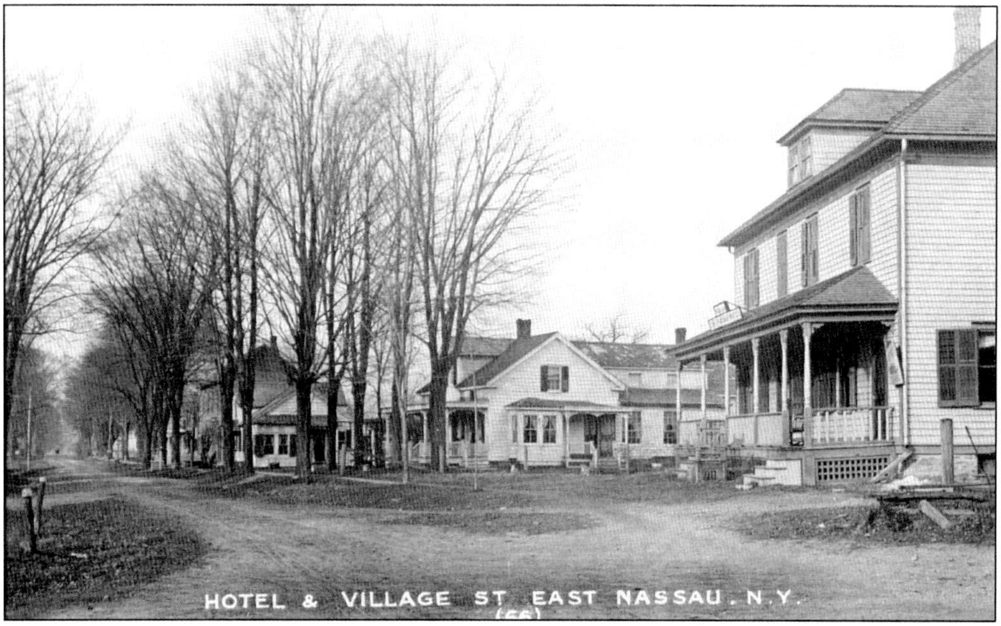

After Nassau village and Brainard, East Nassau was the third-most populated hamlet in the town. Located on Kinderhook Creek, for many years it was known as Schermerhorn's, in honor of John W. Schermerhorn, one of its early inhabitants. Businesses, a hotel, a school, and churches flourished in the hamlet. (Courtesy of Wally Stock.)

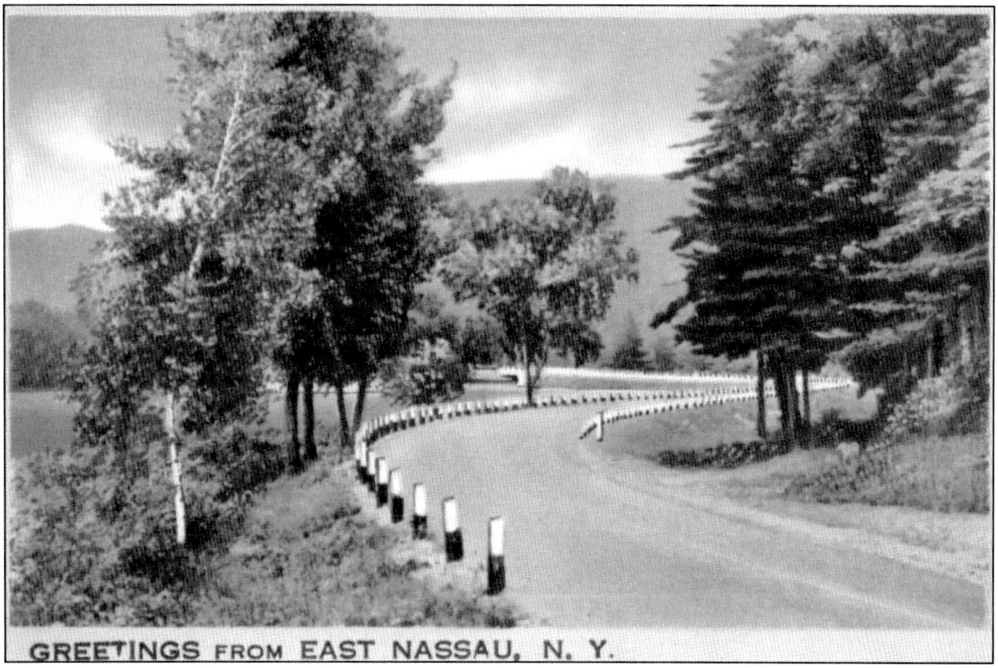

Postcards have long been a popular way to capture the memory of a particular place. This was true in East Nassau as well, as this 1950s original color postcard shares a rather idealized view of the area. Postcards like this also helped local merchants, as they were hopefully able to make a few pennies' profit on its sale. (Courtesy of Harold Schmidt.)

Seven

Veterans and Memorials

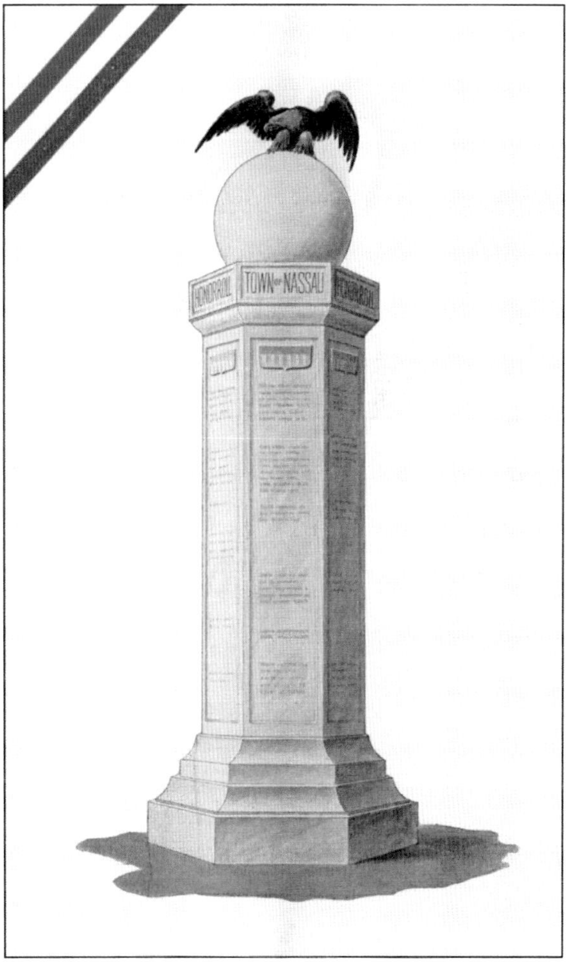

As World War II raged, Nassau citizens joined together to construct an honor roll at the village square listing the names of all town residents who were in the service. The wooden hexagon was designed by F.K. Van Almelo and built by Richard Decker, both local volunteers. Nassau's men and women have served in every military conflict, from the Revolutionary War, the War of 1812, and the Mexican War through both world wars, the Korean War, Vietnam, the Gulf War, and the wars in Afghanistan and Iraq. In 2012, the bridge over the Valatiekill was dedicated in honor of fallen soldier Staff Sgt. Derek Farley, who died in Afghanistan on August 17, 2010, as he tried to defuse a roadside bomb. Farley grew up in Nassau, played on the Little League, and was a member of the Boy Scouts. Large crowds lined Nassau's streets in late August 2010, when the funeral procession drove through the village and past the ball field on John Street before pausing at the village square before an honor squad.

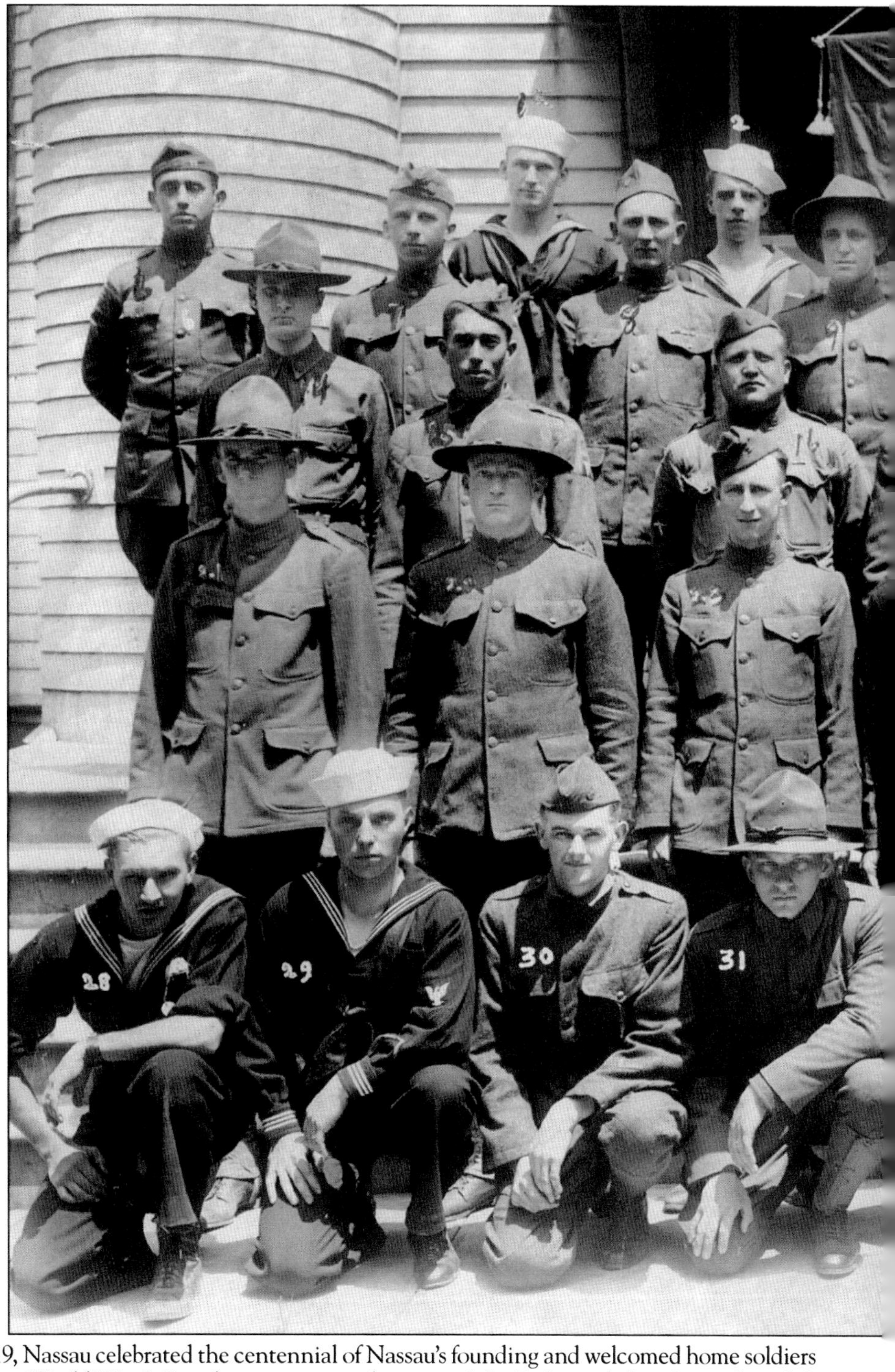

On July 4, 1919, Nassau celebrated the centennial of Nassau's founding and welcomed home soldiers and sailors from World War I. Seen here posing on the steps of the Reformed church are, from left to right, (first row) Arthur Chrestensen, Bernard Canady, William Hughes, Wilber O. Martin, George Larkin, William Green, Minard Palmer, and Oscar Winters; (second row) John Hughes, Fred Phillips, Thomas Lavin, Raymond J. Pierson, Frederick Kosegarten, William McKever, and

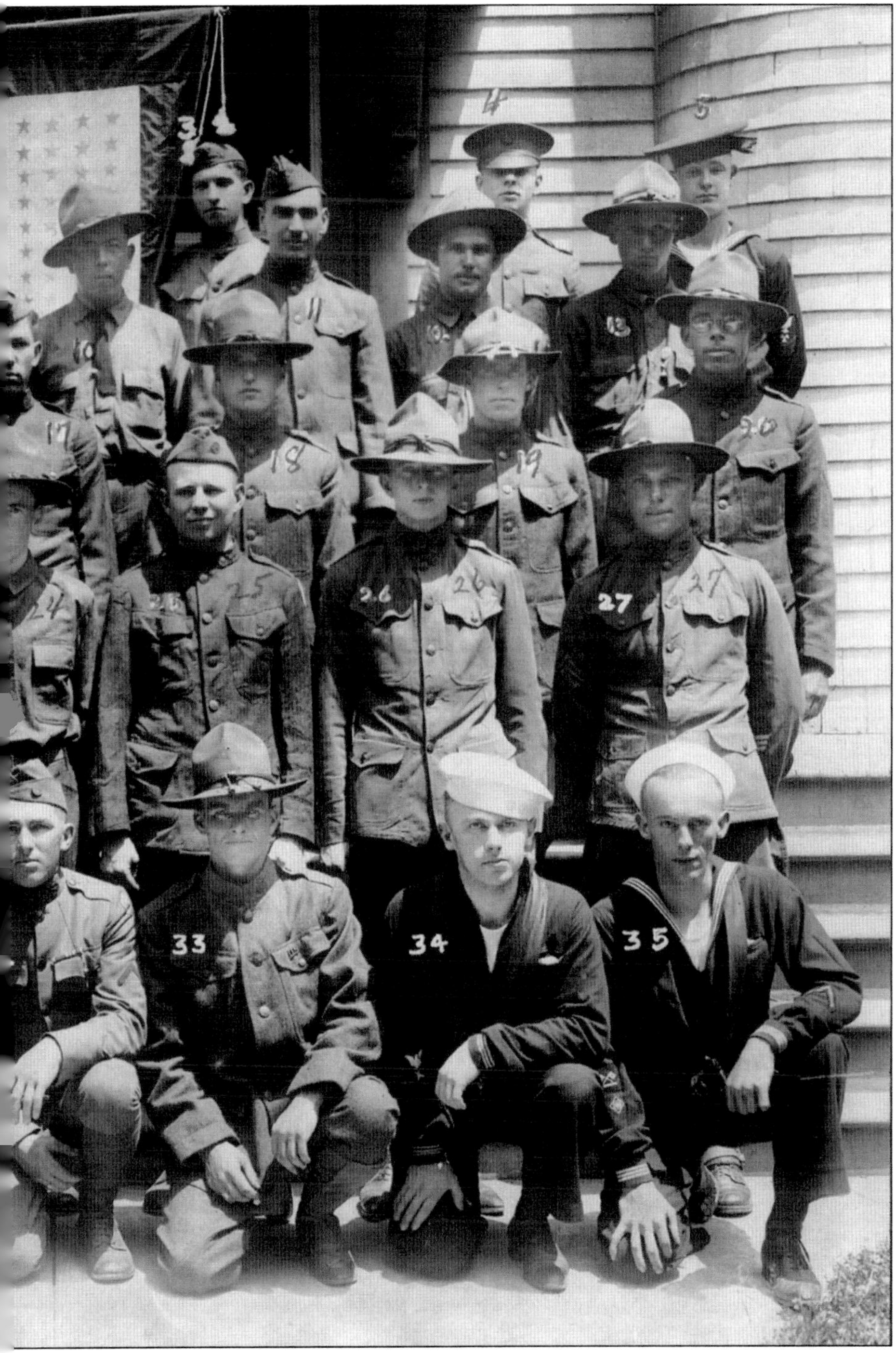

William Canady; (third row) Ezra Goewey, John Kittell, Jacob Mayeroff, Ralph Whitman, Wesley Brault, Chester Finley, and Arthur I. Williams; (fourth row) William Panitch, Andrew Angel, John Clapper, Felix Etman, Warren Knapp, Ira Goewey, Frank Marks, and William Williams; (fifth row) William Sheldon, Robert Phillips, James H. Miller, Robert McClellan, and Elmer Rate. (Courtesy of Nassau Free Library.)

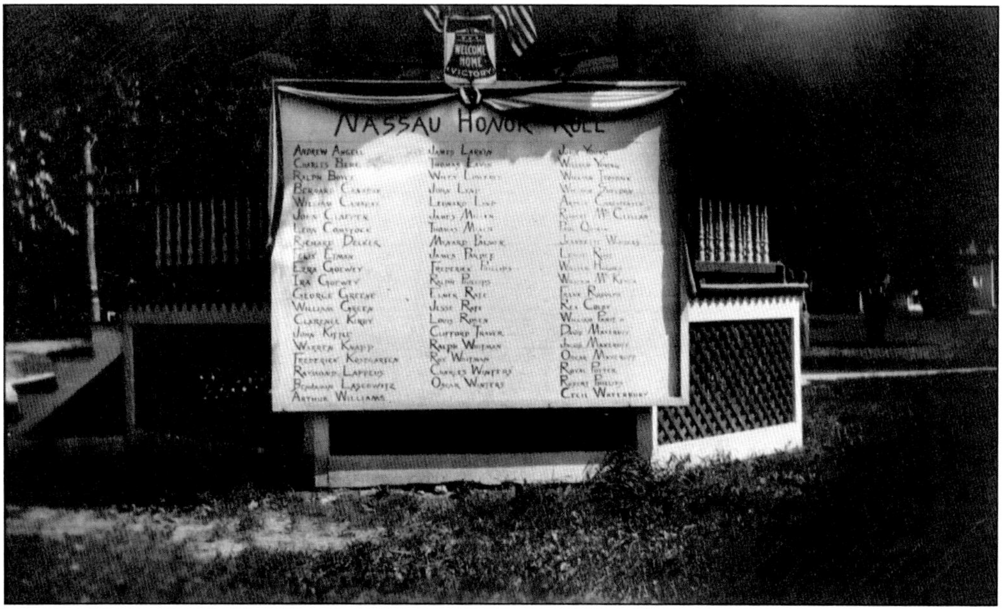

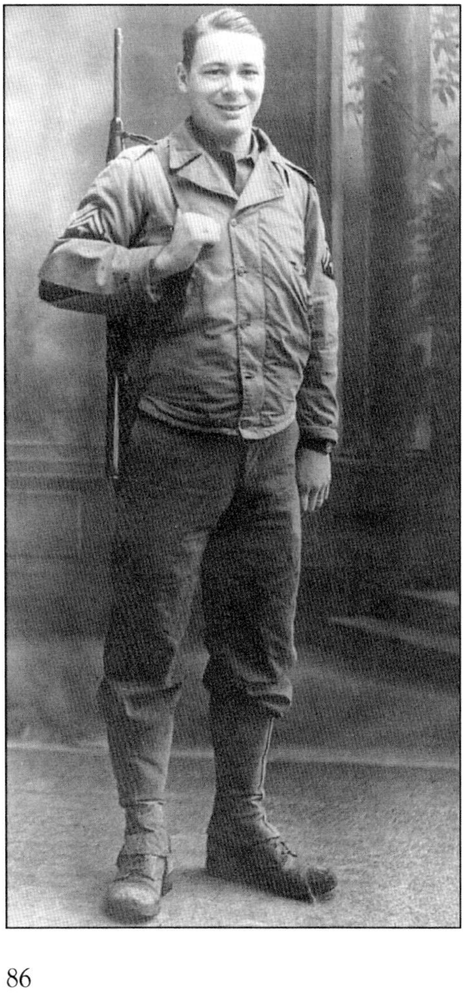

A large wooden sign was affixed to the village square bandstand with the names of the men serving in the armed forces during World War I. At the welcome home celebration for soldiers and sailors held on July 4, 1919, the placard sports a "Welcome Home Victory" message emblazoned on an image of the Liberty Bell. The celebration included a church service of thanksgiving, a parade through the village, a historical pageant, a complimentary dinner for the servicemen, afternoon sports at the fairgrounds, an evening band concert, and fireworks to round out the day.

Raised in Nassau by his grandfather Roscoe Velie, Arnold Lee Velie was one of three million men and women who enlisted in 1942. Pictured after his safe return, Velie achieved the rank of technician fifth grade and lived into his late 60s.

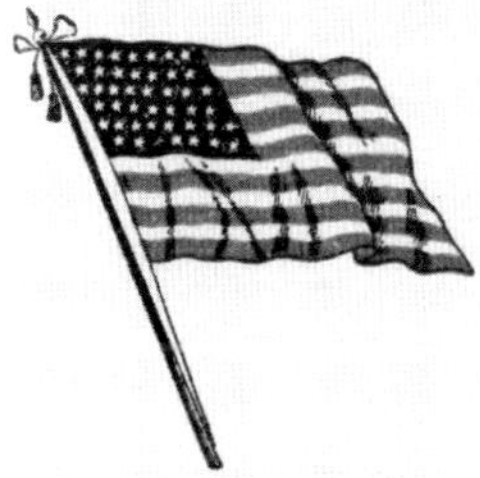

Nassau Boys Who Answered the Call to the Colors

Angel, Andrew
Adams, Walter, *Killed in Action*
Adams, William
Alderman, Edmond
Brault, Wesley
Bartlett, George
Benedict, Sidney, *Died of Disease*
Chrestensen, Arthur
Comstock, Leon
Clapper, John
Canady, Bernard L.
Canady, William
Cummings, Arthur
Deitle, William
Decker, Richard
Deamer, Elmer, *Died of Disease*
Etman, Felix
Finley, Chester
Gaffney, James H.
Gardner, Leonard
Goewey, Ezra
Goewey, Ira
Hughes, William
Hughes, John
Kirby, Clarence
Kipp, Herbert
Knapp, Warren
Kittell, John
Kaufman, Samuel
Kosegarten, Frederick
Lappies, Raymond
Lavin, Thomas
Larkin, James
Lynd, Leonard
Lynd, John
Larkins, George
Minch, Thomas
Mackmin, Raymond
Miller, James Henry
Mayeroff, Oscar
Mayeroff, David
Mayeroff, Jake
Obatz, Harry
Panitch, William
Pierson, Raymond John
Palmer, Minard
Phillips, Ralph
Phillips, Robert
Phillips, Fred
Quirin, Paul
Rudolph, Frank
Rosen, Louis
Rosen, Morris
Sheldon, William
Schilling, Franz Fridolin, *Killed in Action*
Traver, Clifford
Vickery, Le Roy
Vickery, Elmer
Vincent, Floyd
Whitman, Ralph
Winters, Charles
Winters, Oscar
Wright, Irving
Williams, William
Williams, Arthur Irving
Weatherby, Jacob

Boys Who Entered S. A. T. C.

Cecil Waterbury
Royal Potter
Wilbur O. Manchester
William McKeever

This list of names was distributed at the July 4, 1919, ceremony. The notation "Boys Who Entered S.A.T.C." refers to the Student Army Training Corps, a program allowing students to continue their college educations while also receiving military training. Because of the short duration of the war, most corps members did not see service overseas. Walter Adams, listed here as killed in action, died on October 10, 1918, in France. He was raised on his family farm in "the Alps," in the northern part of Nassau, and Averill Park's American Legion post was named in his memory.

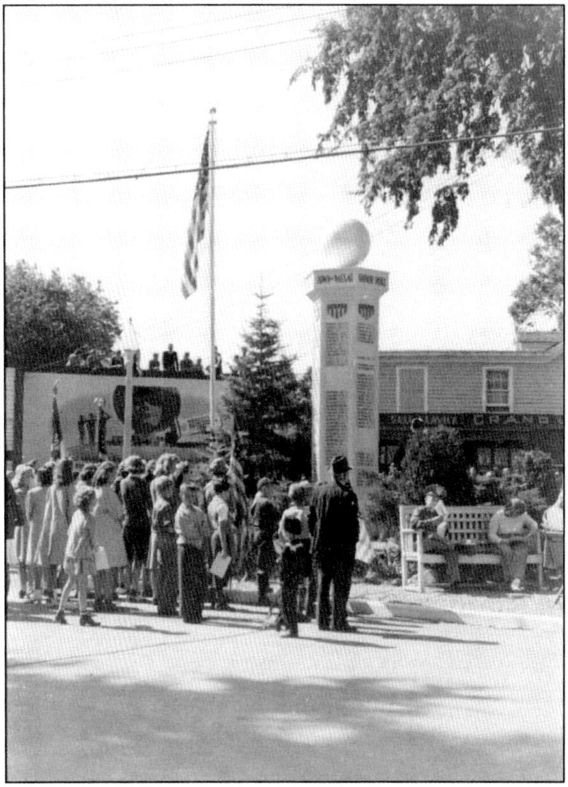

On Sunday, September 12, 1943, Nassau gathered again to honor those serving in the military. Unlike the World War I honor roll less than 25 years previously, the new memorial took center place in the village square. A large wooden hexagon with a sphere on top lists the names of 209 men and women from Nassau who were serving in the armed forces at that time. It also notes one who had died in service, 22-year-old Pvt. David A. Patnode, who died early in 1942 in North Africa. Regrettably, the war would continue for three more years and several others would perish.

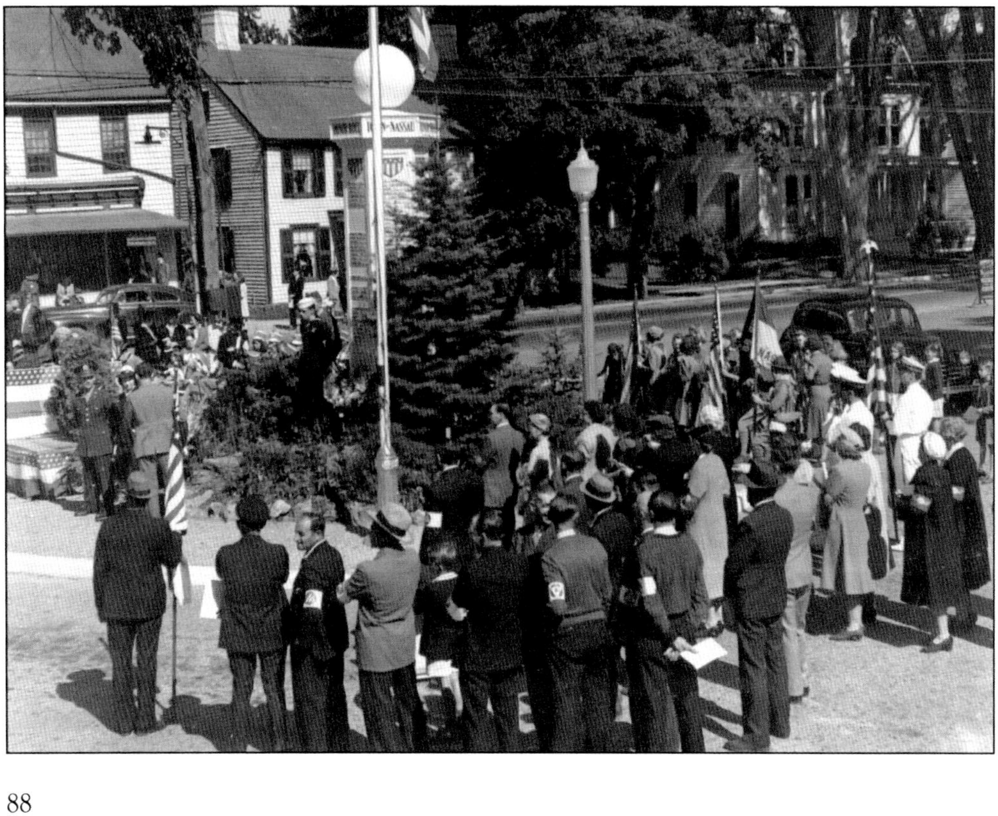

Representing the armed forces at the dedication ceremony were Nassau servicemen Milton "Ace" Thompson, US Army, and George B. Parsons, US Navy. Irene Harrington and Marge Doolittle cochaired the event, and noted local orator Comdr. Jacob Krouner of the Averill Park American Legion dedicated the honor roll on behalf of local servicemen and women. Reproduced here is the list of names included on the honor roll that day.

NASSAU HONOR ROLL

Edward F. Aitken
James Allen
Charles H. Andros
Kenneth Ashley
William H. Ashley, Jr.

Robert R. Bailey
Robert K. Baker
Ralph Balfort
Ralph Barker
John J. Barsalow, Jr.
Robert Bass
Fred Bates
Robert A. Bergeron
Walter Bergeron
Walter Bertram
Benjamin Bicklehaupt
John Biggins
Joseph Biggins
William Biggins
Earl F. Bingham
Raymond Bingham
William Bingham
Frank B. Boyce
Milton Boyce
Herbert T. Bristol, Jr.
Leon S. Brumer
Robert Bushnell

Donald R. Chandler
Harry Chandler
Russell Chandler
Donald F. Chase, Jr.
Eileen Clark
Elmer Clark
Carlton Clum
Morris Cohen
Toni Commerota
Francis A. Conklin
Henry J. Conklin
Earle N. Cooper
Edgar F. Cooper
George N. Cooper
Charles E. Cramer
Malcolm Cramer
Harold Cronin
Harold J. Cummings
Raymond Currier
Sylvester F. Currier

William Daley
Robert M. Dean, Jr.
Eugene Decker
Salvatore De Luca
Roger Dietz
Arthur Druba
Arthur Dubri
Fred Dunheiser

John C. Enseline

Thomas W. Finley
William Finley
John H. Finn

Meyer Garbarsky
Harold Gardner
Irving Gaylord
Ernest G. Gile
Henry Gile
Irving Goldman
Louis Goldman
Samuel Goldman
David Gootz
Harry Grant
David M. Graves
Jeremy H. Graves
George Green
Gordon Greenhill
Wilson K. Griffith
Woodrow K. Griffith

Earl Hall
Leland Hall
Leslie P. Hanson
Wilfred G. Harrington
Cortland Hart
William J. Heintz
Herbert Helprin
Irene Francis Hewitt
William Hilton
Roland C. Holmes
John Hopkins, Jr.
Edward W. Houlne
Ronald Hughes
Jerome Hunt

George Irvine

Walter M. Jeram
David Justus, Jr.

Israel Kaplan
Herbert Katz
Ralph Kaufman
Carl Kellogg
Raymond A. Kellogg
Royden Kellogg
Joseph Kiernen
Ralph Kimmey
John Koenig
Donald Kullman

Arthur A. Laier
Fredericks D. Laier
William J. Laier

NASSAU HONOR ROLL

Clifton Laraway
Robert E. Larkin
Gertrude S. Lashoff
Theodore C. Lawrence
Harry Leberich
Joseph Leberich
Joseph Le Chance
Jack Levine
Leonard Levine
Nathan Levine
Harold F. Lewis
Samuel Lindenbaum
Hazen F. Lord

Donald Manns
Morris Markowitz
James H. Martin
Walter A. Martin
Howard L. Marvin
Clayton Miller
Cornelius J. Miller
Francis J. Miller
Francis W. Miller
Thomas J. Miller
Wendel R. Miller, Jr.
Edgar Monington
Joseph P. Myers

Edward Ozga

George B. Parsons
David Patnode
(Died in Service)
Edward Patnode
Jay Pinkerton
Sidney Placksin
Gerald Ploughman
Abraham Pollock
Herman Pollock
Benjamin F. Pratt, Jr.

Frank Radley
Howard Radley
Wallace Reed
William Reinwald
Winfield Rendell
Howard Richards
David Richter
Jacob H. Roach
Delmas O. Robbinett
Alvin Rosenberg
David Roth
Paul Roth
Edgar J. Rowe

Andrew Sanford
Earl W. Sanford
Ralph Sanford
Helen C. Schaefer
Walter Schermerhorn
Edmund H. Schiller
Emerson R. Schiller
Morris A. Schips
Samuel Schips
Christopher Schwartz
Phillip Schwartz
Raymond P. Schwartz
Kenneth Sears
George Sedgwick
Charles Senricks
Phillip Smith
Seymour Smith
Harold Southard
Alfred T. Sprague
A. Clayton Stanley
Donald P. Sutherland
Dwight R. Taylor
David Terry
Howard Thomson
Milton Thomson
Mathew Tierney
Morris Tolokonsky

Simon Udwary

Fred K. Van Almelo, Jr.
Arthur Van Blarcum

Lester Wagner
Cecil M. Waterbury
Gritten Weekley
Robert G. Weekley
John H. Weest
Herman Weiss
Elmer Wenz
David West
George S. Wheeler
Donald R. White
Harold E. Williams
Donald C. Winters
Stanley Winters
William Wogotske
Edgar Wood
Le Roy H. Wood

Albert Yosha
Michael Yosha
George F. Young, Jr.
Howard G. Young

Louis Zipkin
Max Zipkin
Samuel Zipkin
Irving Zweig
Morris Zweig

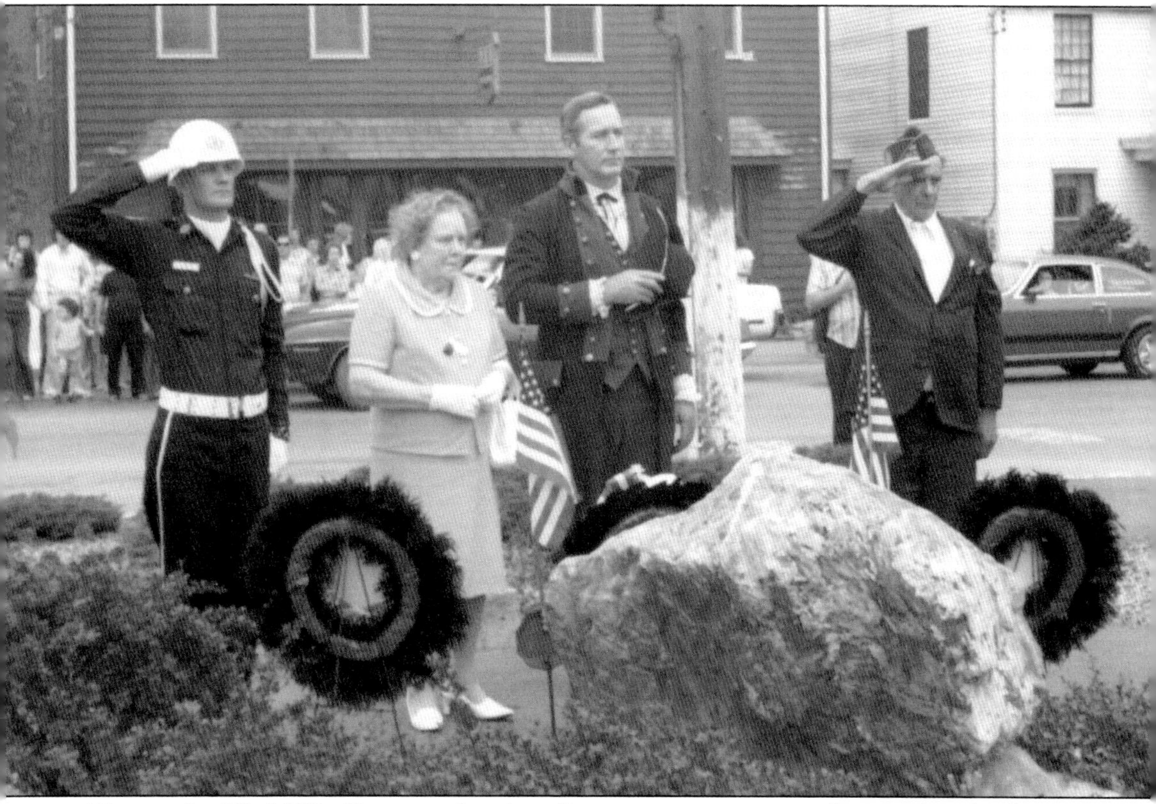

The wooden World War II memorial at the village square gave way to a large rock with a bronze plaque dedicated to Nassau's veterans. Ethel Bingham, a self-appointed civic beautification leader, selected the stone from along the roadside and enlisted Archibald "Archie" Sherman's help in getting it in place. Seen here as part of the 1976 bicentennial year Memorial Day observance are, from left to right, Theodore Bombard, town historian Mary Davis, town supervisor Floyd Hitchcock, and William Hilton.

Eight

Nassau Lake

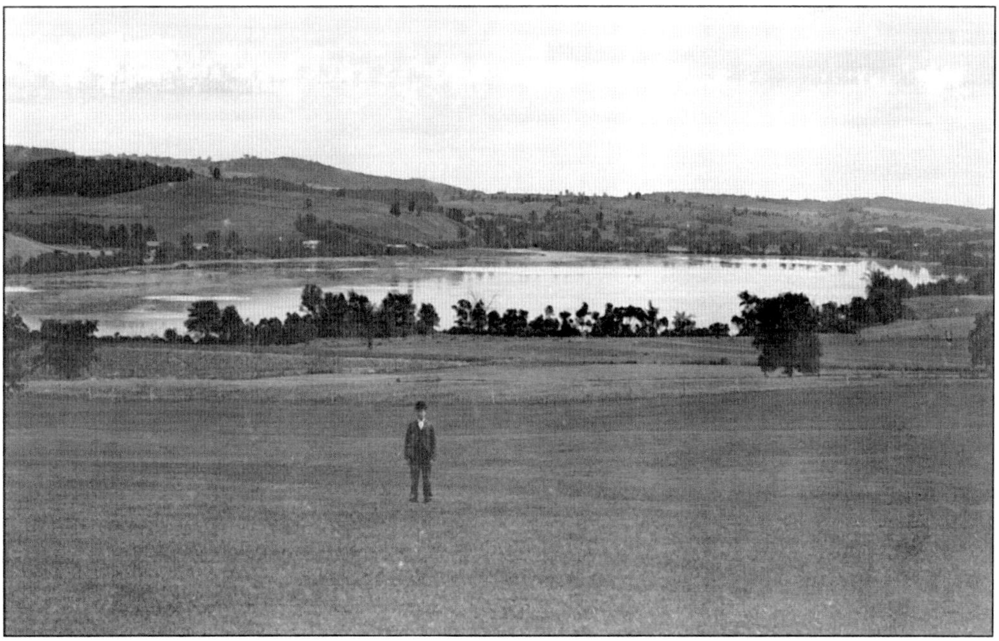

The area known today as Nassau Lake was once hemlock forest and meadowland. Next to a stream running through the area, Mahicans created a settlement called Ontikehomuck. In 1792, Nassau resident Jonathan Hoag purchased several hundred acres of this land. After he built a gristmill and a rough stone dam across the stream, about 150 acres were flooded to create a source of power for the mill and a small lake. As the years progressed, farms ringed the lake, and many of the original families are remembered by the names of roads that crisscross the area today, including, among others, Boyce, Poyneer, and Best Roads. This early image from about 1890 shows the broad farm fields in a view looking south towards Nassau Lake. (Courtesy of Nassau Free Library.)

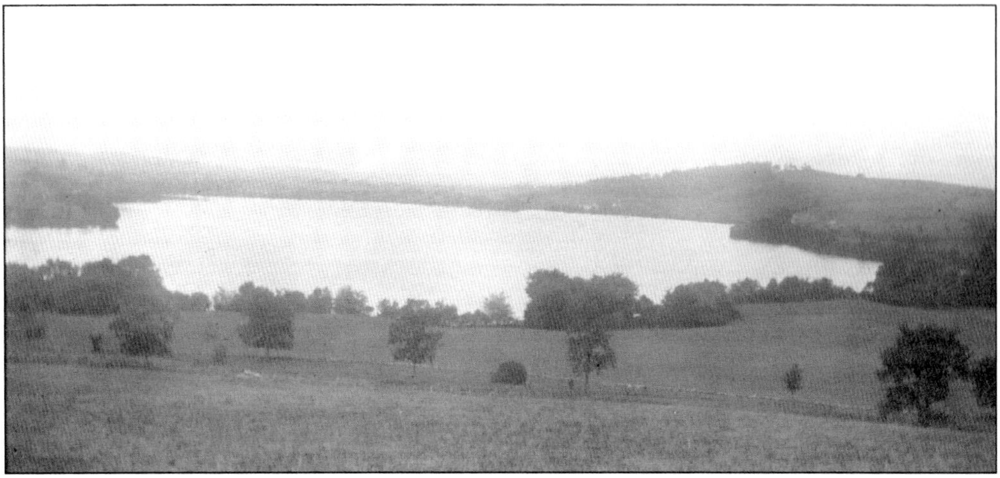

The 1870 Schodack business directory lists the farms of four Boyce family members with a combined acreage of over 400 acres. They were certainly not the largest landowners in the area, but the Boyce family prospered for many years in the Nassau Lake–East Schodack area. Dr. Arlington Boyce practiced medicine in the late 1800s. During this period, it was proving harder to maintain profits at many of the long-held farms. Farmers often took in summer boarders, helping start the transition to a tourism-based economy at Nassau Lake. These two photographs were taken in 1906 from the home of Daniel Boyce. (Both, courtesy of the Schodack Town Historian.)

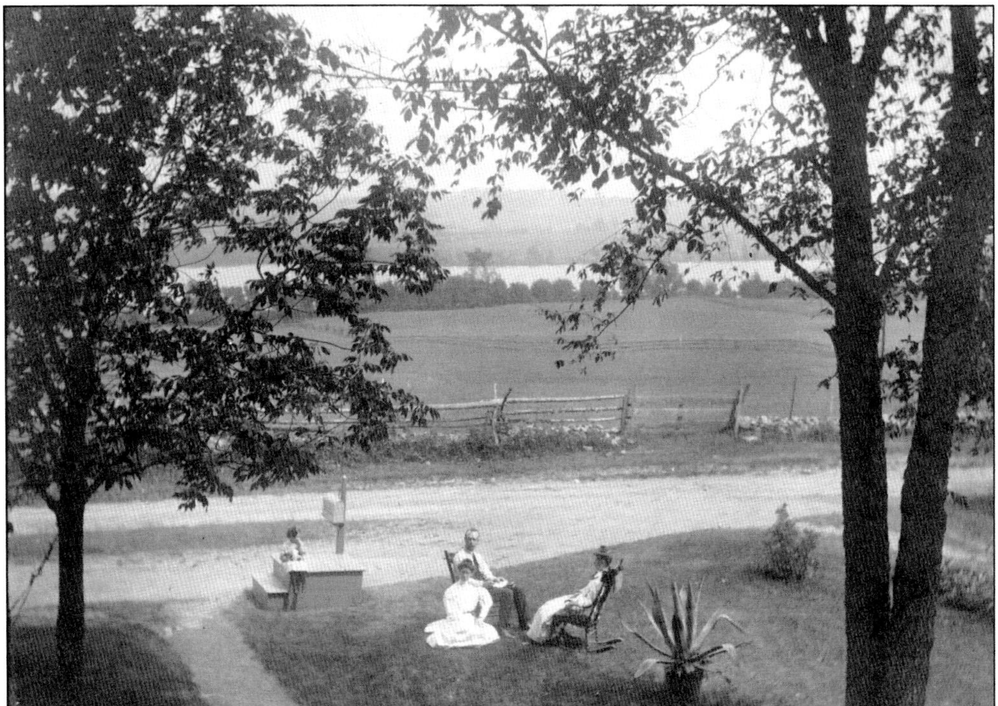

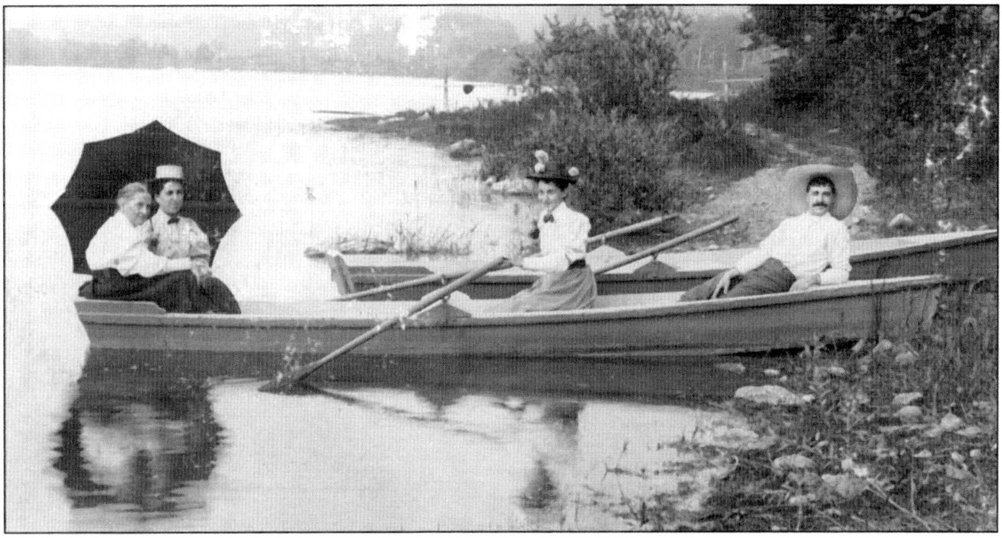

With the construction of the trolley line in 1900, fast and reliable transportation to the west side of Nassau Lake was now possible. With rapid advances in technology and the introduction of laborsaving devices, new wealth was created for some, and leisure time increased for many more. The lake area started changing from being used purely for agriculture, now incorporating recreational and seasonal summer use as well. Above, boaters enjoy a pleasant day on the lake. Several local farmers took the opportunity to rent boats. One of the first summer cottages, shown below, was built by George Welch, the owner of Welsh & Grey Lumber Corporation in Albany. Welch named it Braeside in honor of his Scottish heritage. The name Braeside lived on as a trolley stop and can still be found on some modern maps.

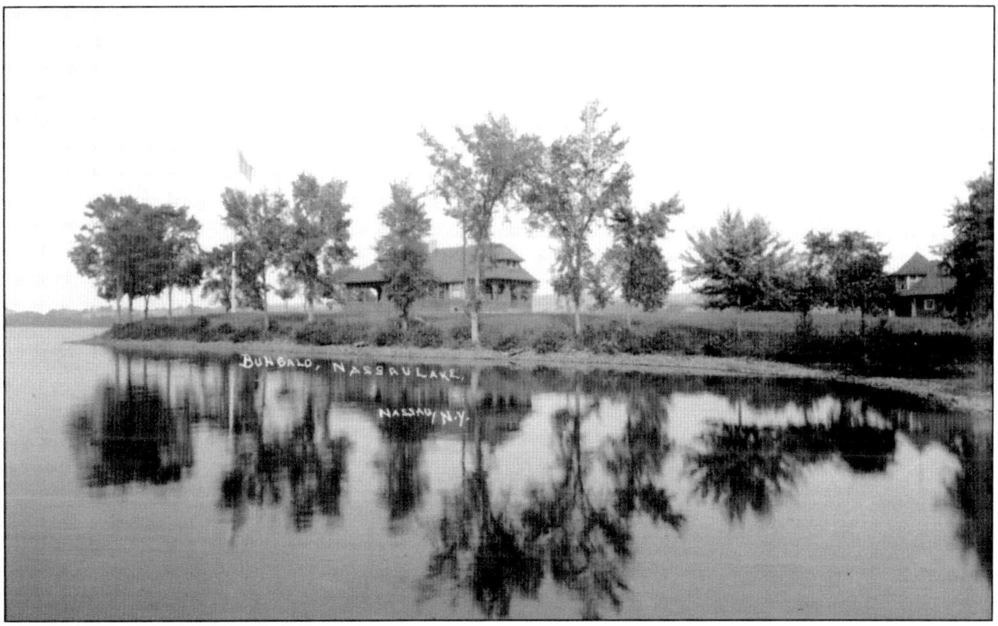

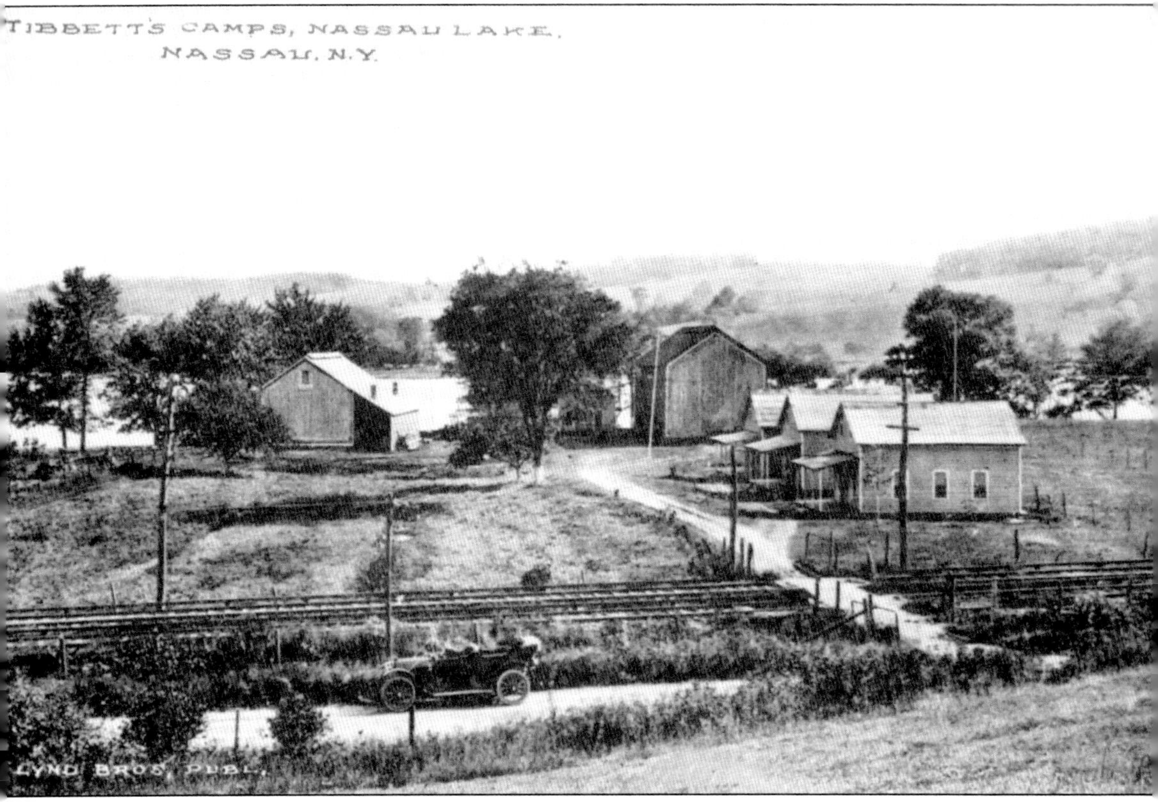

This image shows more modest tourist cottages adjacent to the trolley tracks. There were eight flag stops on the four-mile trolley line between Nassau village and East Schodack. A train would stop at a flag stop only if signaled to do so. The stops were Merchant's Crossing, Rosecrans, Braeside, Nassau Lake Park, Best's Crossing, Howard's Crossing, Kell's Crossing, Garrison's, and East Schodack. (Courtesy of the Dan Smith collection.)

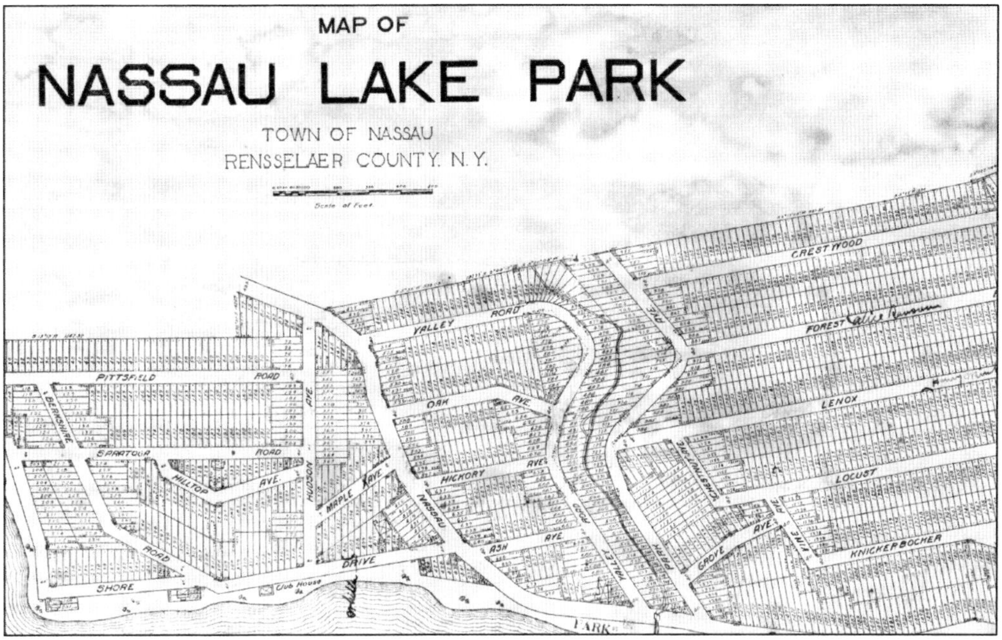

In 1924, the *Albany Evening News* and *Knickerbocker Press*, the forerunner of today's *Times Union* newspaper, promoted the sale of lots at Nassau Lake. Called Nassau Lake Park, the development had three locations chosen to divide into lots, two on the west side of the lake and one on the east side. In all, there were well over 1,000 lots, each 20 feet by 100 feet. The initial sale was for 394 parcels, priced at $67.50 each with $10 down and a $2.50 monthly payment, provided the buyer subscribed to either newspaper for six months. In advertisements at the time, the lots are described as "High and dry lots. All directly on or near Nassau lake road. Free use of parks, clubhouse, piers, bathing houses, rustic summer houses, also lake for fishing, boating and bathing." (Both, courtesy of Nassau Free Library.)

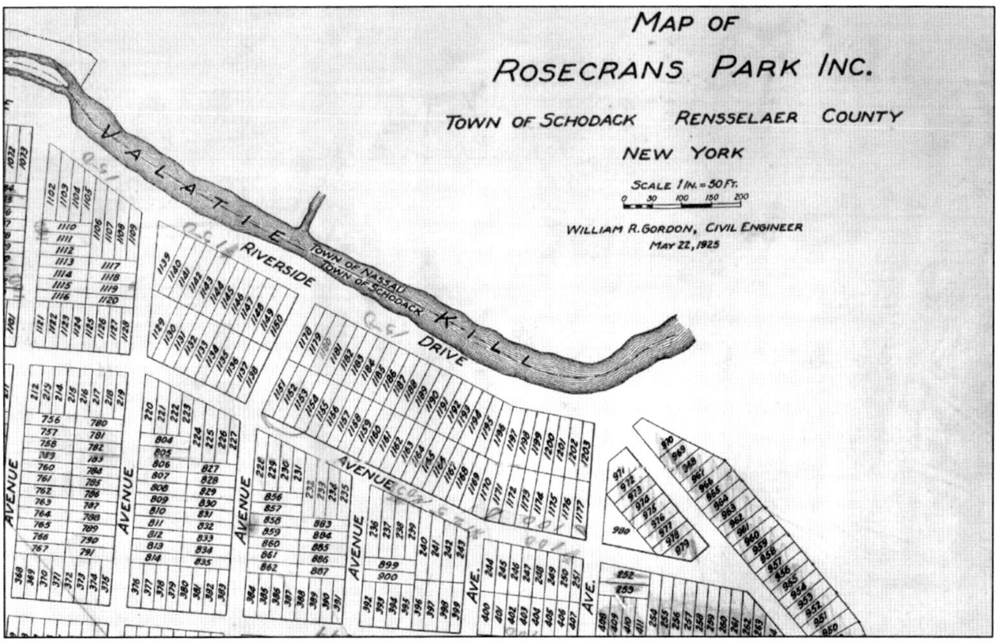

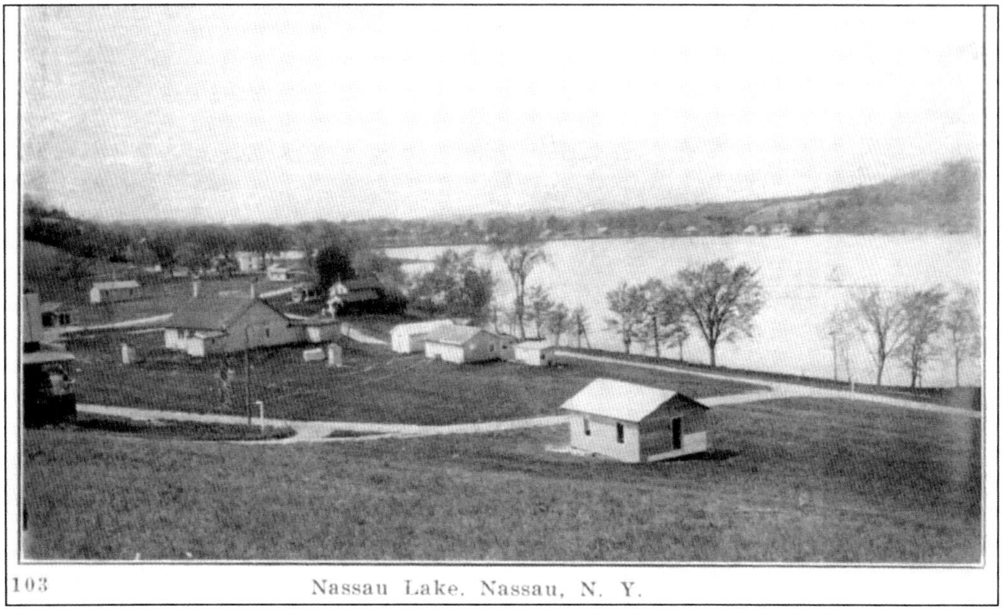

With the popularity of the automobile, Nassau Lake was touted as one of the closest resort areas to Albany for weekend excursions and picnics. Just to the northeast of the lake, the Smith family supplemented their farm income by renting out rooms to Jewish tourists from New York City. Smith's farm continued well into the 1950s and was a well-known summer resort. (Courtesy of the Dan Smith collection.)

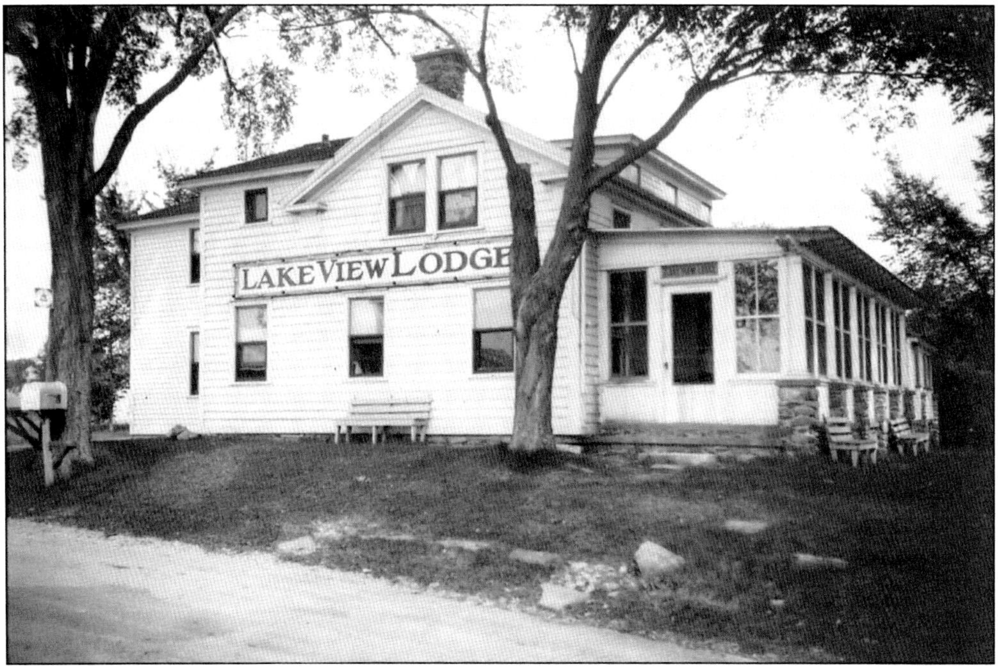

The Lakeview Lodge occupied a prominent location on the east side of Nassau Lake. In 1933, the Albany Printers Progressive Club sponsored a testimonial clambake at Lakeview Lodge honoring Albany's mayor, John Boyd Thatcher, followed by an evening of dog racing at the Nassau fairgrounds. This photograph was taken by Raymond Velie in 1936. (Courtesy of Judith Marquette.)

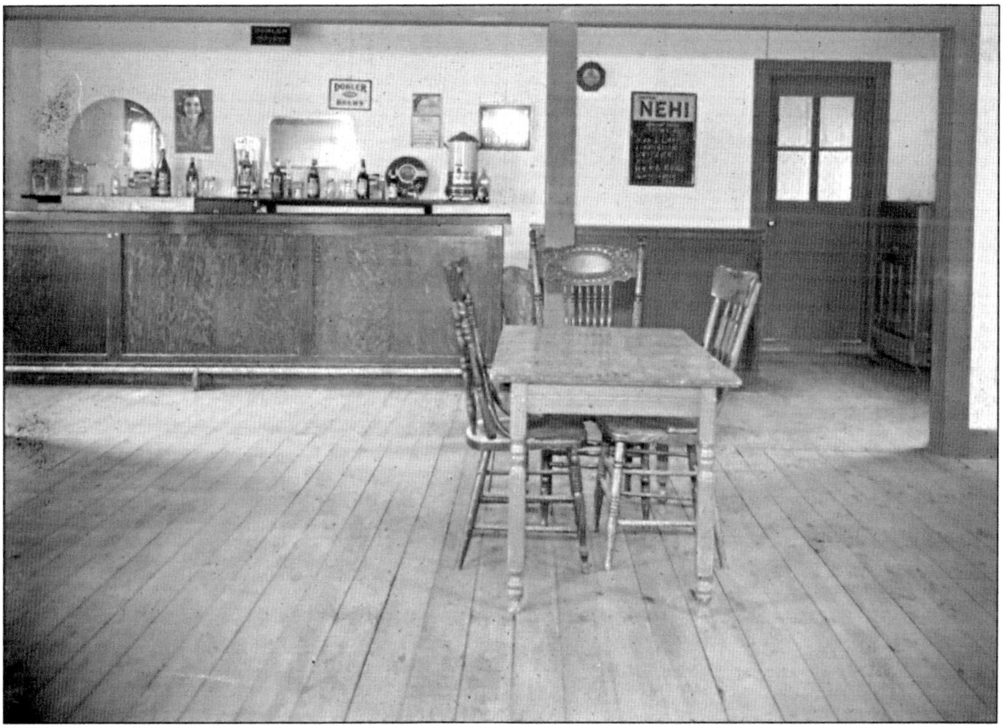

Photographed in April 1937 by Raymond Velie, Kalter's Hotel in Morey Park was typical of the taverns and modest restaurants located at Nassau Lake. The Nehi chalkboard on the wall lists the sandwiches available: ham and cheese, egg, ham and egg, and hamburgers. Owner John P. Kalter also harvested ice on Nassau Lake for sale during the summer months. (Courtesy of Judith Marquette.)

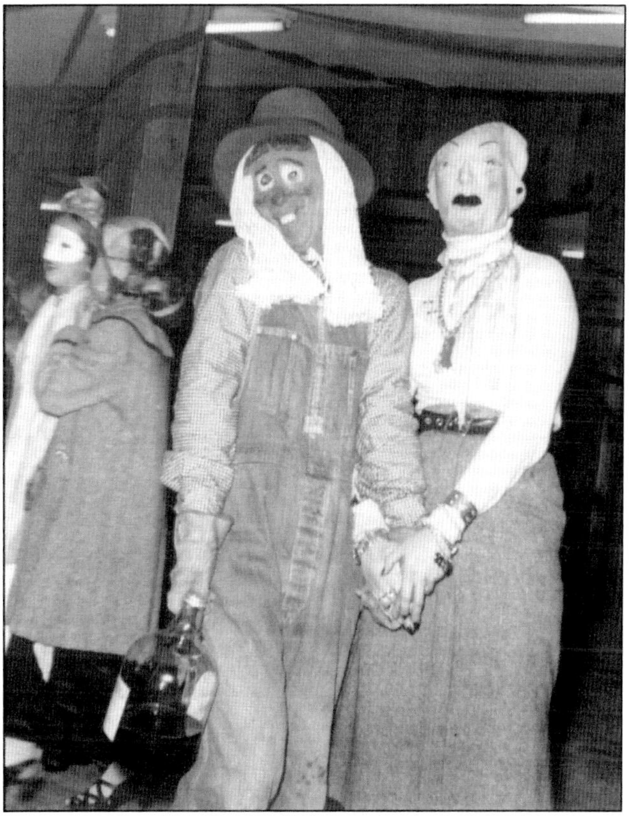

The Nassau Lake Park Association was founded when the newspapers turned over their involvement in the land scheme to property owners in 1926 for $1. A clubhouse was originally built during the land speculation, and it remained one of the only reminders of Nassau Lake Park well into the 1970s. Here, a couple dressed for the annual Halloween Dance at the clubhouse poses in the late 1950s.

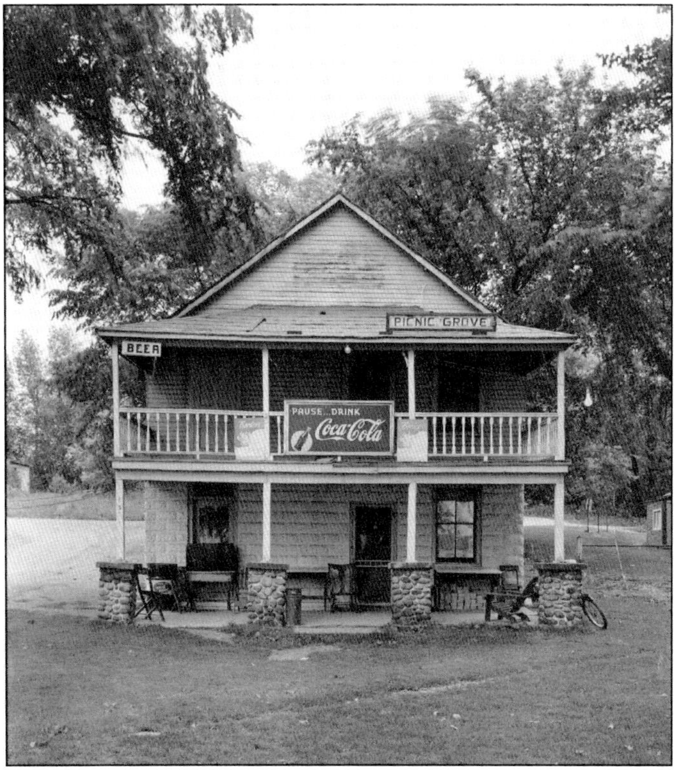

As it became a growing recreational location, business opened in the Nassau Lake area to cater to leisure-time crowds. Among the first was the Lake View Hotel, advertised by the Albany Southern Railway Company as "one of the finest along the line." Seen here is the more modest Allrich Hotel, which was run by the Kenyon family in Morey Park. A number of similar establishments were located at Nassau Lake, most known simply by the owner's name, including Lindemann's, Capron's, Mantica's, Russo's Morey Park Tavern, the Harris Inn, and Herman's. The last to survive was Gene's Fish Fry, which was open into the 1980s. (Both, courtesy of Joe Kenyon.)

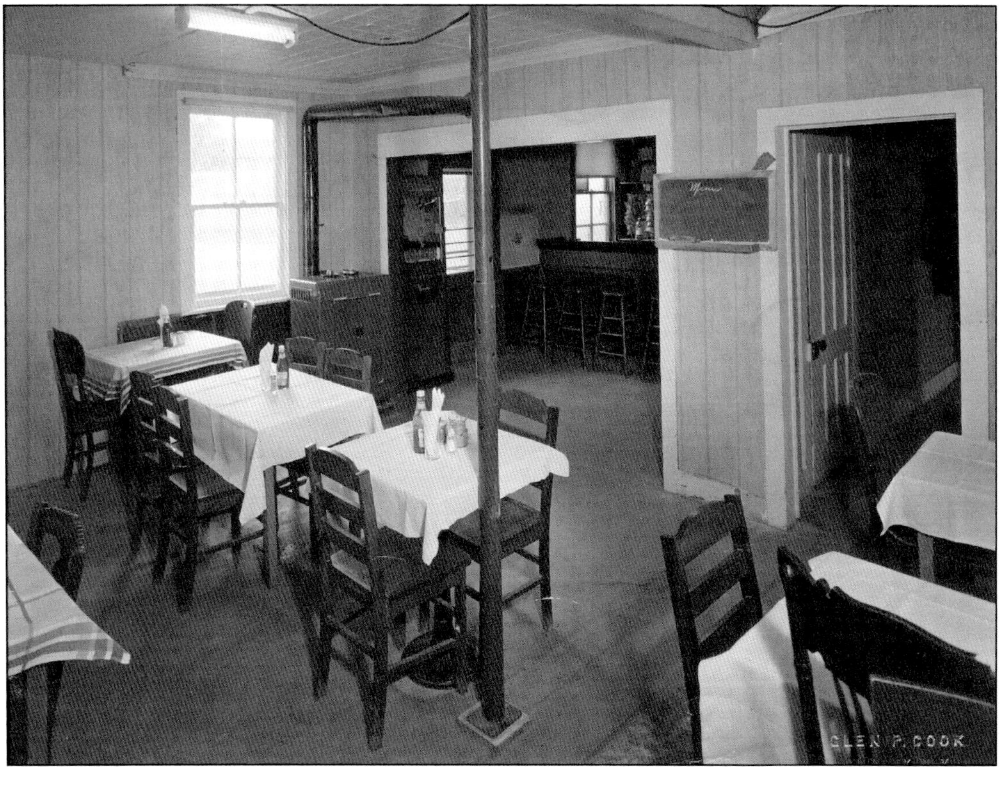

Nine

The Postwar Years

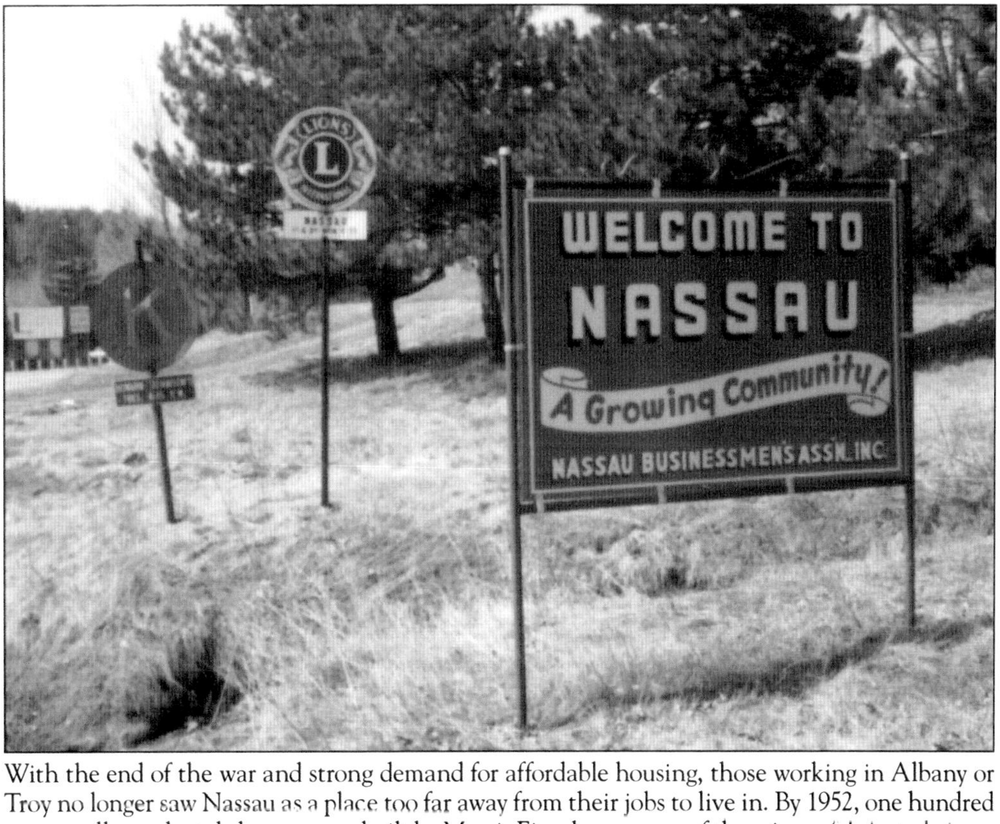

With the end of the war and strong demand for affordable housing, those working in Albany or Troy no longer saw Nassau as a place too far away from their jobs to live in. By 1952, one hundred new, small, ranch-style homes were built by Morris Eisenberg, many of them in prefabricated pieces at the former piano factory. Between 1957 and 1960, the Berkshire Spur section of the New York State Thruway was constructed as an alternative to US Route 20. Traffic between New England and the Albany area now had a faster, safer way to travel, cutting out Nassau. Local business owners joined together to help promote and increase business and growth in Nassau, including erecting blue Welcome to Nassau signs on US Route 20.

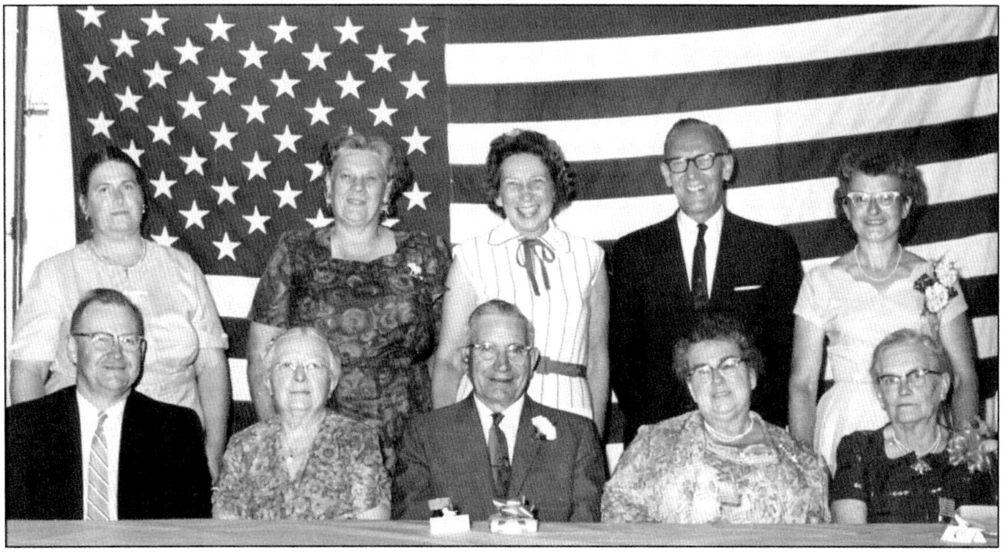

Nassau has a long history of electing Republican candidates to office. Republican Club members and political officials are seen here posing in the late 1950s. They are, from left to right, (first row) supervisor Earle Cooper, unidentified, highway superintendent Clyde Bassett, Ella Sturm, and town clerk Alice Larkin; (second row) Kathryn Larkin, Clara Parker, Dorothy Linton, Douglas Hudson, and Victoria Metzger. Hudson was a member of the state assembly and the state senate.

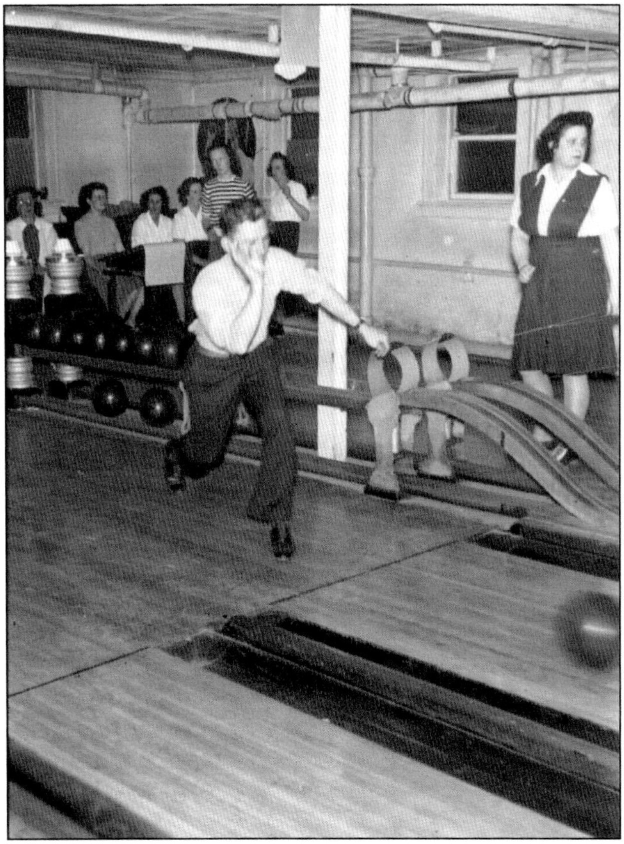

The Nassau Masonic Hall was built on Chatham Street in 1930. In the basement, a four-lane bowling alley entertained many, and league play took place almost daily. Numerous neighborhood boys and girls set pins over the years. Howard Thompson is seen here, possibly with the Thursday afternoon ladies' league. The construction of the eight-lane Bowling Green in East Greenbush in 1958 spelled the end of bowling in Nassau. (Courtesy of Nassau Free Library.)

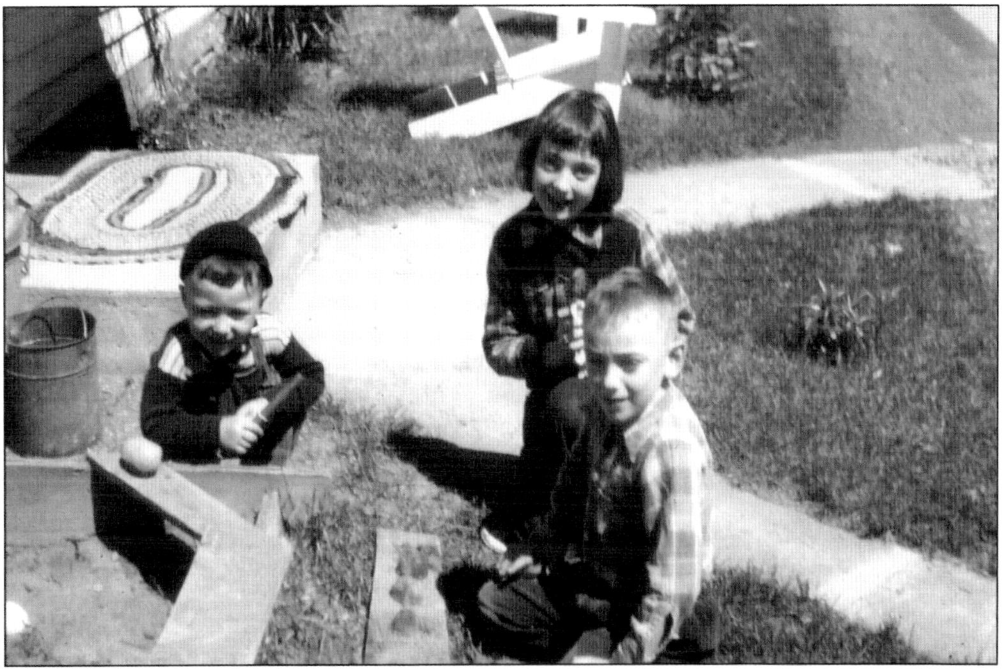

In the 1940s, Burton Bulles accepted a position as head teacher at Nassau School. He and his family moved to 21 Elm Street, where they rented half of the house. Above, the three Bulles children—from left to right, Charles, Eleanor, and Burton Jr.—play in the side yard. At right, their mother, Jean, hulls strawberries in 1945. In 1954, the family moved to 45 Church Street. (Both, courtesy of Eleanor Bulles Coburn.)

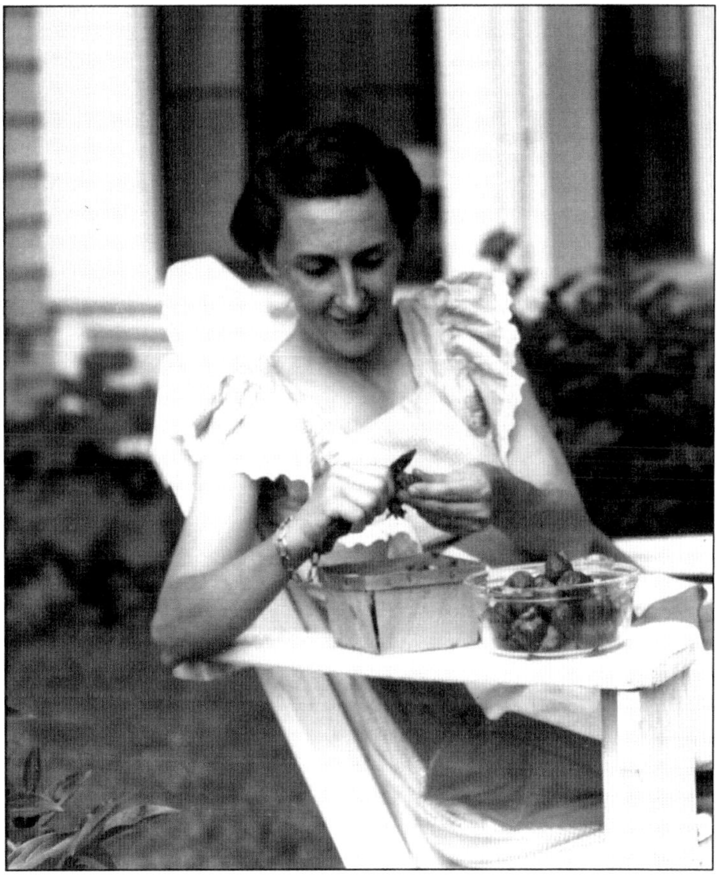

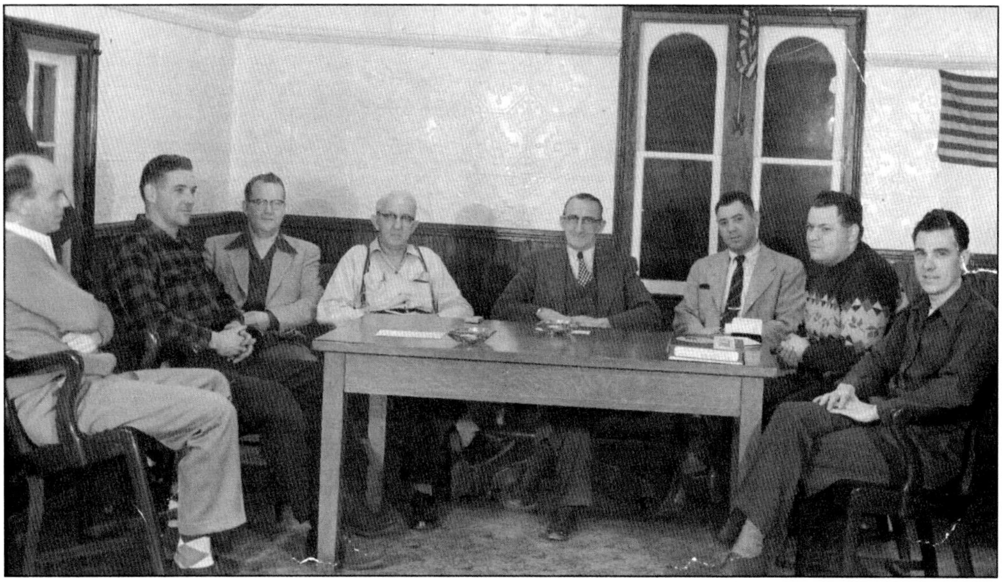

Nassau's village hall was on Malden Street in what had previously been the home of the Nassau Hose Company. The clerk's office was on the ground floor, as was a two-cell jail. Here, the village board and guests pose for photographer Donald Chandler on the second floor in the mid-1950s. Pictured are, from left to right, Clarence Visscher, Matthew Tierney, Earle Cooper, Roy Allendorph, Nassau mayor Christopher Ogden, Samuel Solomon, Gordon Smith, and Russell Decker. (Courtesy of Village of Nassau.)

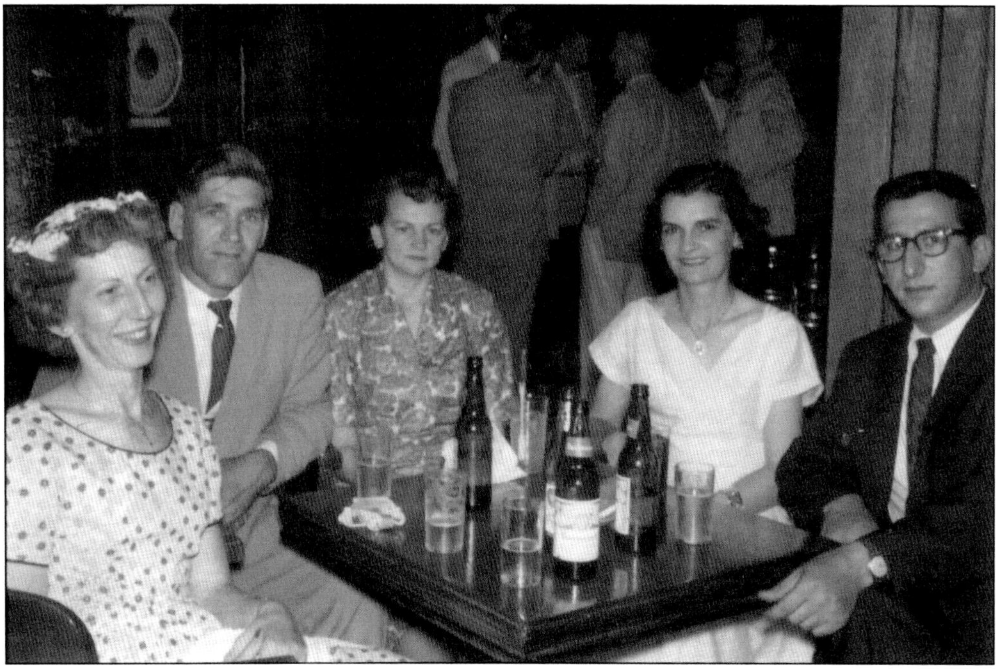

The June 1958 wedding of Bonnie Lee Mesick and James Waters at the Crooked Lake Hotel brought together Westbrook Drive neighbors, from left to right, Elsie Piniazek, Harold and Aurilla Karins, and Joan and Anthony Motta. James succeeded his father, Norman, as the owner and pharmacist at Waters Pharmacy. (Courtesy of the Piniazek family.)

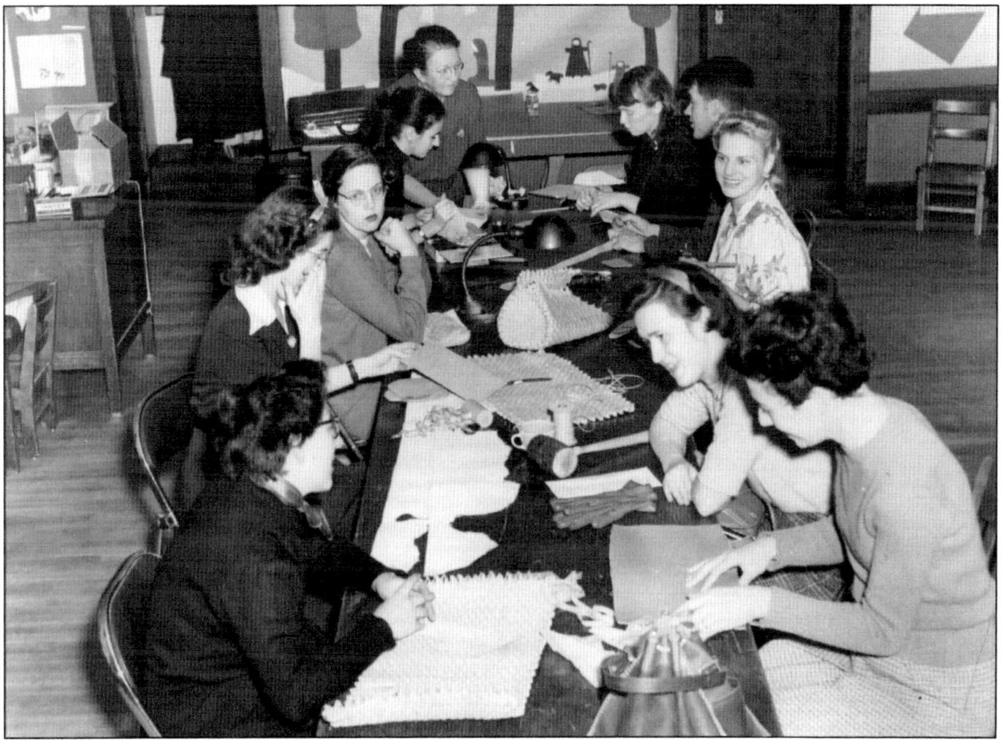

The facilities at Nassau School have been used by many community groups over the years. A leather crafts class is seen here in the early 1950s. The class is led by Corrine Warner, standing at the head of the table. Vivian Hyland is in the right center. The school has been expanded twice since it was opened in 1939—in 1951 and again in 1957. (Courtesy of the Hyland family.)

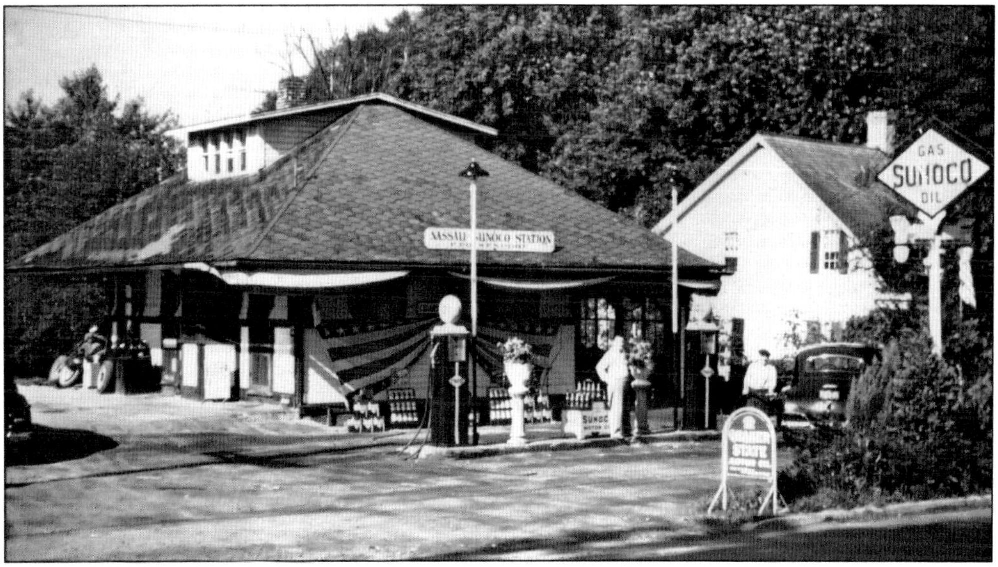

After the end of trolley service, Nassau's former trolley station was converted into a gas station. For many years, Peter Dockendorf ran a Sonoco gas station and garage from the site. The station is seen here decked out in patriotic bunting for July 4, 1946. Dockendorf conveniently lived in the house next door.

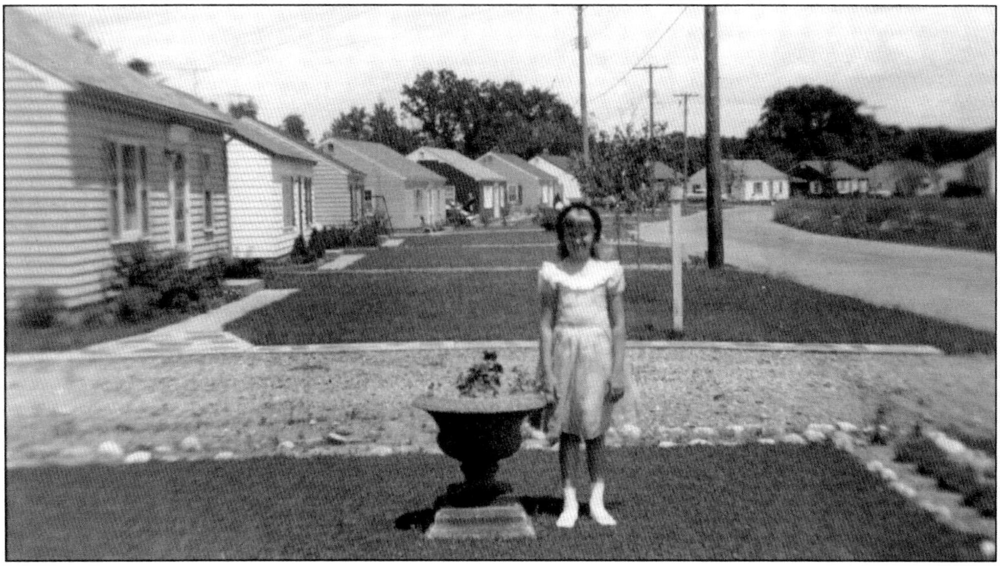

Like many World War II veterans, Edward Piniazek and his family moved to Nassau when new housing became available. Here, his daughter Judi stands in front of the newly developed Westbrook Drive development on June 27, 1956. The Piniazek family lived at 41 Westbrook Drive. (Courtesy of the Piniazek family.)

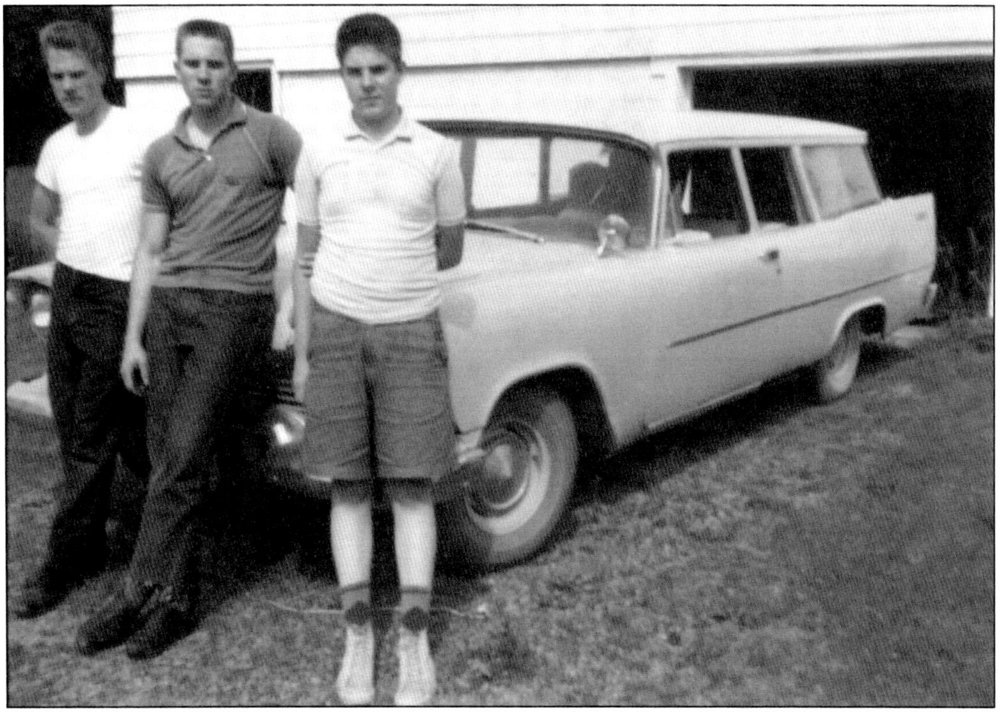

Another of Nassau's postwar housing developments was Orchard Park, built past the old fairgrounds on New York State Route 203. When federal government employee Everman England was transferred to Albany, Nassau was a convenient and agreeable location for him to settle. Here, the three England boys—from left to right, Kenneth, Richard, and Lee—pose for a photograph in July 1963. (Courtesy of Kenneth England.)

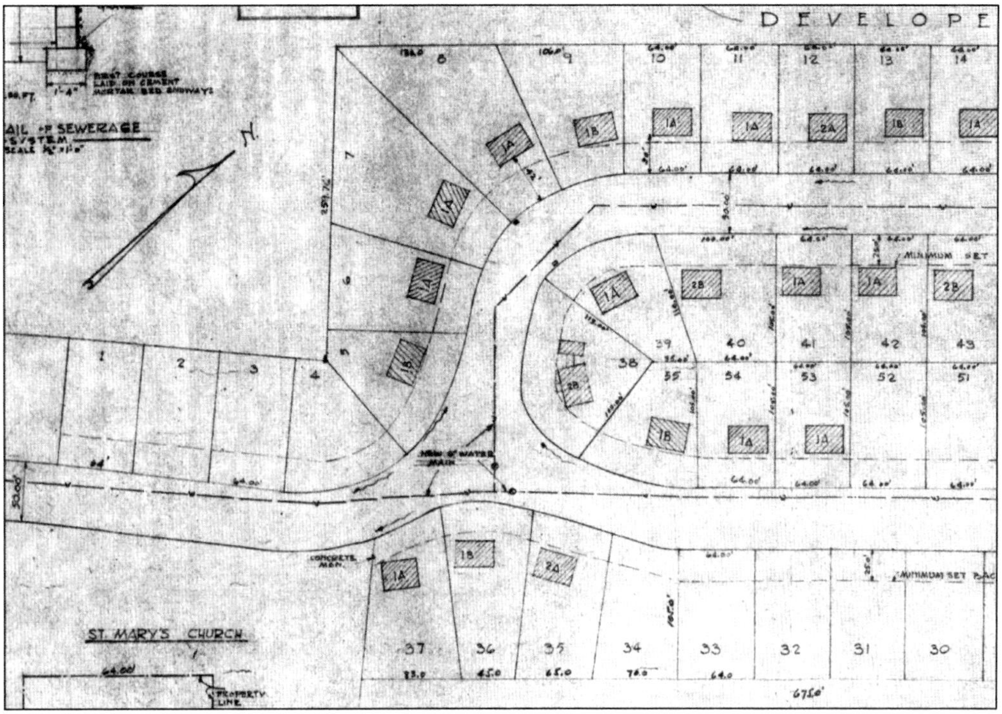

A housing development named Elmwood Acres was built off of Church Street, on the former Phillips farm. Originally, 55 houses were planned, and 25 homes were built in the first phase. At the time of construction, many older residents remembered the area as a popular winter ice-skating site called "the vly," from an old Dutch word. True to nature, in the first spring after construction, the entire development flooded. Many years passed before further development took place. (Both, courtesy of Village of Nassau.)

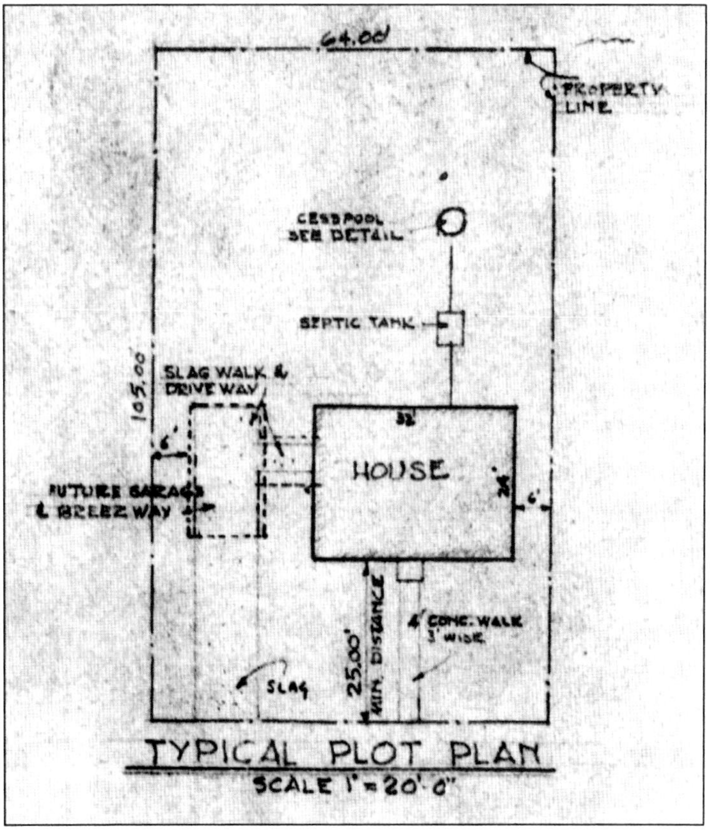

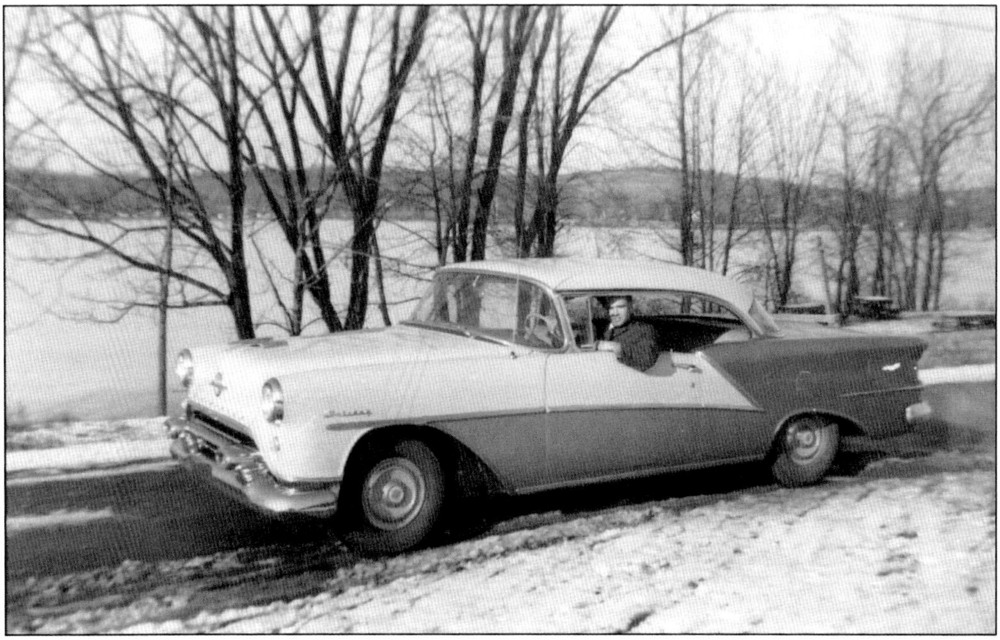

The Hyland family moved to Nassau in 1951 when James Hyland took a job at the Watervliet Arsenal. The family converted a former summer camp on Lake Shore Drive at Nassau Lake into a home, a common cure to the housing shortage of the time. James is seen here proudly showing off his first new car, a top-of-the-line 1954 Oldsmobile 98. (Courtesy of the Hyland family.)

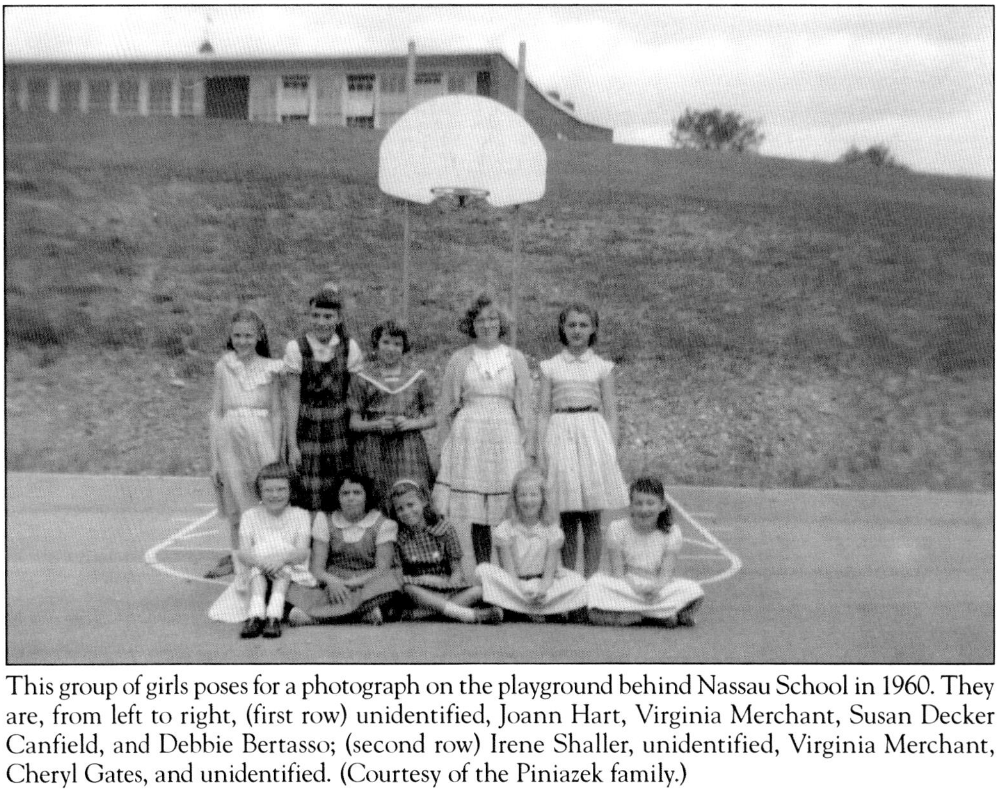

This group of girls poses for a photograph on the playground behind Nassau School in 1960. They are, from left to right, (first row) unidentified, Joann Hart, Virginia Merchant, Susan Decker Canfield, and Debbie Bertasso; (second row) Irene Shaller, unidentified, Virginia Merchant, Cheryl Gates, and unidentified. (Courtesy of the Piniazek family.)

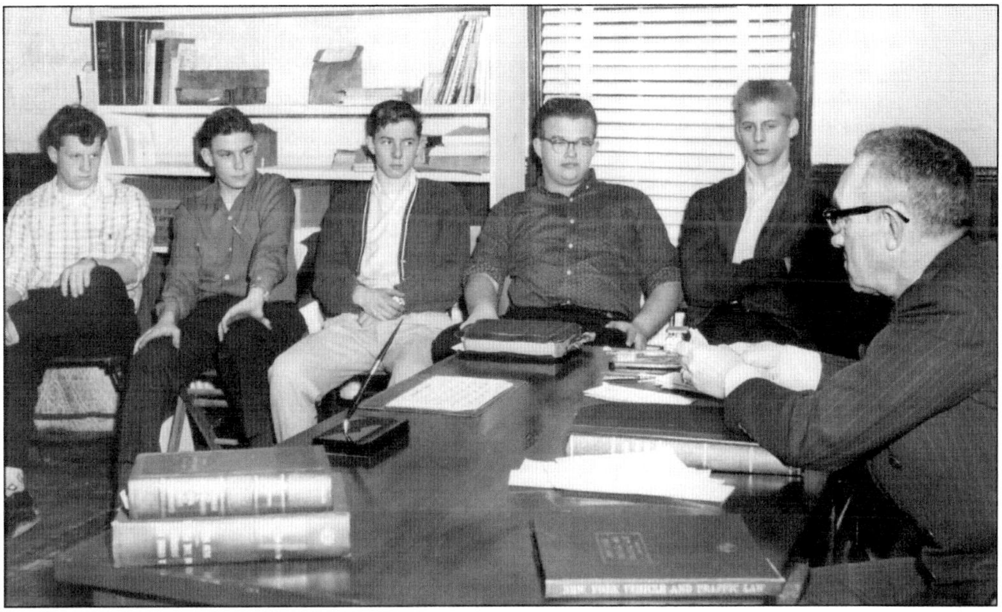

James Lamb was appointed justice for the village of Nassau in 1957, and elected town justice in 1970, at the age of 70. In this undated photograph, Judge Lamb (far right) is seen with, from left to right, unidentified, William Hansen, George Brown, Donald Klein, and Arthur Hull. There is no indication as to why the young men look so glum. (Courtesy of Diane McGrath, Nassau Town Hall.)

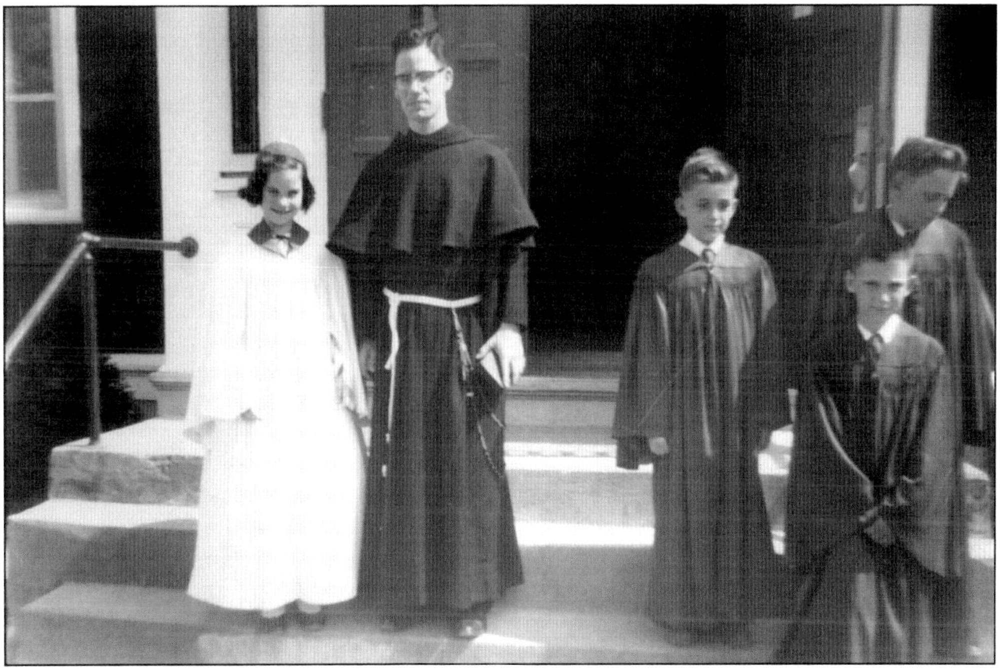

Since 1916, St. Mary's Church has been affiliated with the Franciscan order. Church records show that membership, births, and marriages remained constant for many years. After the war, those numbers rose dramatically. Here, from left to right, Lynn Hyland, an unidentified friar, and Kenneth, Edward, and Paul Phelps exit the church. (Courtesy of the Hyland family.)

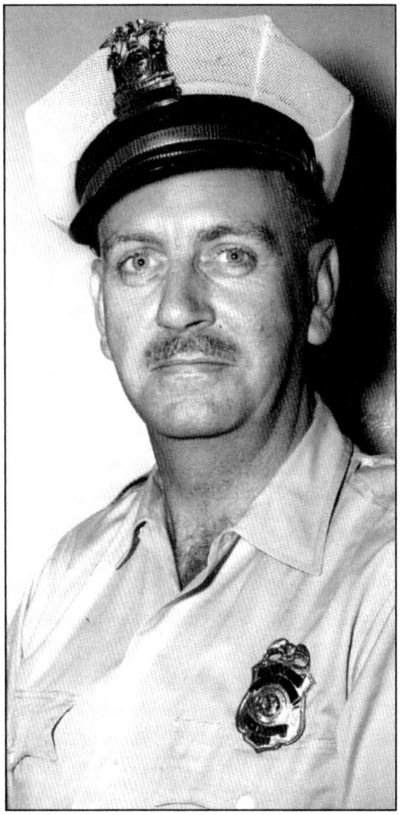

Nassau's location on a major highway between two hills was made for speed. Not long after automobiles became common, residents began complaining about speeders. The first full-time—and most famous—law enforcement officer in Nassau was police chief C. Lowell Avery (left). Affectionately known as "Doc," and not so kindly known as "Wyatt Earp," he exercised tight control of the roads, serving Nassau from 1957 to 1966. When asked by a reporter to comment on the first new car purchased for the police department in 1962, Avery replied, "It's a dandy. It'll really catch them." Below, posing alongside that car are the Avery children—from left to right, Mark, Jack, and Judy—outside their Elm Street home. (Both, courtesy of the Avery family.)

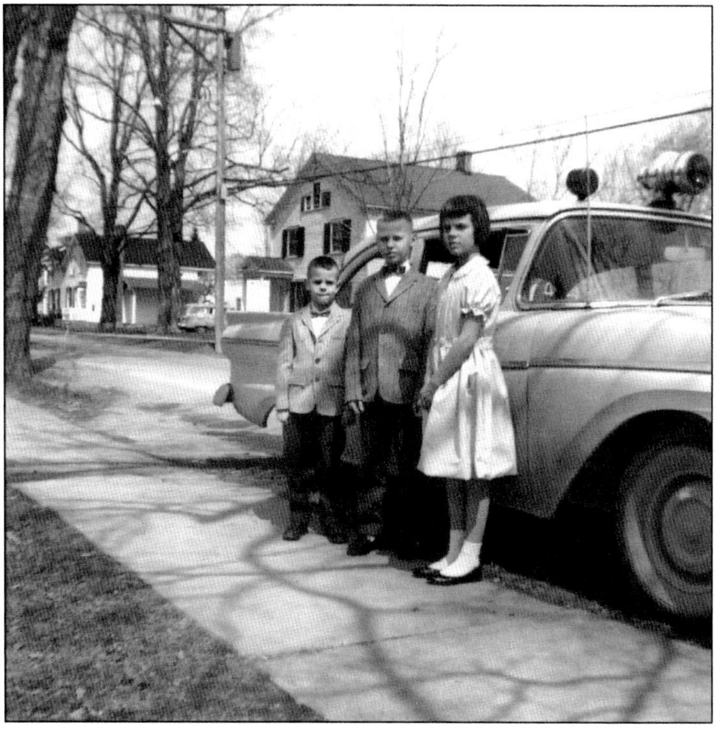

Burr Rowe was a lifelong resident of Nassau and served as a part-time Nassau police officer well into his 70s. Concerned about growing traffic on US Route 20, the village board detailed the police department to provide a crossing guard for schoolchildren and Sunday church services. A conservatory-trained musician, Rowe led the Nassau Band for many years, and, in his early years, played first trumpet with the famed Barnum & Bailey Circus Band. (Courtesy of Norman Rowe.)

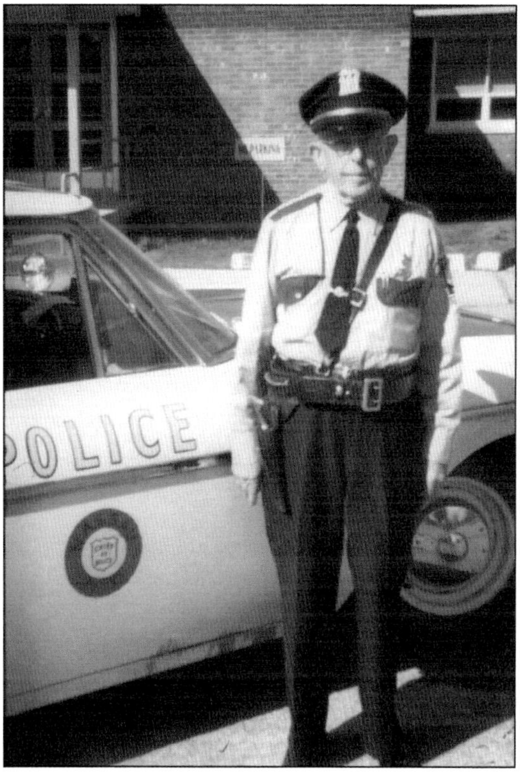

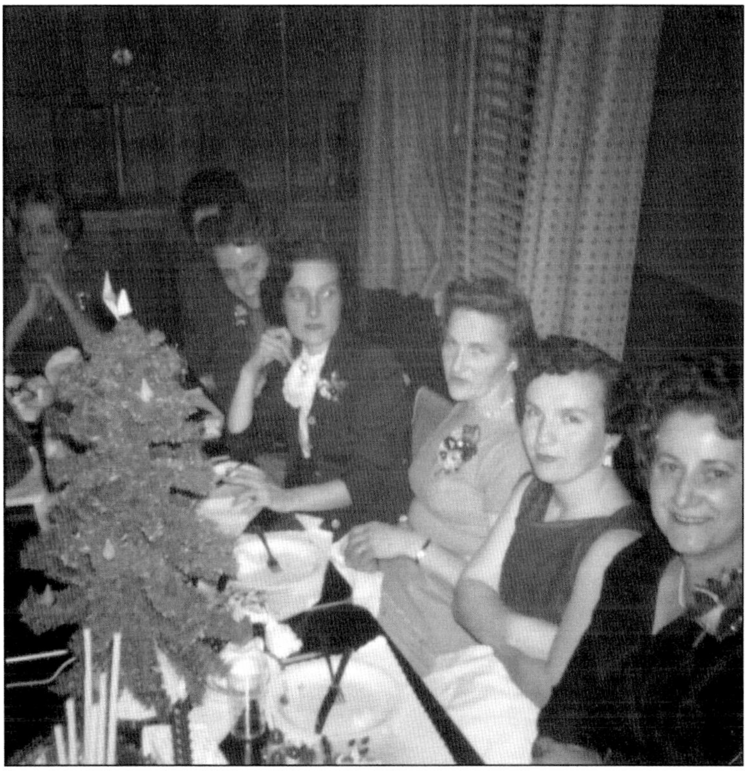

Nassau's Homestead Hotel was the scene for the annual ladies bowling league Christmas party, seen here in the mid-1950s. Many local businesses supported teams, including the Homestead. Shown here are, from left to right, unidentified, unidentified (face obscured), Bonnie Waters, Lois Hanson, Betty Phelps, Kathryn Rickert, and unidentified. (Courtesy of the Hyland family.)

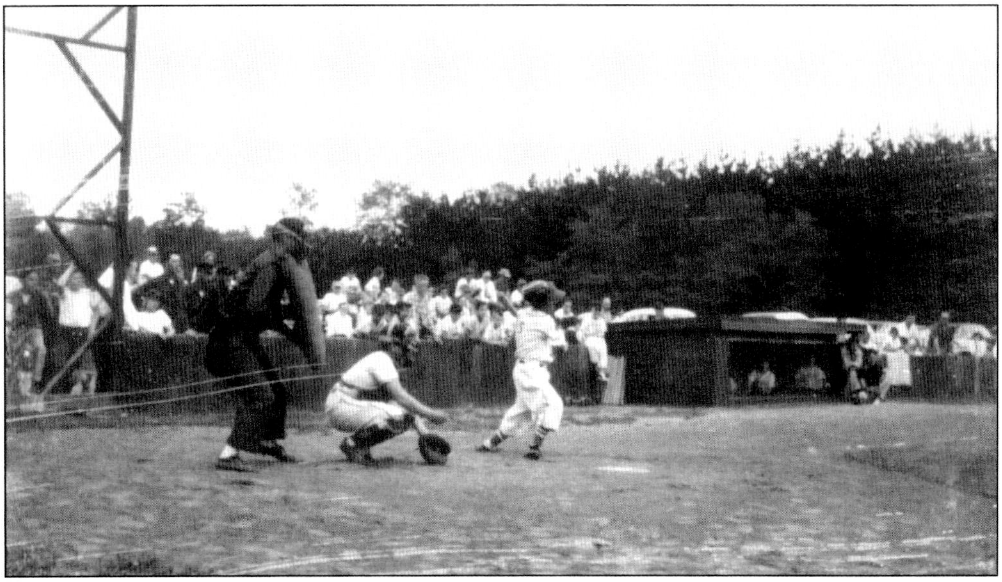

Baseball has a long history in Nassau, beginning in the 1880s. In the early years, men and older teens mostly played. After World War II, the Nassau Baseball Association Little League was founded. Games took place at Merchant's Field, just north of the village line on the Nassau–East Schodack road. Chucky Karins is seen here at bat in the early 1960s. (Courtesy of the Piniazek family.)

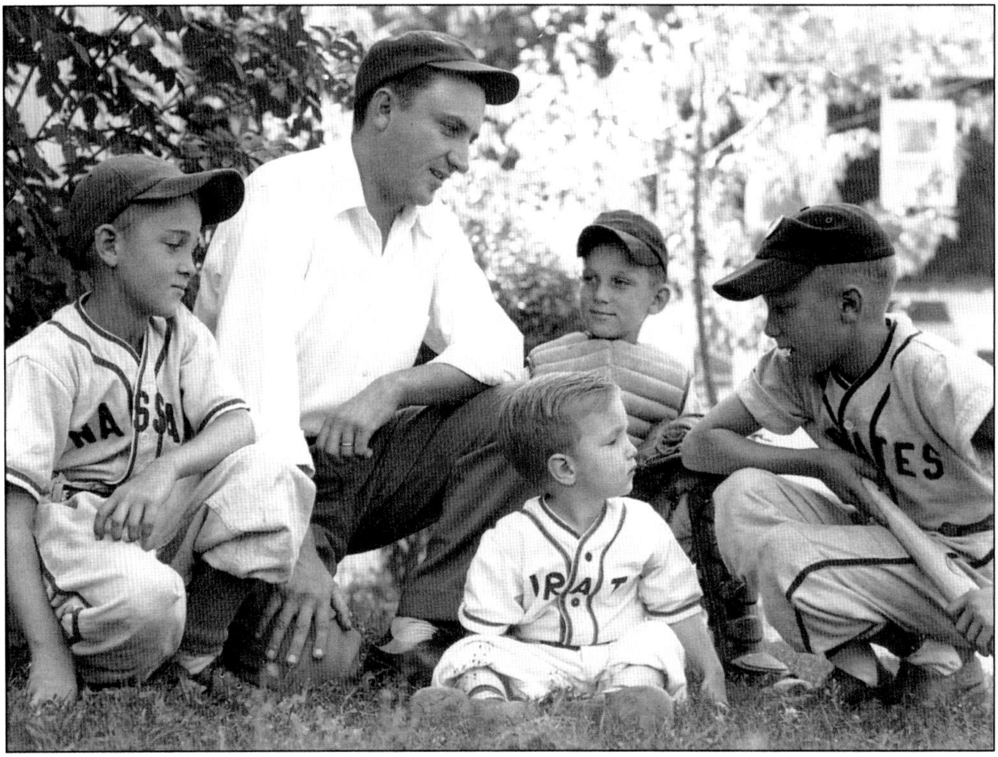

Edward Phelps is seen here coaching his sons in 1957. The boys are, from left to right, Kenneth Phelps, David Phelps (sitting), Edward Phelps Jr., and Paul Phelps. Phelps Sr. operated a successful insurance business from his home at 38 Elm Street. (Courtesy of David Phelps.)

After a heavy snowfall in March 1955, Derek Van Loan (left) and Paul Carpenter (right) pose with Richard Mensing, who fashioned this motorized snow shovel out of a variety of motors and spare parts. The power shovel was a novelty on Fairview Terrace at the time. (Courtesy of the Prior family.)

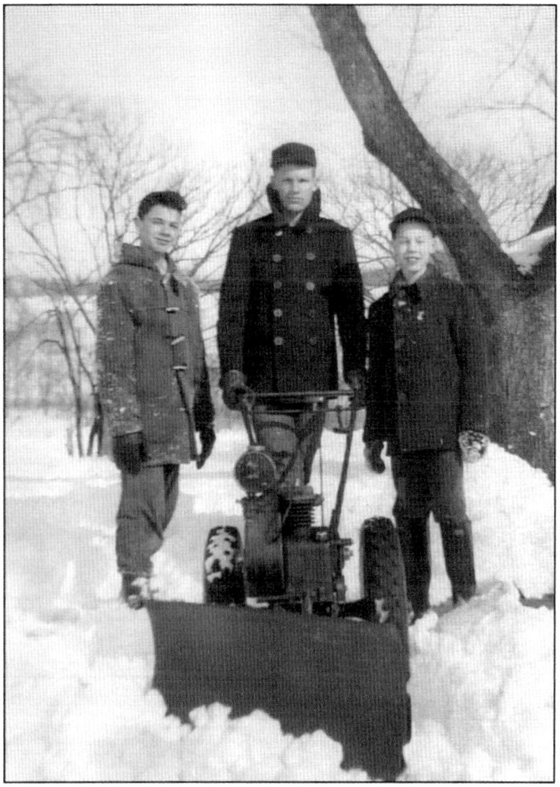

Cub Scouts from Troop 166 pose for a photograph after completing a decorated trash can project in 1956. They are, from left to right, unidentified, James Smith, Tommy Sanford, Larry Cooper, Burton Bulles, unidentified, and Harry Vincent. Scout groups in Nassau date back to before World War I.

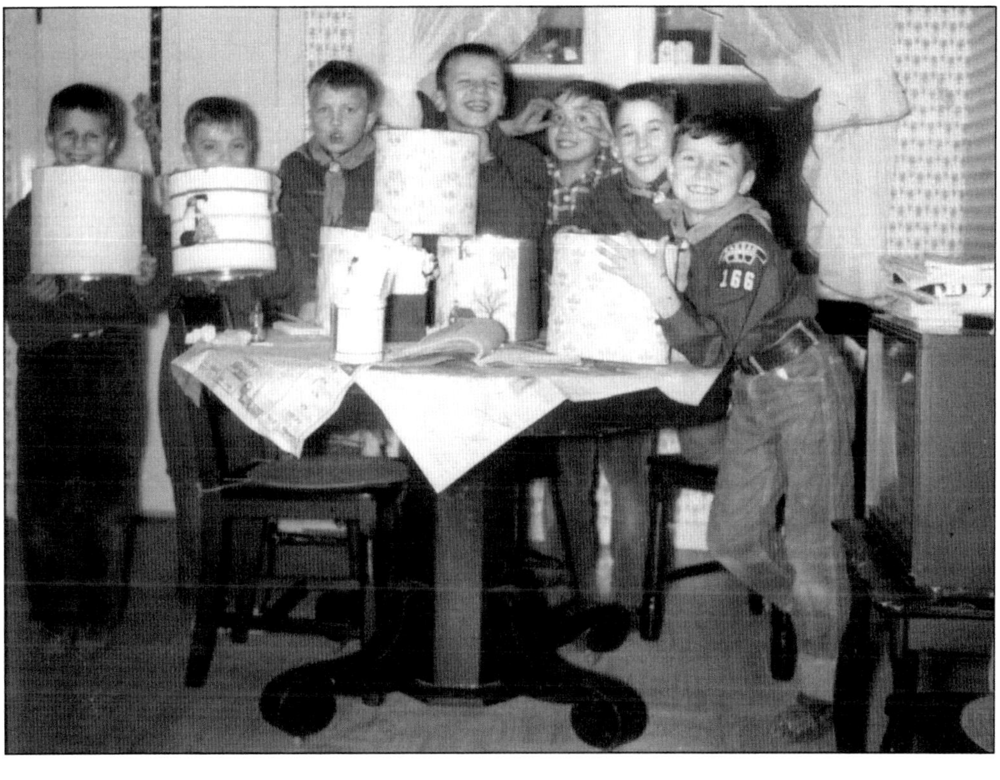

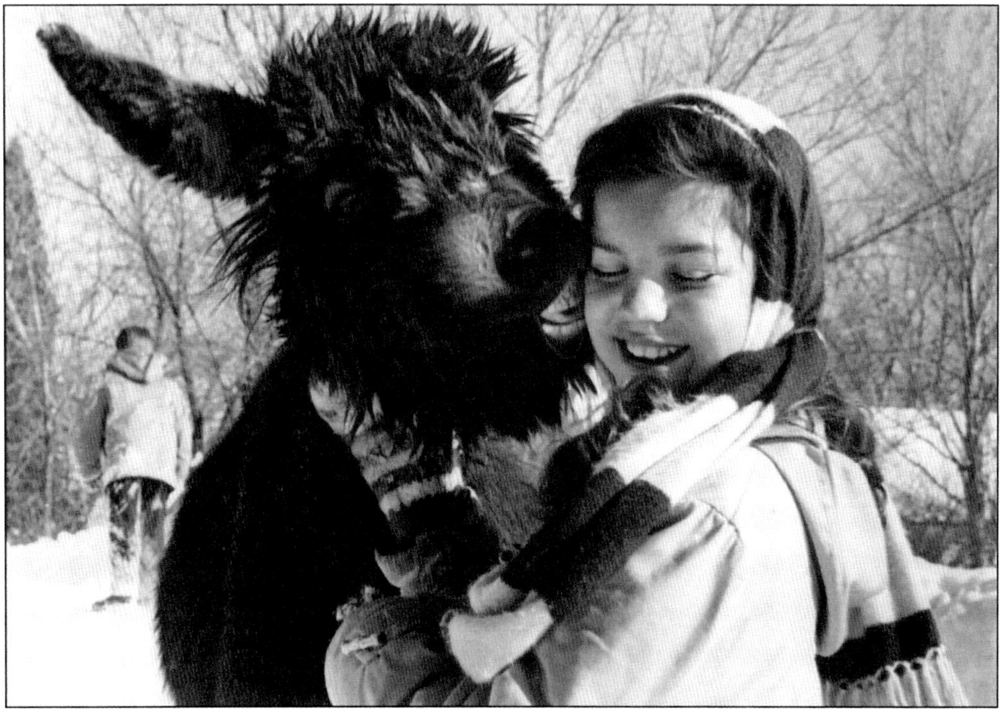

For her 12th birthday, Janis Hyland received a six-month-old donkey as a gift from her aunt Natalie MacEwen. Part of a government program to relocate overpopulated wild burros from the West, Bridget Burro, or "BB" to her friends, was treated like part of the family. (Courtesy of the Hyland family.)

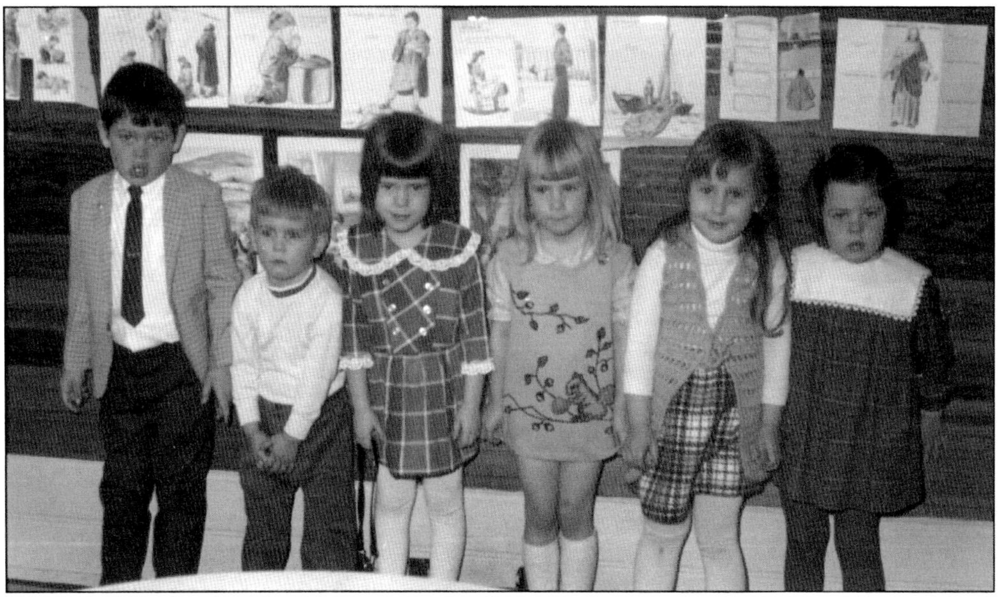

These timid first and second graders from the Nassau Reformed Church Sunday school are, from left to right, Paul Sheldon, Joey Morris, Terry Moore, Ellen Veenandahl, Kelly Morris, and Barbara Sheldon. When this photograph was taken, in March 1971, dressing up for church and Sunday school was considered very important.

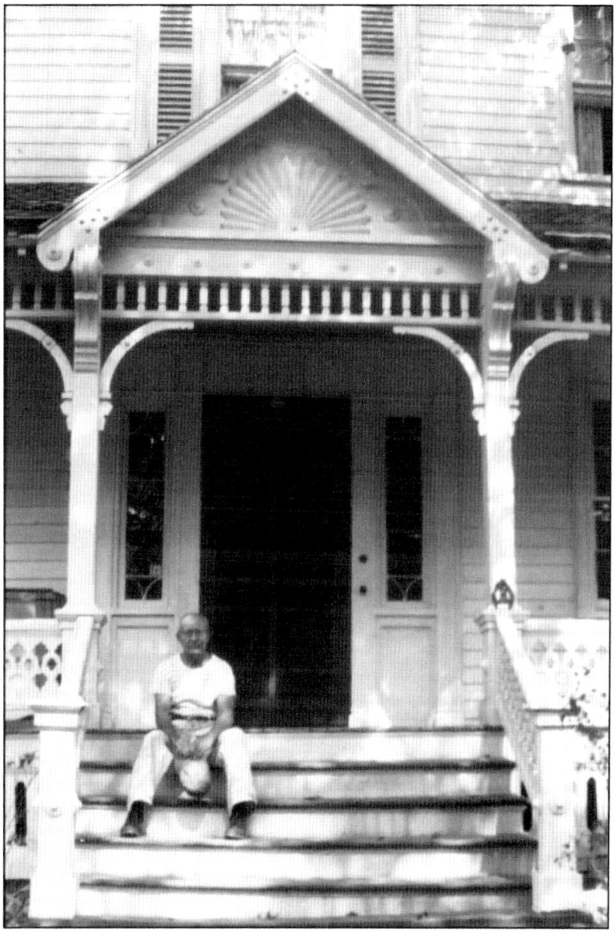

Howard Shufelt takes a break after applying the primer coat of paint to 45 Church Street in August 1953. He was a housepainter in Nassau, as his father, William Shufelt, was before him. On page 12, Howard is seen 55 years earlier, as the groom at a Tom Thumb wedding.

Before it was leveled to make way for the gas station that stands at the site today, the structure that housed the corner pharmacy for years ended its life as a series of food markets, first as a Grand Union, then as an IGA, and, lastly, as an independent grocery store. A pizza shop sign can just be seen to the rear of the building in this 1974 photograph.

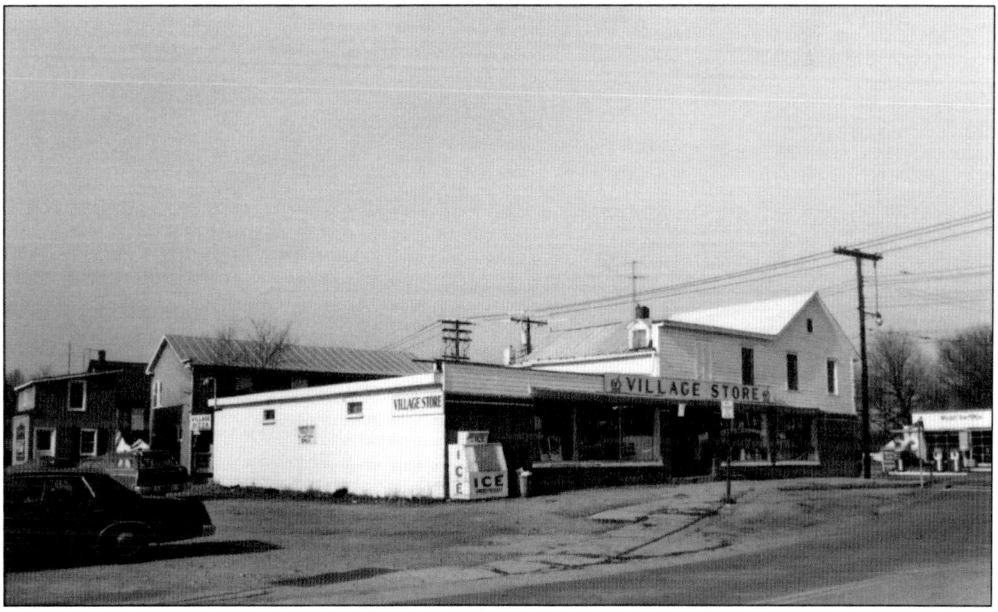

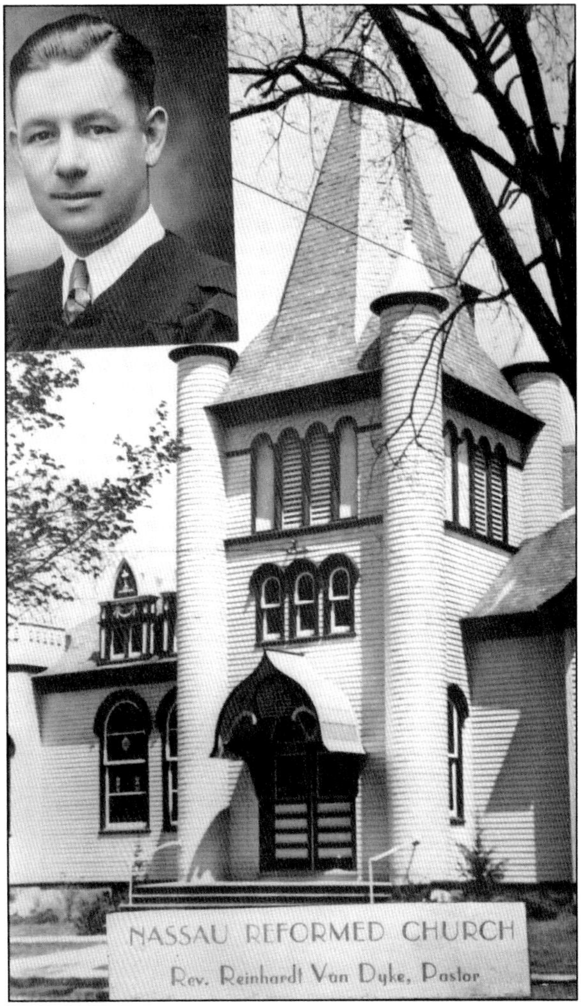

Rev. Reinhardt Van Dyke came to the Nassau Reformed Church fresh out of seminary in the spring of 1938, and remained until 1946. During those years, the traditional Sunday evening worship service was discontinued, and a young people's society, the Youth Fellowship, was begun. Considered the most architecturally interesting of Nassau's churches, its contrasting trim color accented the Queen Anne–style design. (Courtesy of Nassau Free Library.)

In 1955, breaking with the frequent Dutch ancestry of ministers, the consistory called Oklahoma-born Italian American Rev. Carlo Lazzaro to Nassau. The 40-year-old minister served Nassau's congregation for 30 years. Popular with the community and open to those of all faiths, Reverend Lazzaro is seen below at an Easter morning sunrise service. Many years later, the land he stands on became Ye Olde Parsonage Apartments.

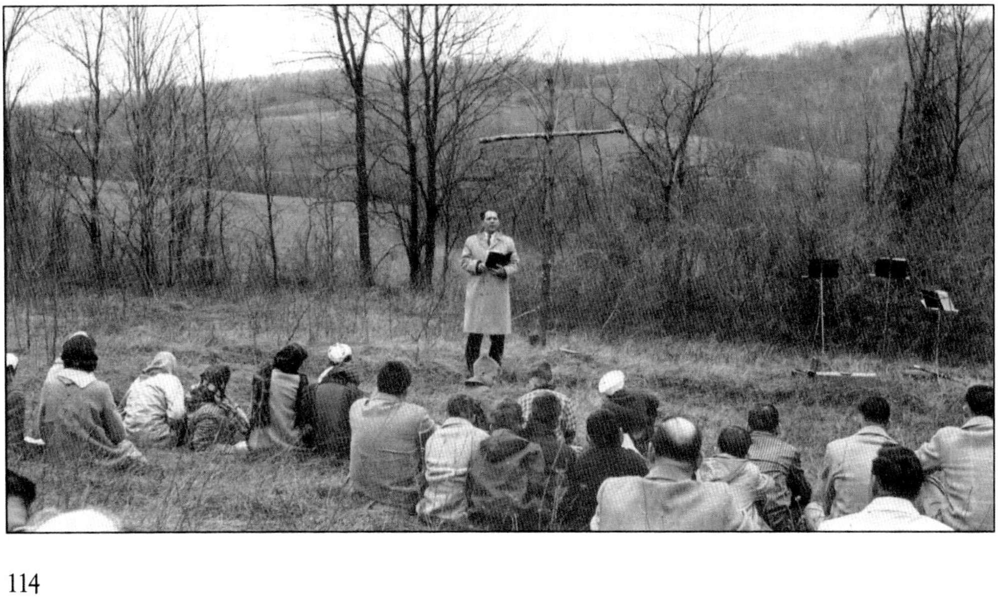

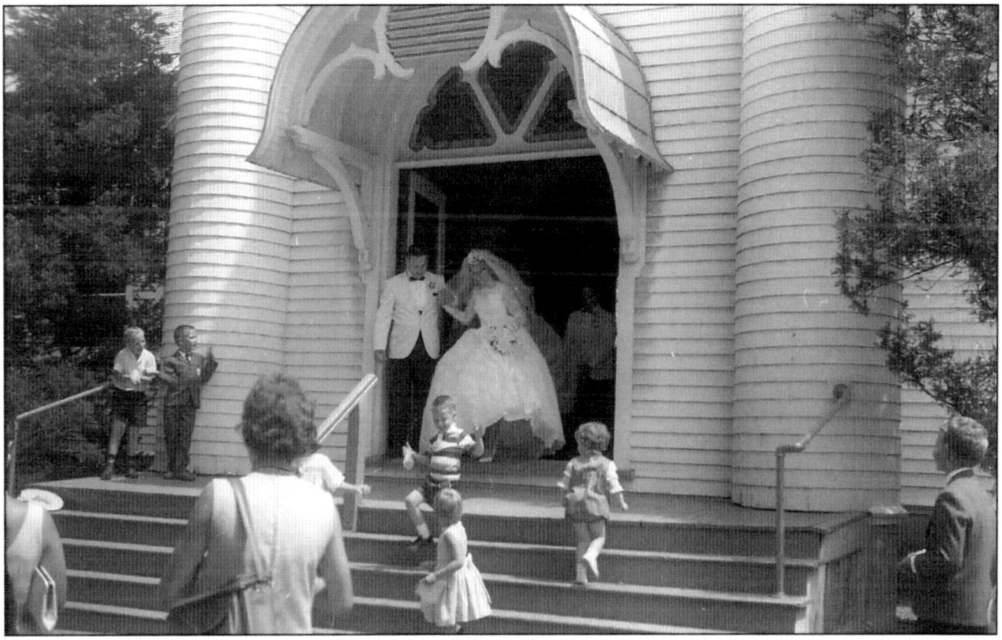

Above, Mr. and Mrs. Robert Bingham are greeted by well-wishers after their marriage ceremony at the Reformed church in July 1966. Mrs. Bingham, the former Diane Druschel, was raised on the family farm on Nassau Lake's east side. Below, Sunday school students are seen outside the church in 1981. Under Reverend Lazzaro, attendance outgrew the capacity of the church building, and a new Sunday school building was constructed behind the sanctuary. Sadly, the 1901 building was demolished in July 2001, after preservationists were unable to convince the congregation to save the structure, which had been victim to years of neglected maintenance and limited financial resources.

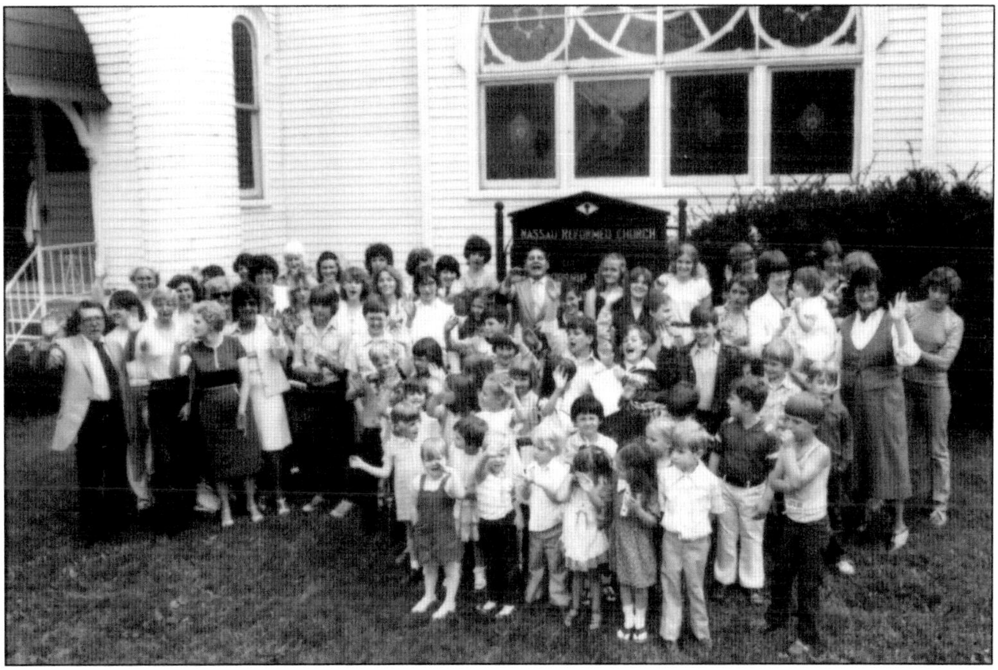

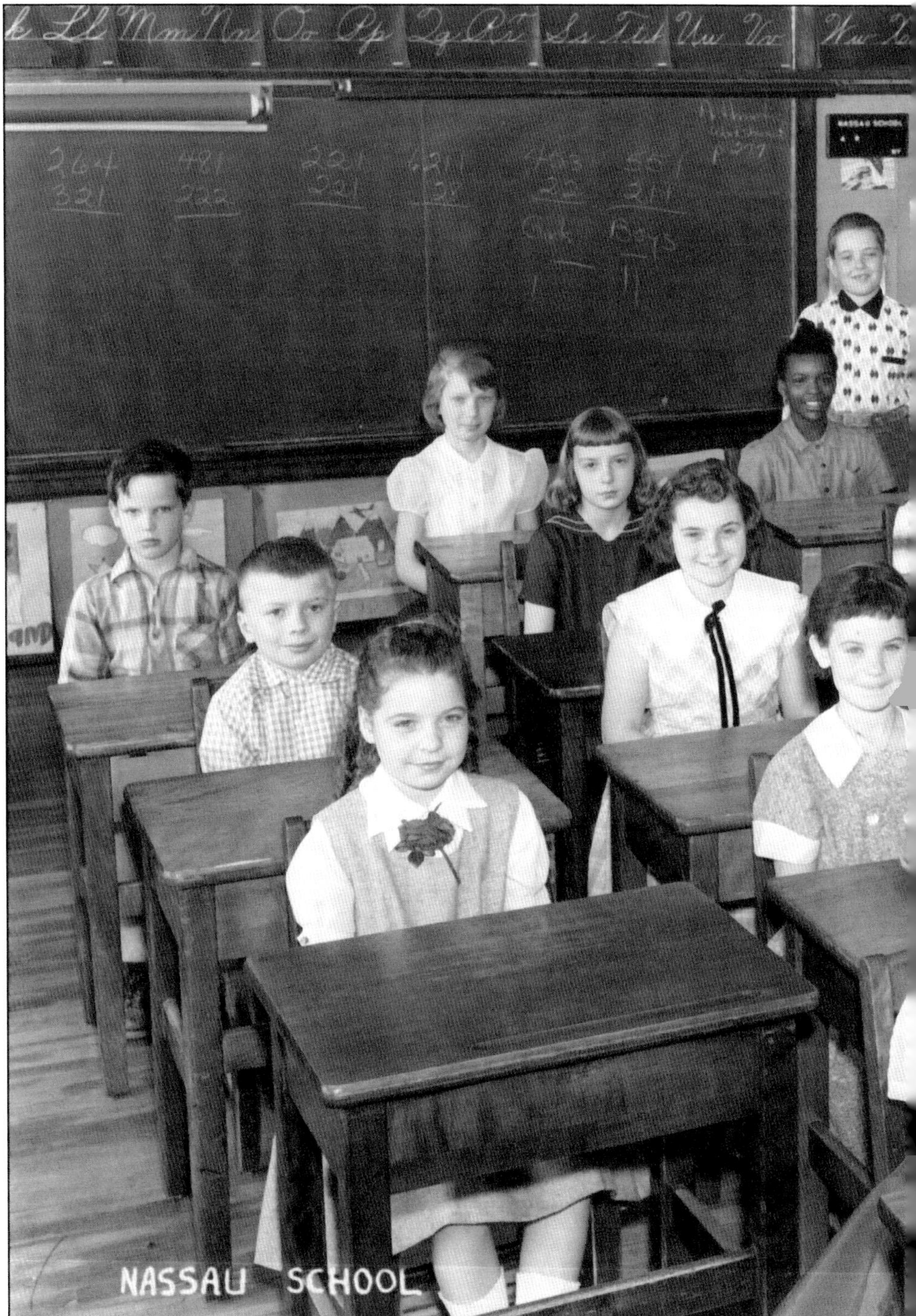

Miss Ryan's fourth grade class at Nassau School is seen here in 1956. At the time, the annual Columbia High School yearbook also included photographs of all the classes in the elementary schools of the district. This class includes, from left to right, (first row) Barbara Murphy and Nancy Clewell; (second row); Donna Decker, Lynn Hyland, Nancy Reed, and Dottie Schmidt; (third row) Tommy Sanford, Marcia Amadon, Bill Cherry, and Jean DeChamp; (fourth row) Kenneth

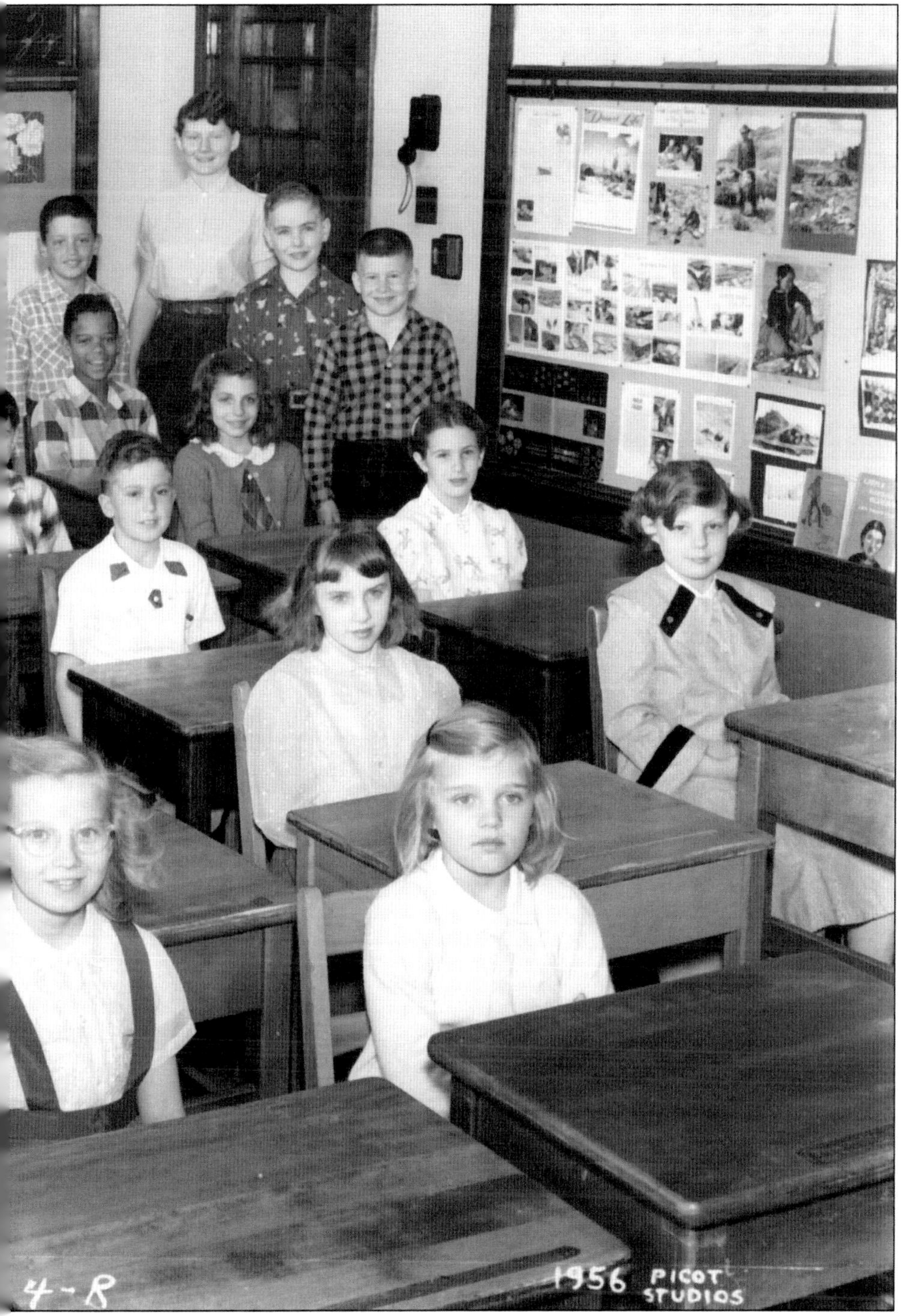

Merchant, Linda Bartow, Harry Vincent, and Loretta Schemerhorn; (fifth row) Gail Montanye, Cheryl DeGroff, and Wilfred Shedon; (standing) Milton Thomson, Frank Visconti, Miss Ryan, Jim Bruck, and Steve Cooper. Absent from this picture were Cheryl Richards, Billy Coonradt, and Edward Gardineer. (Courtesy of the Hyland family.)

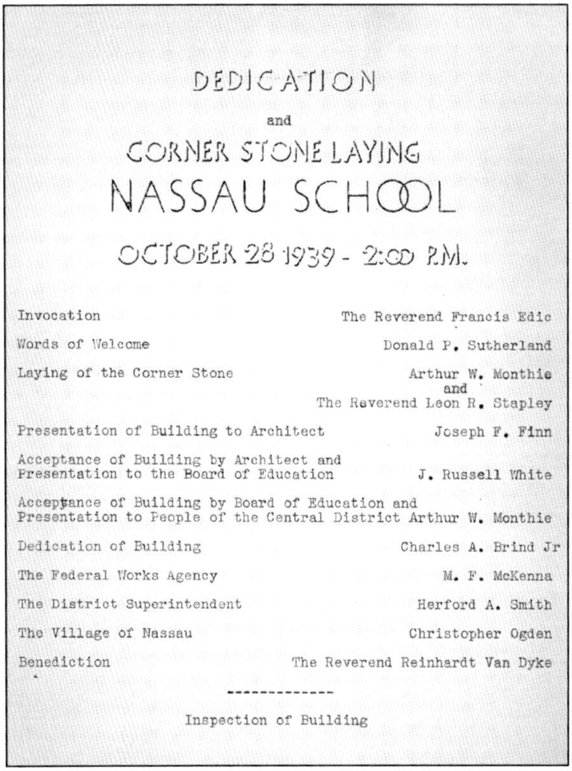

DEDICATION

and

CORNER STONE LAYING

NASSAU SCHOOL

OCTOBER 28 1939 - 2:00 P.M.

Invocation	The Reverend Francis Edic
Words of Welcome	Donald P. Sutherland
Laying of the Corner Stone	Arthur W. Monthie and The Reverend Leon R. Stapley
Presentation of Building to Architect	Joseph F. Finn
Acceptance of Building by Architect and Presentation to the Board of Education	J. Russell White
Acceptance of Building by Board of Education and Presentation to People of the Central District	Arthur W. Monthie
Dedication of Building	Charles A. Brind Jr
The Federal Works Agency	M. F. McKenna
The District Superintendent	Herford A. Smith
The Village of Nassau	Christopher Ogden
Benediction	The Reverend Reinhardt Van Dyke

Inspection of Building

In 1936, Nassau voted to end its own school system and enter into the East Greenbush Central School District. It was opposed by some, but in order for East Greenbush to centralize its own schools, additional students were needed. Nassau was approached with the promise of a new elementary school if centralization was approved. (Courtesy of Nassau Free Library.)

The new Nassau School had six classrooms, a combination auditorium and gymnasium, a kitchen, and a principal's office. Pupils from eight often one-room schools were combined at the new school. The teaching staff in 1941 includes, from left to right, (first row) Carol More, head teacher Berton Bulles, and Carol Mead; (second row) Ethel Decker, Florence Hall, Ruth Kenyon, and Sarah Miller. Kenyon later became principal, serving for many years before retiring. (Courtesy of Eleanor Bulles Coburn.)

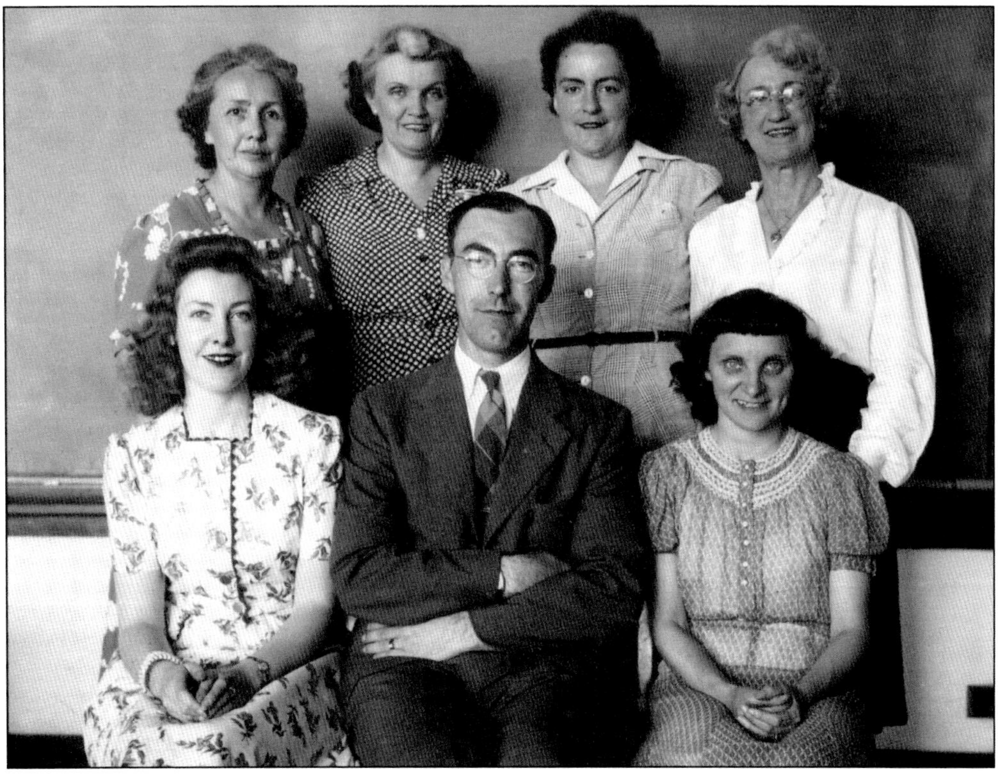

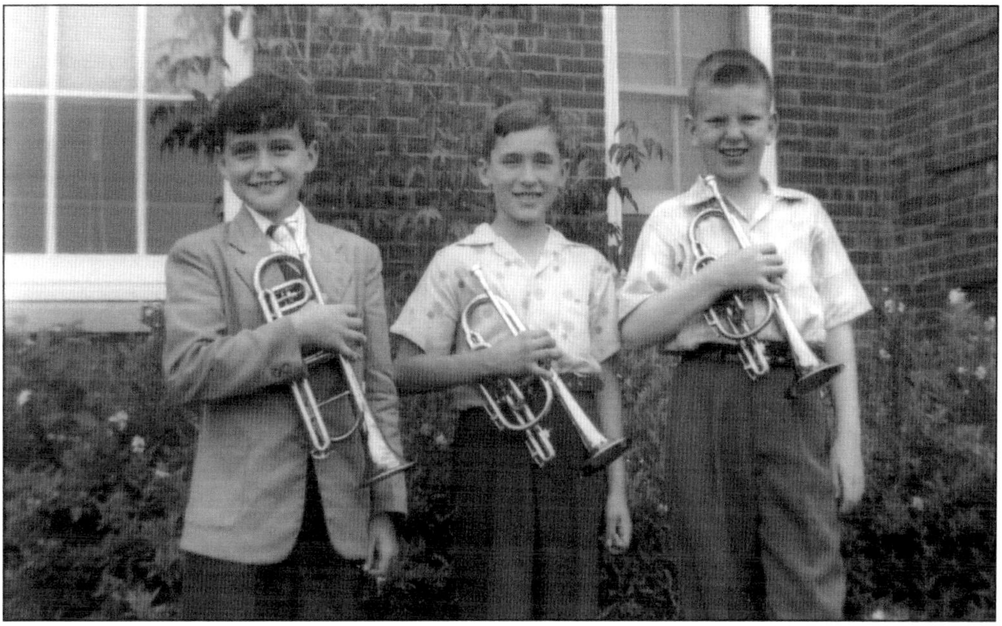

The new Nassau School was positioned on the hill above John Street, and benefited from funding from Pres. Franklin Roosevelt's Works Progress Administration (WPA). Many small local schools at the time merged into central school districts to take advantage of generous government funding. The photograph above shows school band members, from left to right, Harry Vincent, David Bogart, and Billy Mitchell after they performed solos in "Bugler's Holiday." Below, Cub Scouts from Nassau Troop 166 pose after a trip to the Albany Institute of History and Art. (Both, courtesy of Eleanor Bulles Coburn.)

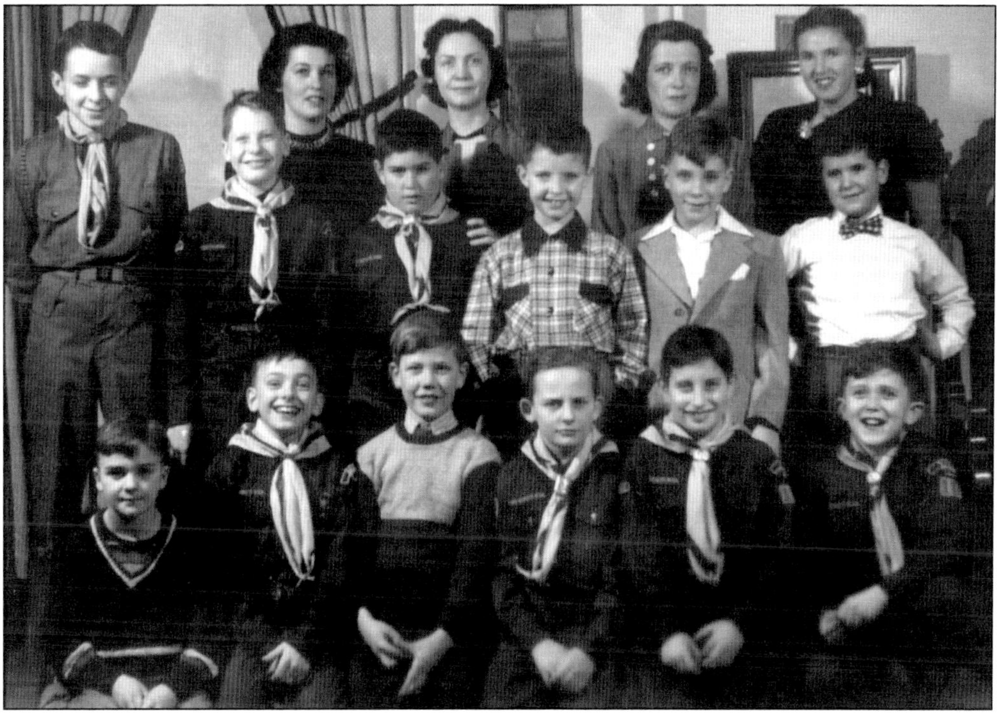

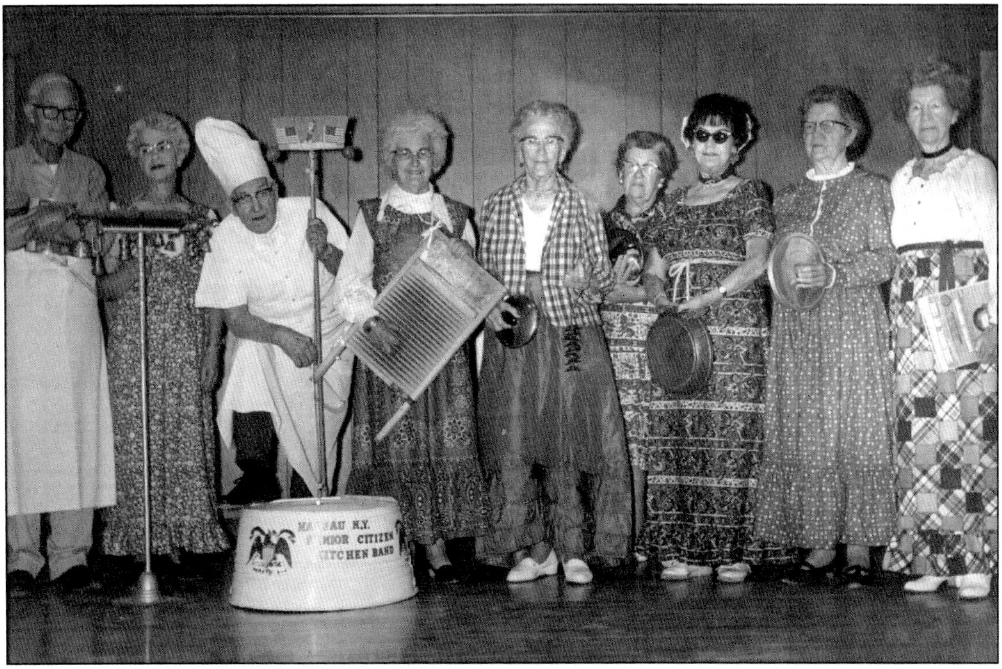

The US bicentennial in 1976 created many opportunities to celebrate, including the formation of the Nassau Senior Citizen's Kitchen Band. The band includes, from left to right, John Casey, Blanche Granger, Daniel Murphy, unidentified, Myrtle Kosegarten, unidentified, Hilda Barrows, Jeanette Winters, and leader Florence Knickerbocker, whose favorite tune was "Pistol Packin' Mama."

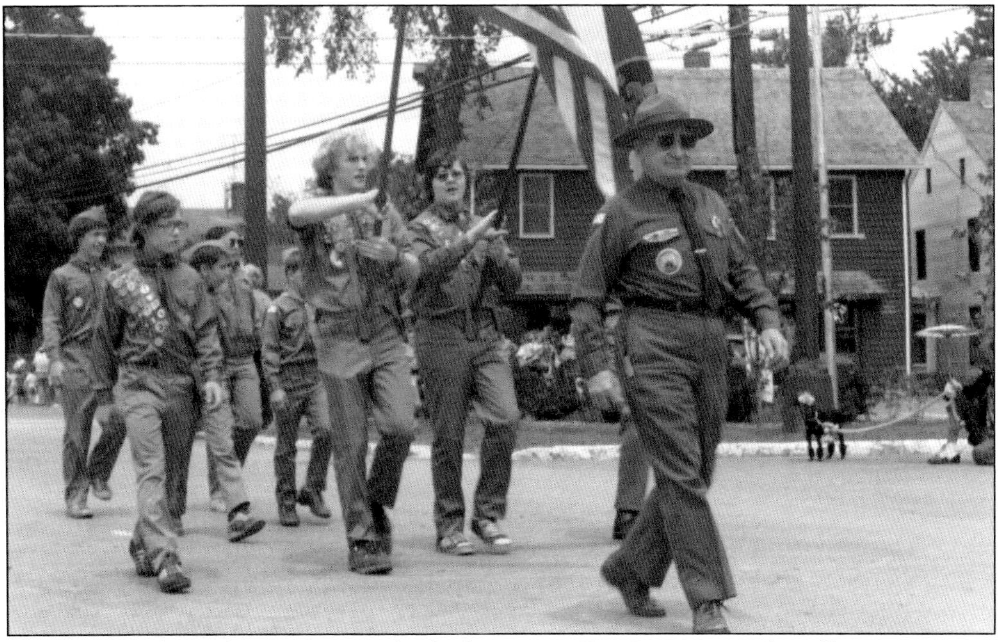

Troop 166 leader Sydney Morrow Jr. leads the Nassau Boy Scouts past the village square in a Memorial Day parade in the early 1970s. Directly behind him are, from left to right, unidentified, Earl Morrow, and James Mesco. Christopher Noeth is on the far left in the back. (Courtesy of Kathy Grossman, Nassau Pharmacy.)

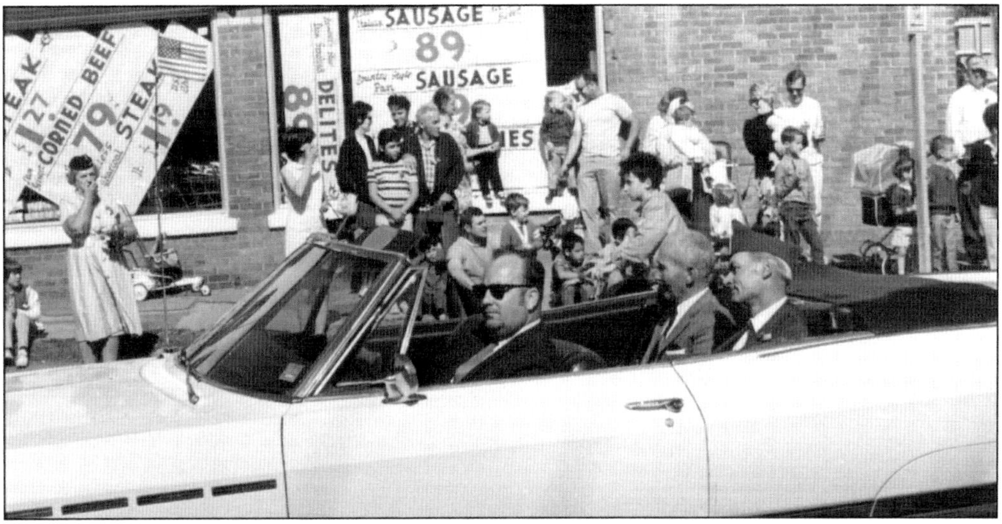

From the 1960s on, the annual Memorial Day parade became the main patriotic celebration in Nassau. Wearing a cap in the backseat of the car is Ralph Mensing, one of many Nassau veterans honored as grand marshal of the parade in the 1970s. Mensing was elected village mayor in 1969.

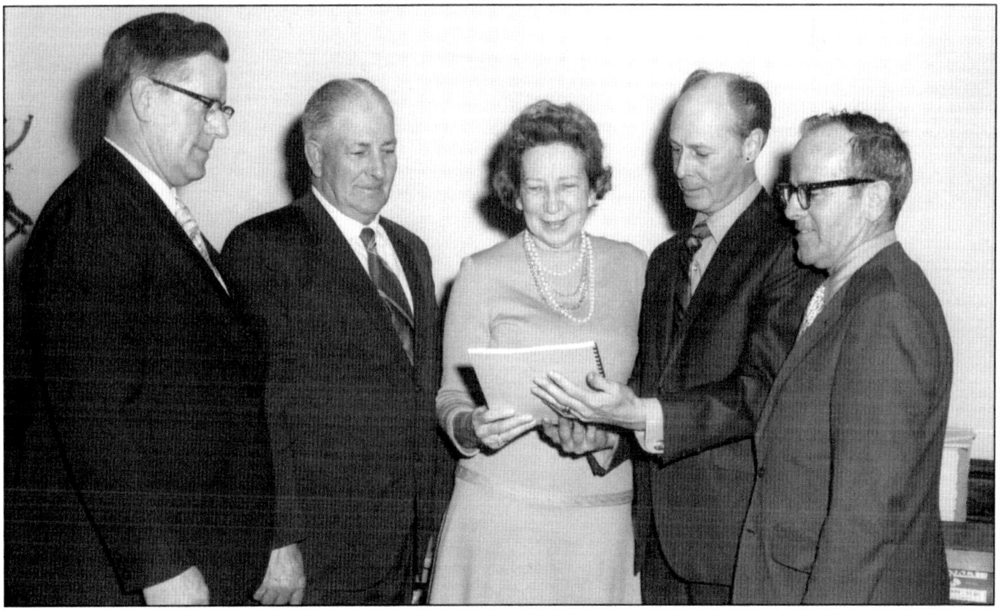

Town officials congratulate Dorothy Linton Quinn on her work with local civil defense preparation. Pictured, from left to right, are town supervisor Fred Bates, councilman John Kie, Quinn, councilman Clarence "Red" Visscher. and Rensselaer County legislator Joseph Warren. After the conclusion of World War II, the threat of possible war with the Soviet Union spurred local governments to prepare for the possibility of invasion or nuclear bombing. Duck and cover drills were carried out in schools at the time, starting with the elementary grades. Students were instructed to lie on the floor beneath their school desks with their hands over their heads to survive a possible explosion. Adult volunteers were recruited to serve as spotters in case enemy planes passed overhead. Nassau's proximity to assumed air routes for the possible bombing of the Watervliet Arsenal or the General Electric factory in Schenectady made it an important reporting site. (Courtesy of Diane McGrath, Nassau Town Hall.)

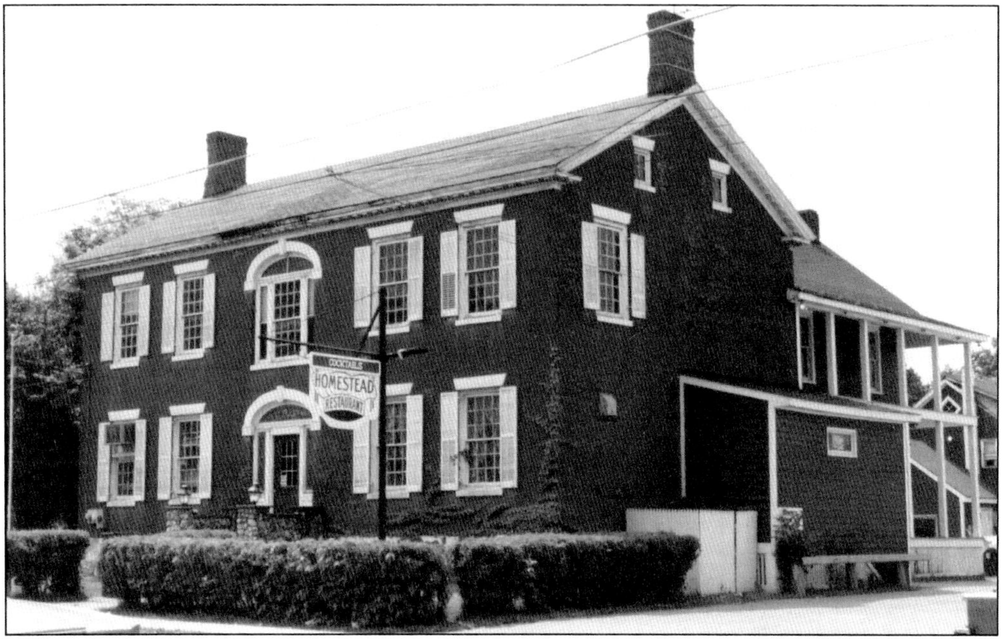

The Homestead Hotel, at 8 Church Street, was originally built by Thomas Hoag in 1808. Many a Nassau schoolchild was shown the basement, which reportedly had a tunnel that crossed to a cellar on the opposite side. Prior to the Civil War, escaped slaves used the building as a stop on the Underground Railroad as they made their way to freedom in Canada. It remained a private home for many years. In 1951, genial Irish couple Patrick and Helen Dunleavy turned it into the Homestead Hotel. (Courtesy of the Schodack Town Historian.)

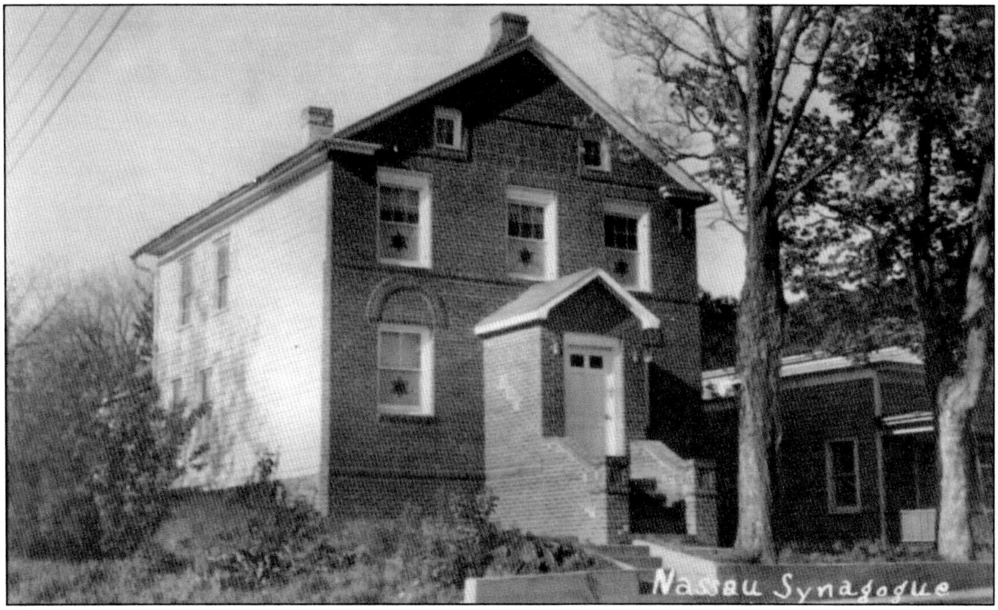

Many are surprised to learn of the long Jewish history in Nassau. By the 1920s, there were an estimated 200 Jewish families living in Nassau, Schodack, and East Nassau. Nassau had a kosher bakery and two kosher butchers. The synagogue on Albany Avenue, seen here, has been a center of community life for almost 100 years. (Courtesy of Nassau Free Library.)

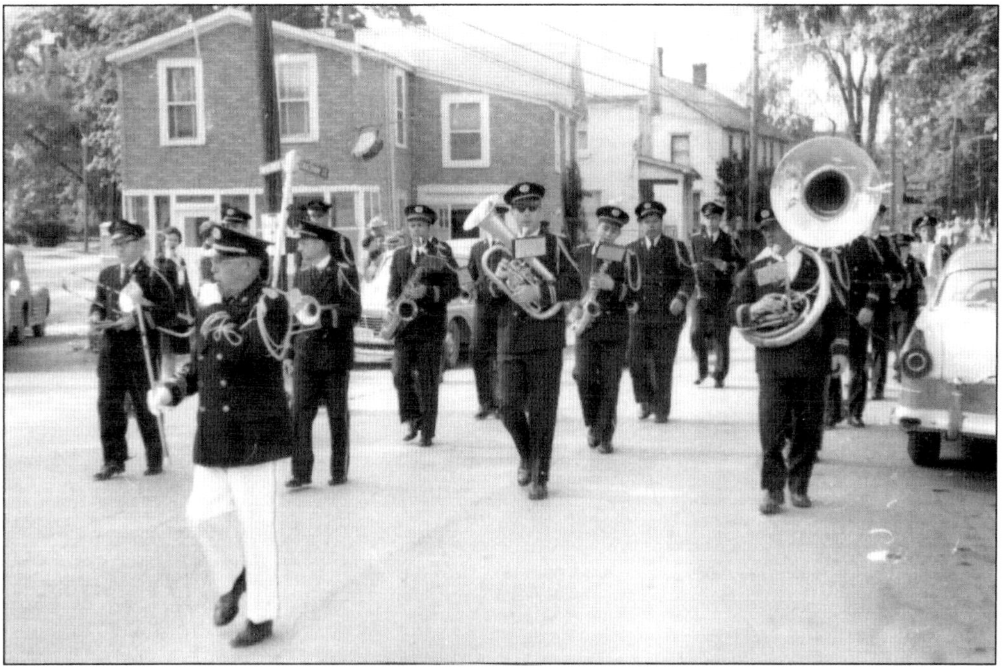

The Nassau Band, under the direction of Burr Rowe, marches from Chatham Street towards the village square around 1960. Visible behind Rowe are, from left to right, Harry Vincent, Frank Parks, Austin Lansley, Berton Bulles, Norman Rowe, Bruce Rowe, Barney Krebs, and George Demeur.

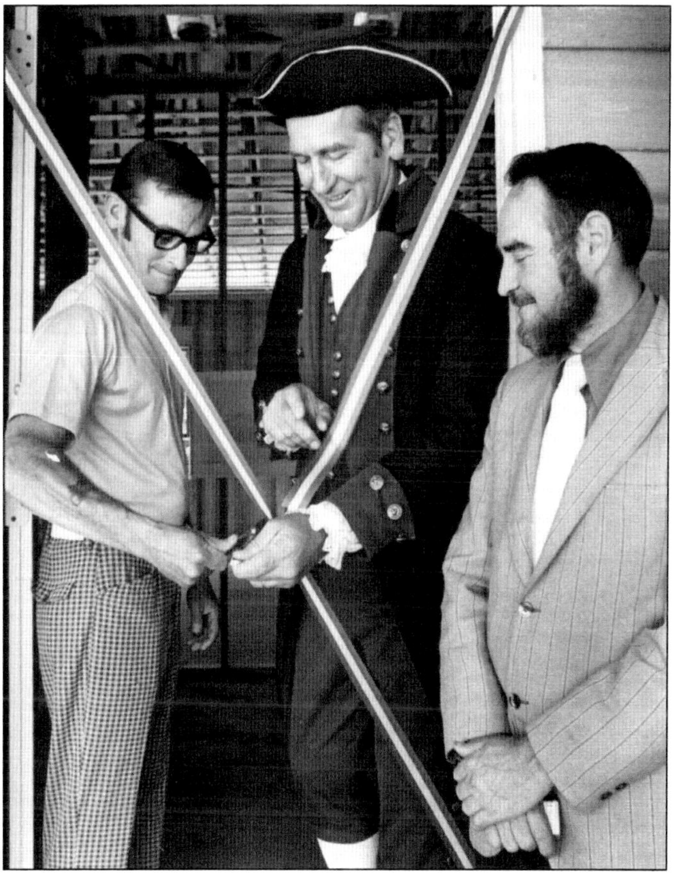

In 1976, the Nassau Free Library cut the ribbon on a new addition to the then 85-year-old institution. Seen from left to right are Nassau mayor Jerrold Van Deusen, town supervisor Floyd Hitchcock (in bicentennial attire), and library board president Kenneth Smead. (Courtesy of Nassau Free Library.)

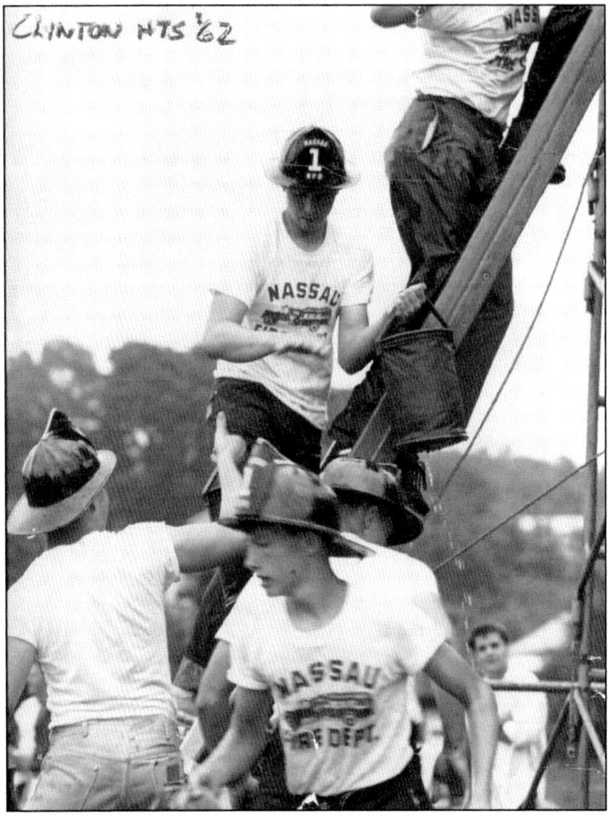

Established in February 1903 with 26 members, the Nassau Hose Company No. 1 has served the community for more than 100 years. Members are seen here enjoying a friendly rivalry with neighboring fire departments in a 1962 Firematics competition. They are Larry Cooper (on ladder), Robin Dingman (with back to camera), and Jimmy Fitzpatrick (facing camera). (Courtesy of Nassau Hose Company.)

A mid-1970s image of the hose company includes, from left to right, Donald Chandler, Charles "Chic" Andros, Michael Banks, Al Richards, Wilfred Harrington III, Thomas Colligan, Jean Fletcher, Archibald "Archie" Sherman, Thomas Jones, Wilfred Harrington II, Richard Becker, Barbara Ayers, Barbara Becker, Jack Coonrad, Thomas McShane, and Larry Cooper. (Courtesy of Nassau Hose Company.)

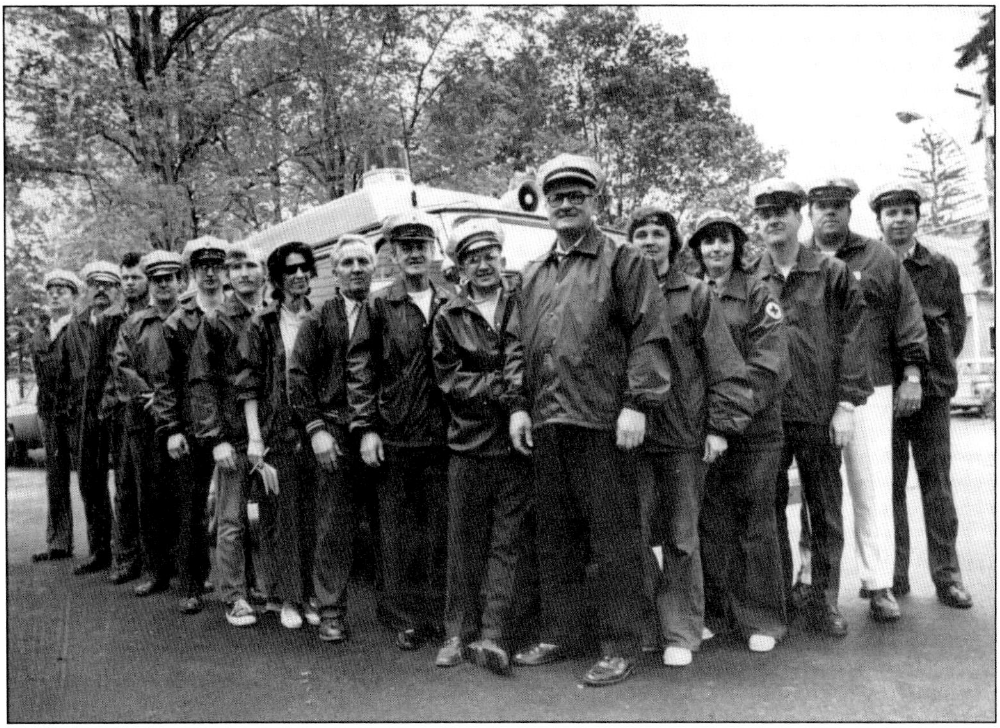

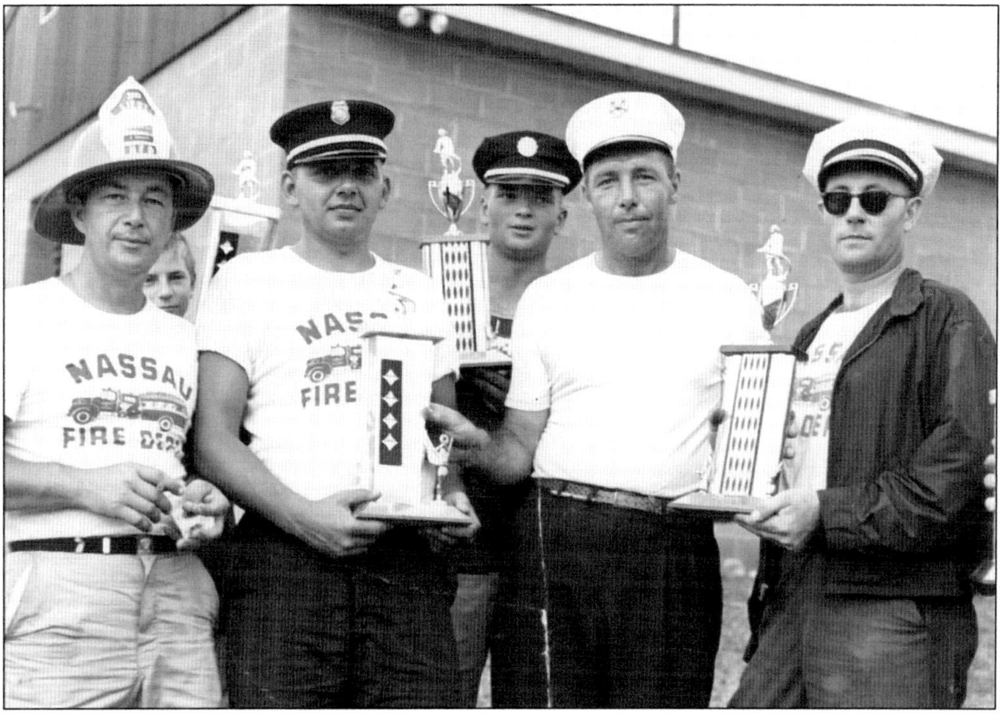

After the demise of the Nassau fair, the fire company held weekend field days on the old fairgrounds in the 1950s and 1960s. Seen here receiving their trophies in the summer of 1963 are, from left to right, Norman "Bucky" Senecal, Karl Bennett, an unidentified bystander, Harold Coons, and Donald Chandler. (Courtesy of Nassau Hose Company.)

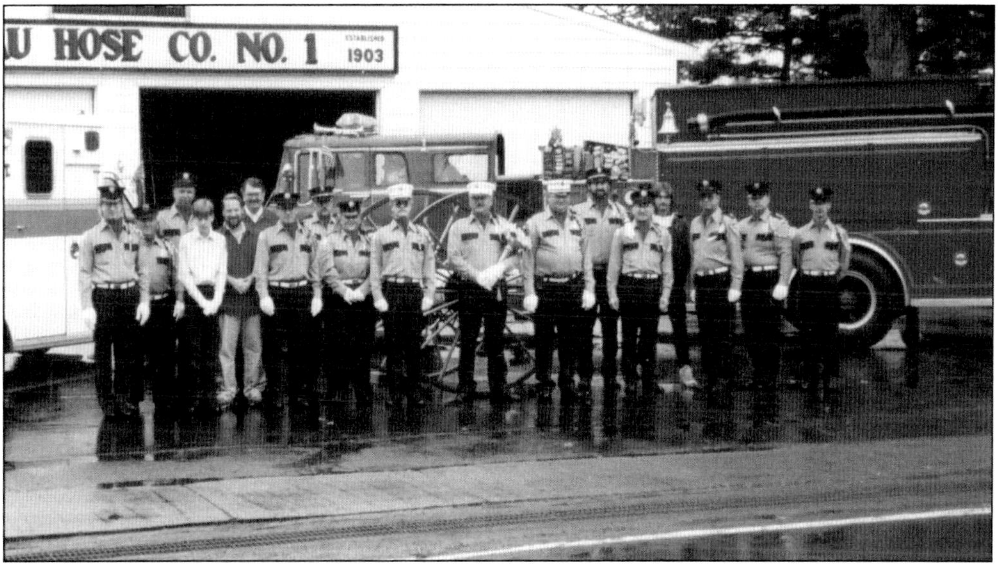

Members of Nassau Hose Company No. 1 pose in 1992 in front of their 1974 Ford fire engine. Established in 1903, the company services approximately 1,000 households in the village and town of Nassau, and contracts with Schodack to service an additional 800. In 1953, a rescue squad was formed as part of the fire department. Previously, ambulance calls had been answered by Bruen Rescue Squad in East Greenbush.

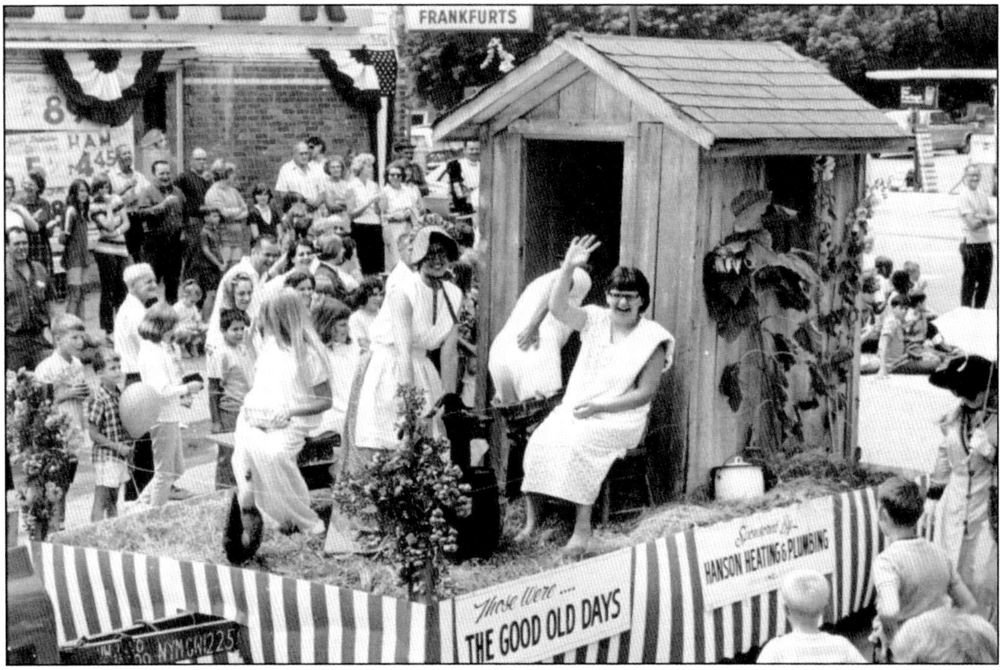

Area businesses were encouraged to take part in the 1966 Home Town Day parade, part of Rensselaer County's 175th anniversary. Above, the Hanson Heating & Plumbing float passes US Route 20 towards Chatham Street at the village square. Buntings decorate the IGA grocery store, which had been the town pharmacy for decades before that. Lenora Kahnle was crowned queen of the festivities, and Edger Rowe, 93, and Cora Bliss, 92, were saluted as Nassau's two oldest citizens. Another celebration is seen below, this time for the 1976 bicentennial, which also featured community floats. The Women's Republican Club reenacts the roles of Nassau women of the past. The two women in the center looking at the camera are Verna Orr (left) and Laura Cooper. (Above, courtesy of Nassau Free Library.)

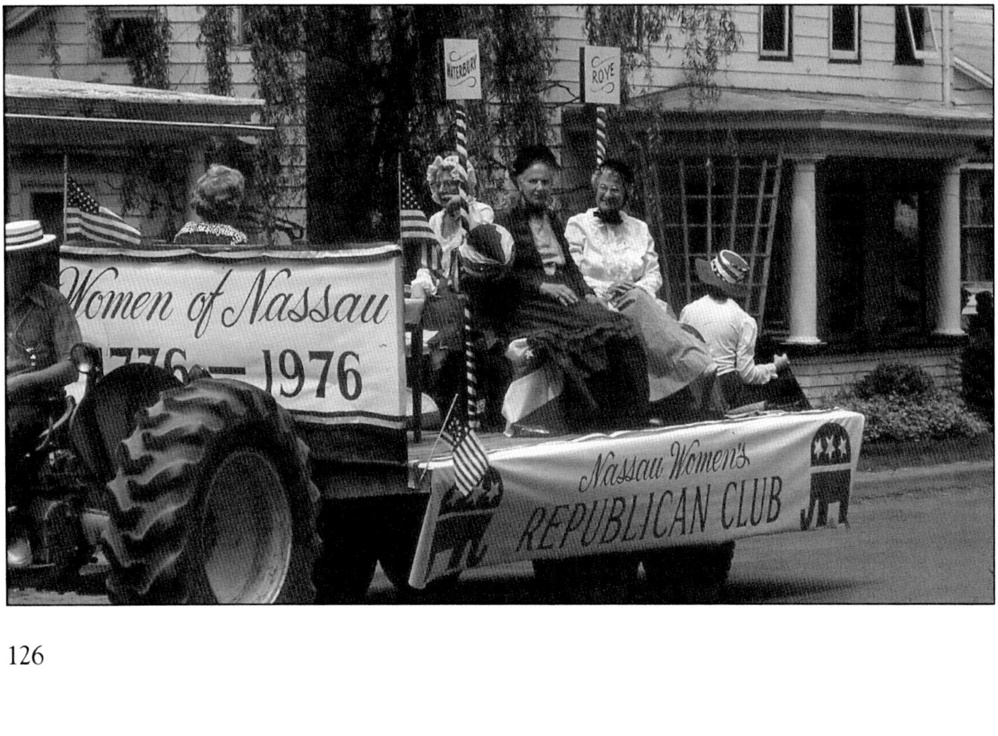

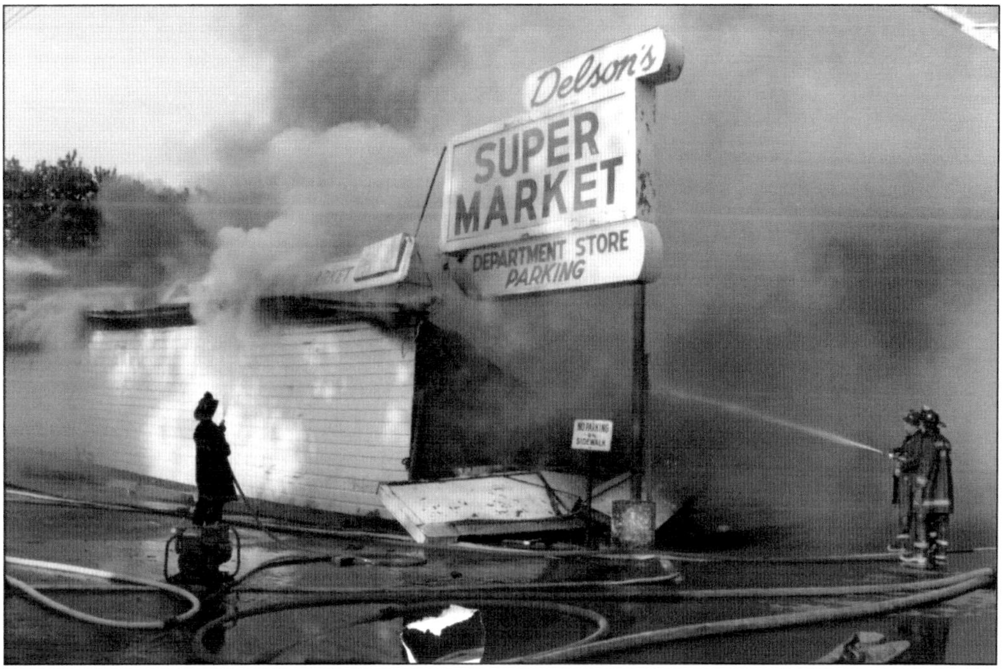

B.H. Delson's "economy store" was considered by many to be the heart of Nassau. Its slogan, "If we don't have it, you don't need it," reflected an expansive product line, including groceries, a full-service butcher, clothing, dry goods, notions, toys, tools, and hardware. Russian immigrant Louis Schwadelson started the business in Nassau around 1910, and his son Benjamin later expanded it to include stores in Chatham, Millerton, and Saugerties. The family later shortened their name to Delson. On July 29, 1982, the store and a house on Lake Avenue were set ablaze by a teenage arsonist. More than 30 firefighters were injured in the two fires, less than a mile apart. In all, more than 100 firefighters from 20 companies responded to the fires. The business never rebuilt in Nassau, and, citing a lack of profitability, all the other locations folded in the 1990s.

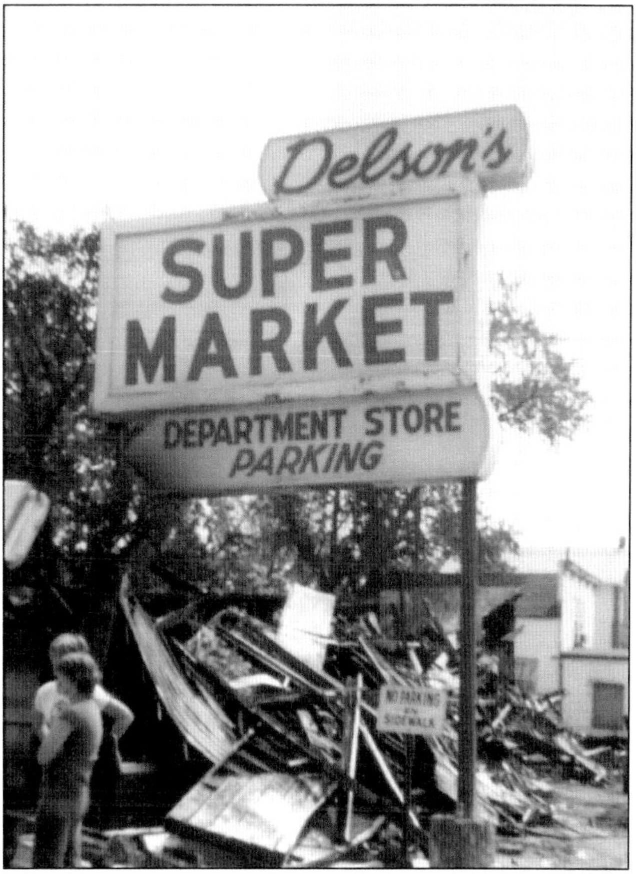